Viveka ... Viveca

Viveka ... Viveca

by
VIVECA
LINDFORS

New York   EVEREST HOUSE   Publishers

Library of Congress Cataloging in Publication Data:

Lindfors, Viveca, 1920–
  Viveka—Viveca.

  Includes index.
  1. Lindfors, Viveca, 1920–   . 2. Actors—Sweden—
Biography.   I. Title.
PN2778.L53A38   1981   792'.028'0924   [B]   81-12563
ISBN: 0-89696-125-7   AACR2

Published simultaneously in Canada by
Beaverbooks, Don Mills, Ontario
Manufactured in the United States of America
Designed by Judith Lerner
First Edition
RRD981

TO MY FATHER WHO GAVE ME WINGS. . .
TO SWEDEN WHO OPENED MY EYES TO STEPMOTHER VIOLETS. . . TO
JEANNA WHO TAUGHT ME TO DANCE. . . TO MY BROTHER WHO MADE
ME AWARE OF MAN'S FRAGILITY. . . TO G.R. WHO INTRODUCED ME
TO THE WOMAN IN ME. . . TO G.T. WHO LEFT FOR A NEW LIFE
WITHOUT ME; HAD HE NOT, I MIGHT NOT BE THE WOMAN I AM
TODAY. . . TO H.T. WHO HELPED ME DARE TO BE AT A TIME I NO
LONGER THOUGHT IT WAS POSSIBLE. . . TO AMERICA WHO TAUGHT
ME TO BE SENSITIVE WITHOUT BEING VULNERABLE. . . TO MADAME
AND I.B. WHO HELPED ME RESTORE MYSELF. . . TO ALL INDISPENSABLE
ASSISTANTS IN VARIOUS PARTS OF THE WORLD WHO PATIENTLY
HAVE TYPED DRAFT UPON DRAFT. . . TO GEORG SVENSSON, MY
SWEDISH PUBLISHER AT BONNIERS, AND TO BILL THOMPSON, MY
AMERICAN PUBLISHER AT EVEREST, FOR SUPPORTING MY OFTEN
CRUMBLING BELIEF ABOUT FINISHING THE BOOK. . . TO ALL THE
WOMEN IN MY LIFE, KNOWN AND NOT KNOWN, WHO WITH WORDS,
FEELINGS, AND DEEDS HAVE HELPED ME BECOME WHO I WANT
TO BE. . . TO THE AUDIENCES WHO KEEP AFFIRMING MY VITALITY
AND JOY, TIME AND TIME AGAIN. . . TO PAUL AUSTIN, FRIEND,
PARTNER, AND CO-WORKER. . . TO JOHN, LENA, AND KRISTOFFER,
MY THREE CHILDREN WHO ALWAYS ACCEPTED ME. . . TO NATASHA,
KATRINA, NICHOLAS JOHN, AND NORA ELIZABETH, MY GRANDCHILDREN
WHO REASSURE ME OF THE PAST, THE PRESENT, AND THE FUTURE. . .

※

AND LAST, BUT NOT LEAST, TO MY MOTHER,
WHO DID NOT HAVE A CHANCE
TO BE FREE, AS I DO

CONTENTS

INTRODUCTION

*"I wanted to see what was
there for me once, what is
there for me now . . ."*
LILLIAN HELLMAN
Pentimento

T IS ABOUT a woman removing her mask," I explained to
the customs officer who was going through my red, beat-up
theatrical trunk, covered with a pink sticker, *I Am a Woman*,
the name of my one-woman show, ready to be performed any
time, any place.

I am at Logan Airport in Boston . . . U.S.A. . . .

I am coming home from home . . . from way up north, from
Sweden where the stepmother violets are blooming at this time of
the year . . . where I was born a female and where I chose to
become an actress.

I am holding the exquisite silver mask made in the shape of a
bird in front of my face. "Like this," I said, making the gesture
revealing my face, slowly, deliberately, as I do in the opening of
the play, and gracefully, so much more gracefully than in my life.
The mask torn off the impostor, as Strindberg puts it, is a better
description. The gesture takes only a few seconds. In my life I am
finally accepting the "unmasking" as a daily routine as essential as
brushing my teeth.

Long ago, in order to survive, perhaps, I created two perfect
images of women for myself. One the wife, the mother, the friend
—always loving, dependent on intimate relationships only; the
other the actress, the lover, the breadwinner, always active, dependent upon work and the wish to change the world today. Those
two images, far apart in their goals, in a constant tug of war with
each other, left me, the real woman, neglected, frustrated, ambivalent, and incapable of open and lasting intimacy. When my
fourth marriage broke up, after eighteen years, I faced it. I had
thought only death would do us apart.

"*I Am a Woman*, that's the name of the play?" The customs
officer's eye has caught one of the brown paper brochures in the
PR kit.

"Yes," I said. "I am the woman and the actress."

"Oh! Viveca Lindfors, of course. I recognize the voice. I used to see you in the movies."

"You still will," I said. He looked surprised. "How old are you?" I ask. I can't help myself.

"Like it or not, I'm fifty-five," he answers.

"I like it," I say, "just like me." I quickly continue, not giving him much of a chance. "I am glad you are still working; wouldn't you hate to retire at this point in your life when things are really coming together?" He looked at me half seriously.

"I got you, lady. I loved you in that movie with Errol Flynn. I am glad you are still active."

His reaction is not uncommon. Most people think that actresses retire at the age of thirty-five, while our leading men, opposite younger and younger females, get better and better parts, their temples graying in distinguished style as we are dyeing ours. We are not allowed to grow old with them, and the line at the unemployment office in Hollywood is long and filled with actresses over thirty-five.

Not only in Hollywood. A producer in Sweden complained about the lack of parts and the frustration among his middle-aged actresses. "They would tear my eyes out if I hired you," he said.

When I began my career in Sweden thirty years ago, I had no such worries. I zoomed to the top in no time; I was box office number one after my second film. I was a sex symbol. "She was way ahead of her colleagues because of her sensuality," it says in the Swedish Film Dictionary. I believed them and gave them what they wanted, off as well as on screen. People flocked to see my films for the love scenes. I was good at it like Garbo, and when the City of Angels called it never occurred to me not to follow in her footsteps. I went with the wind and gave little thought to what it meant to leave behind me a career as a serious actress at the Royal Dramatic Theatre in Stockholm and two tiny children—John was four and Lena two and a half. Leaving their father, my husband at the time, I considered less serious. I thought, "He could be replaced."

I would be away for three months. It turned out to be nine. When I began to forget my own children, I got scared. What were *their* fears? That I was a ghost mother and Nana, their nurse, the real one? That I had gone on a plane with the wind and would never come back? Or were these my fears? It took me forever to feel I had the right to exist both as the artist and the woman, and it was here, in the U.S.A., that I began to let go of my vulnerability without losing my sensitivity.

Boston Airport is busy. I am looking down the hall and catch Doug, my stage manager, the indispensable, still hassling about our sculptured set. Every time we cross a border we have to prove that we are not selling *them*, only the show. I suddenly feel exhausted. We have been on the road for two years. The map on the wall in my office on 95th Street looks like an airline route. "Hop on the plane, baby, we play Chico, California Wednesday night and Virginia the next. We are picking up a couple of grand. They love you, baby." I can still hear Doug knocking on my door at 7:00 AM, "Get up, Viveca, got to make a plane."

I love Doug. He works like a vaudeville actor, with the same creative intensity. It's in his blood; it can't be taught. By 7:00 PM the set is up and the stage is painted with lights—pinks, blues, mauves, whites. "We've got to create magic, Viveca," he says.

Jet lag or no jet lag, it's my turn. I turn on the tape recorder to do my exercises. I hear Gui, my dance teacher's voice, over the rock and roll: "One, two, one two bend and stretch. Come on, Viveca, move that body, bend and stretch." On the other side of the tape are my voice exercises with Joe. He makes up the weirdest words to the scale: "I love you so, I love you so" or "Come, go with me to my house." They boom out over the empty theater.

At 8:30 I take my place in the dark—I, the Woman, the Actress —and as the haunting melancholy music fades and the lights slowly come up on me, I remove the mask and begin the journey of one woman and many women—mine too. Two hours later I have affirmed myself again. I am reborn.

"We wanted to wake the wonder in us all," Paul Austin, my friend and director, said during a dialogue that followed the performance. The wonder of Anne Frank, age fourteen, and Anais Nin, age seventy-two. The wonder in me, too. I didn't think it was possible five years ago when the work began; when G.T. left for a life without me; the year my mother died; and I was alone for the first time in my life, afraid I couldn't make it.

"Tabori?" The customs officer is putting the stamp in my passport. "That's my married name," I explain. He seems relieved that I am not one of those freaky ladies living alone. I don't tell him I am, but I am making a mental note to get my passport changed. The separation year is soon up.

We had discussed long distance, G.T. and I, about my going to Germany to see him and his theater. But I had given my last performance in Sweden and spent days packing up some old furniture from my mother's house. I carefully packed the old dining room table that I had dinner at all through my childhood—I never liked dinners—I wanted to use it to write on in my Long Island cottage and one day I will give it to John, hoping his dinners will be more joyful. There were some paintings of my mother and grandmother, too. I wanted them on the walls in my cottage by the sea.

I was exhausted from it all. Above all, I had felt during the entire six weeks' tour in Sweden an overwhelming need to have a day by myself! With nothing scheduled. Maybe take a look at my past. Take a look at the place where I spent some of the most vital years of my life.

I called G.T. in Bremen, explained my decision, hoping he would understand, and suggested we meet in London instead.

"Maybe," he said.

"We'll split the expenses," I said.

It was heavenly beautiful in Stockholm. Everybody had gone to the country. I took my bicycle and peddled through the empty city, through the parks where tulips and daffodils were blooming, along the waterfront where I could see the old city on the other side of the harbor. The houses, each one unique, as if they were extensions of human beings.

I walked into the building where I lived as a child. I stood in the courtyard and looked up to the third floor and saw myself behind our kitchen window—round-faced, thick reddish-brown hair, serious, listening to the gypsies.

In those days, they went around from one courtyard to another in Sweden, singing strange old songs, tragic ones, accompanying themselves on the accordion. I would wrap up, carefully, in a piece of newspaper, two or three pennies and throw them down to them. If a child was with them, I added a cookie. They would bow and thank me. I felt I ought to have gone down and given it to them—touched their hands. I didn't. I was afraid I might pick up some illness. Or they would take me away—or I would choose to go away with them forever. Intimacy is only for the family! Sweden is a security-hungry country, and so I stayed at a distance until I knew I too was part gypsy.

That day in the courtyard I put my hand out to her, Viveka with a "k," the red-haired little girl in the window caught by the shabby music of the gypsies. I could tell she didn't trust me. I didn't blame her—I had ignored her a lot. I started to sing in a croaky old voice, songs of unrequited love. Suddenly she fell, or jumped, but it didn't matter for I caught her in my arms and she joined in with me! One tone here, a word there. I danced a bit, too, awkwardly, for she was heavy in my arms, but then she put her hands around my neck making herself lighter and it helped. We both knew that love and intimacy are not easily come by and that without them nothing is worthwhile.

When I came out of the building, the sun was still warm, the trees were tenderly green against the blue sky, bluer than any place in the world, it seemed.

On my bicycle I continued along the harbor and ended up on the steps to the Royal Dramatic Theatre. I was only seventeen when I became a student in the school located on the top floor. In those days I had no opinions—nor felt the need to have them. I was a sexy dame. I started to laugh, thinking about it all. I had forgotten how strong the image had been in my childhood country.

I was soon reminded of it. VIVECA LINDFORS IS SHOWING HER BREASTS FOR 1.500 KRONER IN THE SCHOOLS were the headlines that stared me in the face the day I got off the plane in Stockholm to do my one-woman show. But by the end of the tour they wrote about me as the woman, the artist. They had discovered the change—a change that had taken me twenty-five years to achieve. I realized it was important to me that they had, more so than I had known.

It felt good thinking about it all, sitting on the steps to the goldcupoled building by the harbor where my life had begun as an actress, where everything had come together and life had seemed crystal clear.

G.T. didn't show up in London. Couldn't make it or didn't want to. I don't know.

It's been five years now since we have touched each other, cared for each other, or had an effect on each other. There is no reason why the divorce should not go through.

The customs officer is handing me back my American passport. The green-covered little booklet symbolizes a gesture so complex it took me years to catch up with it. I no longer torture myself with questions such as "Am I an American or a Swede? Should I live here or over there?" I have made my peace with the fact that I have two countries, that I have my roots now in the U.S.A., too, where my children and grandchildren live. My home is in New York on 95th Street. We all have lived there for twenty-five years. There is much of my past, all of the present, and promises of the future within those four walls. And within *me* live all the people that I have been or still am intimate with.

I suddenly long to go home and root myself, feel my own walls around me, get closer to everybody, take Brandy, my dog, for a walk, talk to Kristoffer, my actor son, about our show *My Mother*

13

. . . *My Son,* and with John, my son the politician, about Ronald Reagan, my ex-co-star in the movies, becoming the President. I long to feel the arms of H.T., my lover after G.T. left, around me, to sit with Natasha and Katrina in the Long Island house of Lena, my daughter the Vice President, and make up stories the way my father did—one about the brave Bjarne, my brother, and one about the tough Margaretha, my sister. Why did he want us to be so brave and so tough? What we needed was love, easy love, every-day love, I'm thinking as I put the passport in my purse.

The customs officer is about to close up my trunk. He has checked everything: the brown traveling cape for the woman on her journey, the slouchy hat for the wives, the money bag for the whore as well as Mother Courage, the wigs for the entertainers, the role players, the white cape for the woman at peace, and, last but not least, the blue scarf symbolizing the purity of Anne Frank. All the paraphernalia—all the props, the make-up, the tapes—that helps me make the magic. I hand him back the mask. "Be careful with it," I say. "It's fragile." He wraps it up in Anne's scarf. I like him even more. "Come and see my show," I say. "It's for every-body—men too!"

He laughs. "Okay. I'll bring my lady."

"What's your name?" I say.

"George," he says and shakes my hand. He has clear blue eyes and he looks straight at me, as my father did. I started to laugh.

I wouldn't have laughed five years ago. I was in a dilemma so corny, so disastrous it lived up to every cheap novel I had ever read. In my wildest dreams, I never imagined it could happen to me.

14

Viveka ... Viveca

Five Years Ago

"Out with the carcass . . . out
with it . . . I am going to bathe . . .
I am going to wash myself clean . . .
If it is still possible . . ."

AUGUST STRINDBERG
Alice in Dance of Death

I DON'T MIND BEING a grandfather but I don't like being married to a grandmother," George quoted from an article in *The New York Times* one morning five years ago.

We were having breakfast around the green dining room table on 95th Street where we had lived for eighteen years—the writer, the actress, and the three children.

As an actress I was used to the dilemma of being over thirty-five. That the problem would pop up its ugly face between us I was unprepared for. That he would fall in love with someone more mature or more giving had frightened me at times. I was not always as loving as I thought I ought to be, or wanted to be, and since I didn't always get out of our marriage what I had expected, I figured he didn't either. I had had one or two lovers but nothing serious. I knew about a red-haired girl one summer who adored him like a father and when I found the slip from a motel I realized he was more or less than a father, and it hurt. I knew he was intoxicated by my daughter Lena when she began to show signs of becoming a woman, but *Lolita* was popular and G.T. was a writer with a rich fantasy life.

But she was married now and had given birth to her first baby. We were grandparents, and I wrote it all down under the experience of marriage, or just life. Bittersweet memories that one could smile at. But this gray February morning nothing seemed funny, not even bittersweet.

He had told me about the girl from Berlin. She was the same age as my daughter Lena.

Six weeks later, our marriage was over. I was replaced.

Once I knew of her existence, the cocoon began to unravel. It horrified me that it had gone on for so long and I had known nothing.

I had been away all fall doing *Mother Courage* by Bertolt Brecht for the Arena Stage in Washington. I had wondered why G.T. didn't come down for New Year's Eve. I thought it had something to do with the fact that he and Marty, Lena's husband, didn't direct the production. I had been angry about that, too. We had done the play, the three of us, together a year before in Vermont.

When Zelda Fichandler, the artistic director of the Arena Stage, asked me to do the part, I suggested our team to her. It seemed natural that she should take advantage of the work already accomplished. "I have my own director," was her answer. One can only guess why. Teams generally are not popular in the theater. Too threatening, perhaps? But *Mother Courage* is for an actress what *King Lear* is for an actor. It was too hard to pass up.

I went up to the Berkshires to discuss my dilemma with G.T. and Marty, who were doing a workshop production of *Pinkville*, G.T.'s latest play. They were generous and told me to go ahead. I was still nervous about having to deal with a new director and a new production concept. "Can I count on your being with me?" I asked G.T. "Do you have the time?" They were using his adaptation so there was no reason why not. He seemed uptight about it. I understood. I was uptight about it too. But he did say yes.

Driving back to New York with Lena and Kris, G.T. had been crying, Lena told me. "Mommy doesn't trust me anymore," he had said to her. Why did he bring in the word trust? Why to her and not to me? All I wanted to know was would he have the time? Perhaps he knew that he wouldn't and couldn't.

Uschi—that was the name of the girl—was living around the corner up at Jeffrey's that weekend.

As it turned out, he spent most of the fall in Berlin "preparing a new production." I had to call overseas to get his O.K. on any changes in the text for the *Courage* production. I was upset that he didn't come down and spend New Year's Eve with me, but then I knew that he was in production with *Pinkville* and was going to open soon at the American Place Theatre. We were both working. I was used to that. I still didn't suspect anything.

It seemed everybody knew about her but me. Lena knew. So did Kris, for nearly a year. They didn't take it particularly seriously. "Daddy is having a fling. Why not?" He went too far when he brought her to the house for Christmas and New Year. John, my eldest, had met her now, too.

The children confronted G.T. "If we know, Mother must know, too. If you don't tell her, we will." They didn't have to. G.T. did it himself. Eventually.

He came down to Washington. It was the end of the run. He stood in the dressing room while I was taking off my makeup, as he had done many times during our marriage. He looked at me lovingly, tenderly. Why did I feel so tense? Was it the performance or was I still angry at him for not having come down for New Year's Eve?

"You two love each other; why are you playing so many games?" Jane Alexander, another actress in the play, said to me.

"Why don't I feel it?" I had answered, thinking it was my fault.

I had rarely been home that fall and when I was I was either busy with the house or thinking about the part. It never leaves you. "Maybe I haven't given G.T. as much attention as I should," I thought, forgetting that he hadn't given me any.

After the performance we went to a cast party. By the time we came back to my apartment we were both exhausted. "Let's go to sleep in each other's arms," I said, "and then we'll have the morning together."

"I have to leave on the 7 o'clock flight," G.T. said. I was surprised. Usually I was the early riser. I was disappointed, but I wanted to avoid any negative feelings, any old patterns of possessiveness. I was in analysis. I did not want to fantasize, either in pink or in black. I wanted to accept his way without imposing mine and expected the same in return. In some ways, it blinded me. But I would rather have it that way. I still do.

We went to sleep holding each other, and when we were standing by the elevator the next morning outside the apartment and he said we must talk, I felt a flood of warmth for us, for our love, for our marriage. I hugged him. He was dressed in a white Swedish military coat, like the one my father used to wear. I felt close to him.

"Yes, yes," I said.

"I will be home in ten days' time. It can wait." He closed the door and the elevator went down.

He couldn't tell me about the girl, and I still believed that only death would us part.

Ten days later I left Washington for home. When the cab pulled up in front of our orange-colored house on 95th Street, G.T. opened the door. We hugged each other. "Lindfors," he said. "Tabori," I said. We always used second names. He took my bags upstairs. I got out of my traveling clothes and into my wine-colored gown. It felt wonderful being home. I started to unpack. He was standing by the fireplace in our bedroom, leaning against it, as he so often had. He was an attractive man, tall, elegant, with soft hands, a writer's hands. Behind him he had placed a picture of the two of us embracing. Everything seemed perfect.

"Viv," he said, "I have a girl. I want to confront you with it in order to bring us together," and then he added, "I think."

I sat down on the bed. Our bed.

I believed him. I wanted to believe him. "I'm glad it's in the open. It's better that way," I said. Perhaps I lied, but it was the only way I could cope with the growing spasm of panic in my groins.

Eighteen years ago, life had seemed so full of promise. Now he was in love with another woman. "We must build a fire around our love," he used to say. "I feel your penis always inside of me," I used to say. Now our life together was all in question. I had had lovers, too. We were both going to shrinks—I on my second. But right now I was a woman, dealing with my man face to face. It is between two people, never three. And that is good.

That night we did talk for hours. All blame was gone between us. It suddenly seemed so easy to say, "I was angry with you or I got uptight or I withdrew. I was a shit. Forgive me; I'm sorry. I will become more aware." We never left each other's side for a moment. When I took a bath he sat on the toilet seat and talked to me. Then he dried me as if I were a child. We made love and fell asleep in each other's arms. I had no doubt that he felt the way I did and everything was going to be all right.

The next morning he disappeared. I must have been deaf, dumb, and blind. The girl was still in New York and he had no intention of sending her back to Berlin. Not until he could leave, too.

A deadline for our marriage began to stare me in the face. The spasm of pain threw me into an abyss of emotions. Feelings raced through me like wild horses or petrified mice. From panic to fury, from tenderness to revenge, from passion to violence. I had no control. My fury with him for abandoning me was as deep as my fear of being abandoned.

I suffered from the female sickness: If a man loves me, I am worthy; if he doesn't, I am worthless.

I was stuck. Stuck the ancient way. The female way.

During our last pathetic six spasmodic weeks of our marriage, I often wished G.T. were dead, for then I would not have to make a choice. I would not have to answer any questions like "Should I continue to love him in spite of the girl or should I give up? How far must I go? How long must I wait? And if I don't, will I find another man? A man who is willing to put up with my 'allergies'? And if so, will I put up with his? And if it doesn't work out between us, will I fall apart again? Will I behave again like a whimpering child, without pride, without sense of self? Will I be stuck again not knowing how to live, desperately afraid of being abandoned once more?" Oh God, oh God, oh God!

Making love became my last resource. A flood of desire burst forth in me.

Sensuality had brought us together eighteen years before. It would work again. It erased any rage, any rights about myself, any standards I wanted to set for myself in regard to this shabby situation. All doubts about our love, or mine, were gone. I wanted him over and over again.

"Do we have to fuck every night?" he finally said to me.

"I thought that was a woman's line," I answered laughingly, feeling totally sure of myself now when I had satisfied myself, now when I had satisfied him, as if that was all I ever needed to do as a woman. For, oh yes, those nights he gave in to the passion between us.

It didn't last long. The next day he seemed to vanish again, as he did the morning after he had told me about the girl, as he did many mornings following. "At least I am confusing him," I thought furiously, blinding myself to all other circumstances that drove him away, circumstances that had little to do with me or us or the girl.

"I have to go to London for a story conference," he said one day. "I'll be gone for three weeks." *Pinkville* had opened to lukewarm reviews. Even I sensed our time was up.

By now we were both exhausted from endless arguments where blame had become the name of the game. Even our dog Brandy was ashamed of us. He would sneak upstairs, tail between his legs, confused about which side to take, whom to love.

It was a cold spring morning when he and I saw the car turn the corner of 95th Street where we had lived for eighteen years— the writer, the actress, and the three children.

I was wearing a silver fox coat. It was stolen from me a week later as if they knew, the robbers, the invaders, that there was a woman living alone, no man in the house, just an old dog. I came home after a performance. As I put the key in the door, I saw that the lock was broken. I went upstairs. I discovered that the radio was gone. I didn't care; it was a German radio. Then I realized

21

about the fur coat. I minded that a lot. It was old and worn out but I loved it.

"I'll be back," had been G.T.'s last words. I didn't see him for four years.

I was forty-nine. It was my fourth marriage. There had been many changes in my life already. Also for the children. Although now grown up, they had experienced different fathers, different names, different places. I felt my quota was up.

And so, in spite of fame and fortune, creativity, four marriages, life on two continents, love affairs, I reacted no different from any other woman, no differently from my mother.

Two weeks later, I sat by her deathbed in my childhood country.

2

"I want to feel you, Viveca; I can't feel you," my mother said. It was the day I arrived. I had thought she was asleep. I put my hand in hers. Her palm was warm in spite of the pain her body was suffering. It was strangely peaceful. I gave in to a comfort I had run from for years!

I had received a cable from my sister two weeks after G.T. left. "Mother is dying. Come home." I decided to take the plane to Stockholm the following evening. I didn't want to be late this time, as I had been for my father's death. I was always more careless about him for he was the stronger.

It was lucky that I was free to go. The night before, I had closed in a play by August Strindberg, a Swedish writer and a contemporary of my mother's and father's. It was ironic that I should have been doing *Dance of Death*, a play about two people, the Captain and Alice, battling out their love/hate relationship with no relief until "death do us apart," at a time when I was finally to accept my mother's commitment to my father, at a time when G.T. and I were at our last gasp of ambivalent struggle in our marriage.

I could use it all in the performance: the madness, the possessiveness, the passions, the fears.

When the Captain's heart breaks before hers, she spits at him in fury. Yet, a few seconds later she utters a silent scream of loss, of longing, as the image overwhelms her of a young man in the middle of winter without an overcoat. "I must have loved that man," she mumbles. In spite of the hate, there was love. I identified with it all.

At times I felt as if Strindberg himself was on the stage but split into two halves, the female and the male, the controller and the submissive, the yes-sayer and the no-sayer, my mother and my father, G.T. and myself. Only I was a different-generation woman and he was a different-generation man.

I sat by my mother's bedside in a home for old people outside of Stockholm for three weeks. I kept a journal of what went on between us. She was going in and out of the life that I was part of and another that I could neither see nor hear, yet it seemed so much more real to her. Must have been for me, too, for I never forgot those moments. They became a lifetime of clarity.

One late afternoon, the time of day I loved most, the shadows were dark and strong. It was too late for more efforts, and darkness would soon embrace us. She had been gone for quite a while when suddenly she was with me again. "Thorsten is crying," she said.

"When?" I asked, for I had never seen my father cry; he was a proud and strong man, a Swede, a winner of prizes and a charmer of women, a joyful man who talked of strong family links, who loved life.

"He had gone to identify the body at the police station. I couldn't make it. When he came out of the . . ."—she fumbled for words —"morgue, he was crying."

My brother had drowned himself in the river one day in March. When they discovered the body, they estimated it had been in the icy water for two months. The coldness made it easier for my father to identify him.

I picked up a book of poems written by my father on my mother's dressing room table the day she told me of my father's tears. In the foreword he writes: "What they call depression today, to our generation meant lack of courage." He had written this after my brother's suicide.

My father died a few years after my brother. He drowned in his own saliva; the medical term is emphysema. I began to understand about men's fragility now when I was beginning to accept my own.

My brother was the number one victim of the goddamn masterrace syndrome. He had always felt obliged to follow in my father's footsteps. He tried to be a military man like my father but failed. He tried to be a partner in my father's publishing house but failed. He wanted to be a doctor but never dared to.

23

When his marriage failed, too, he began to break down. There were two children involved. After the divorce he lived alone. He locked himself in for weeks, in his apartment, and surrounded himself with human filth. He was six feet tall, a grownup man, no longer a baby to be wiped and washed and bound in swaddling clothes. He tried to starve himself to death, for he didn't feel six feet tall. My father tried to reason with him through the locked door. My father didn't know what else to do. In those days, one did not know about curing the mind or helping the mind cure itself. And so he called the police and the door was broken down. My mother sat on the steps crying and shaking. Together they watched the police bind him into a straitjacket. Yes, they saw their once soft and loving sweet baby boy, now red-faced, eyes bloodshot from broken veins—for withheld tears are like sharp knives —crushed, imprisoned, overpowered.

The identification with one's own flesh and blood is a fact. It must have been as if, in their anger, their frustration, their own will was bent, destroyed, broken, defeated, betrayed.

A year later, my brother disappeared into black water. It was a cold night in January and I never saw him again; no one saw him.

I was in California where the sun shone day in and day out. As I walked into the low bungalow where I lived with Don, my third husband-to-be, John and Lena, two Swedish maids, numerous cats and dogs, and chickens, too, I found a yellow envelope from Western Union. The message was simple and clear. It informed me about the time and place of the funeral.

I didn't go. Did they tell me too late? Was I in the middle of a film? I don't remember why, only that I felt nothing, only that I remembered vaguely that I had loved him once, when I was five, before he disappointed me, before I thought of him as a man, and before frailty turned into weakness. And after that he became less and less real in my life.

The conditioning hurt us all, but I survived and Bjarne didn't.

"A soldier's daughter never cries," my father used to say to me. It certainly wasn't allowed for a son.

Once I began analysis, I couldn't stop crying. "Why?" I asked my analyst.

"Withheld tears are like old wine in a bottle," she said. "If not aired, they explode, Viveca."

"Are you and George divorcing?" I turned around. My mother was with me again. It was that same afternoon. She had been

24

gone for a while. There was a tray with untouched food. I was standing by the window. How could she have known? Nobody in Sweden knew and nobody could have told her. She must have felt my pain. She was such an expert on women's pain.

"No," I lied; I was still allergic to her pain. My father had mistresses. I remember hearing my mother cry at night. My room was next to hers. I didn't want to identify with her. I took the side of my father, the side of the stronger. I understood him for I, too, wanted to leave her. She was the martyr, the victim. I would rather be the mistress. I knew now I had been shortsighted.

My father never left my mother. Only death did do them apart.

"Are you crying, Viveca?" my mother asked, making one more effort.

But I was still caught in the role of the stronger. "No," I lied again.

Now at the end of her life, when we were finally on common ground, two women, I still couldn't share my pain with her, with whom I had once shared everything.

My mother had no time for hypocrisy at this point. She closed her eyes and went back to her life with my father. Despite the endless conflicts between them I used to see with the insensitive eyes of a child, I sensed what I had never sensed before, the depth of her commitment. I had run far from everything that had reminded me of it and her and yet here she was, in front of me, inside of me, around me, wanting what I wanted, succeeding where I failed. She was on her way to him, my father, her husband, her lover. He was waiting for her. Mine was not. I envied her.

3

"I love you, I love you, I don't want to let you go," I had told G.T. For the first time in my life, I fought for a relationship.

It was a few days after I learned about the girl. She was still in New York and, although her existence had little to do with our crumbling marriage, it confused the focus in our struggle. Every time we were about to break through the sound barrier, he could or would escape to her soothing arms. Or so I felt. I was like a hamster in a cage, and every move I made increased the speed, weakening me, confusing me, making me a partner in our crimes. And I had wanted to be a mature woman!

"I don't know what to do. I am at a loss," I cried. I was having a drink with a friend.

"What do you want to do right now?" he asked.

"Kill them both," I answered.

"Well, why don't you?" he replied softly.

I got up, ran to the phone, called Lena and Marty. "Is George there with her?" "Yes . . . no . . . well . . . but . . ."

I slammed down the receiver, ran out to Eighth Avenue, and flagged a cab. I told the driver to go fast. "I am going to kill somebody," I said. He drove as if fire was behind us, intrigued by the idea. Not only did I want to kill her, but also confront her. How ridiculous. What did I hope for? Understanding? Sisterhood? Had I forgotten what it was like to be twenty-five, when all women over thirty-five seemed like old hags? Or was it just safer to revenge myself on her? After all, I wanted *her* to leave, not *him*.

"Where is she?" I said quietly to Marty. "I am going to kill her." They had already smuggled her out. Too late.

I went for G.T. All I could say was, "Fuck you, fuck you, fuck you, fuck you," as I beat him up. He struck me back. Finally someone separated us. The silence was broken between us. Once more I could speak without shaking. "I love you, I love you, I don't want to let you go," I cried out.

It must have been unbearable for Lena. She was walking around the apartment making order where chaos was all around her. When she offered me tea, I cried out, "No, no. I want to go home with Georgie. Just he and I." Natasha, her firstborn, started to cry, for the first time Lena told me later. She had just given birth to her. I had no thought for either of them. I was filled with one need only. To save my marriage. At least Lena saw a woman fighting for a man. I never had. Maybe I would have had more hope if I had.

"I love you, I love you, I don't want to let you go," I mumbled to him once more. We were walking down 72nd Street. It was the last snowfall before spring took over. He was wearing his white military coat. He stopped. We hugged each other.

Again it looked as if we were getting closer. Again that night we made love as if eighteen years hadn't passed.

I didn't want it to be over. The eighteen years of sharing, children growing up, and now grandchildren, opening and closing of plays, sickness, love, hate, and dullness, too. It felt good to tell him without caring what the answer would be.

The next morning, he disappeared again. "I'll call you later," he had said. But this time I knew where he went. I waited. "I'm putting the girl on the plane back to Berlin. I'll be home later," he called. It would be just the two of us now. I was full of love for him, also of anxiety.

He came up the stairs. He put the paper on the table and went over to the stove to make himself a cup of tea. I was sitting on the sofa. I was ready to understand him, even to understand his ambivalence. And I kept repeating to myself his words, "I wanted to confront you about the girl in order to bring us together." I had believed him then and I wanted to believe him now.

He turned to me while he was fixing the tea. "Let's go to the movies," he said. It was a perfectly normal idea for a perfectly normal couple in a perfectly normal marriage, but our marriage was not normal, not then. Neither were we. He was telling me clearly: "I want no dramas, no confrontations."

That was unfair. I didn't want that either, nor did I want a sophisticated conversation about the house burning up while we were choking from the smoke. I wanted to get back to the kind of trust we had felt the night before and the night before the night before. I wanted to be his lover, his friend, his wife, in sickness and in health. I wanted to grow old with him.

Did he with me? The question was already answered. "Let's go to the movies," he had said.

I saw a film that spring. One scene stuck in my mind. It took place in a concentration camp. Jews were packed into cattle cars on their way to the gas chamber. The Nazi officer was closing the heavy wooden doors. The door got stuck—too many human bodies pressing against it. A Jew stuck his head out through the opening, and with a smile on his face offered, "Can I help you?" He didn't grasp that the Nazi was his enemy. He thought that by his being nice and helpful, things would turn out all right. Together they pulled the door shut, the Jew's smiling face disappearing behind it. The Nazi, his face unmovable, gave the sign to the conductor and the train took off. I cringed when I saw it. I had done the same. I too felt that he who had caused me the wounds was the only one who could soothe my pain.

The only time I saw G.T. cry was when our dog, Lady, died. She was fifteen. She could barely make it up the steps and was peeing all over the place. I resented making the decision but if I didn't, nobody else would. I called the vet. I held her as he put the needle into her. I felt the body in one flash of a second get cold and stiff. That is when I looked up and saw that G.T. had started to cry. We were sitting on the steps when the ASPCA picked up the body and carried her out the door. Lady was an extraordinary dog and deserved tears, but I felt G.T. was crying for something else lost between us.

27

Soon after, G.T. wrote a play called *Nigger Lovers*, the story of a man who kills his beloved dog, a European bitch. She stopped him from living the life he wanted to lead. I played the part of the dog. In the end of the play, her master shoots her. It upset me as if it were a personal warning toward me, but I dared not ask him.

The work helped me get over it and might have helped G.T. if the play had been a hit. The previews were sold out for weeks, and the opening night party was feverish. Around 2 AM people began to disappear and there were few of us left when the public relations man heard the one and only review over the phone. His face made it clear: *The New York Times* was devastating. The next night the house was half empty, cold, and unresponsive. The difference from the night before was extraordinary. And then there was the very real question, "How do we eat tomorrow?"

"Every time we work together, it turns out to be a disaster. Why do I insist upon it; why this constant yearning?" I asked myself. He must have asked himself the same. The next play that G.T. wrote had no part for me. It was *Cannibals*, a play about sons' fantasizing over their fathers' deaths, victims of the Nazi regime. It took him to Berlin and the girl.

It was strange and yet not strange that G.T. of all people would choose to settle down in Germany, a Hungarian Jew brought up in Budapest who had fled his country to escape the destiny of his father, a famous Hungarian journalist killed in a concentration camp under circumstances one can only guess. His death haunted G.T. until he finally wrote the play. It was a moderate success at the American Place Theatre in New York, but it was a sensational hit in Berlin. During our eighteen years of marriage, he never wanted to put his foot on German soil nor buy a German product. Those he had hated now loved him.

I had paid little attention to his involvement with the Germans. I was careless. They offered him money, contracts, a theater of his own—everything he wanted. And then there was the girl, waiting for him, adoring him, in a way I no longer could or would. She was the daughter of a Nazi. He was a Hungarian Jew whose father had been killed in Auschwitz. The road back to those one had once loved is long and winding, and no one can live with hate. Or fear.

4

I am closing the windows in my mother's room. It gets chilly after five when the sun goes down into the lake here way up in the north. I am drinking with my eyes the sight of early Swedish spring. When I come home from abroad I always go to the woods; the smell of the air from the dark-leaved trees and the moss in my childhood country makes me drunk, makes me feel I never left. It feeds my whole body, fresh and uncluttered, as it must have done when I was a newborn babe.

When I was little, my mother saved me from drowning. I have sensual images of her white skin against mine, of being kissed, of my grandmother's arms holding us both, older, thinner. I wanted to pick a water lily for Moa, that's what I called her. (I loved her the way I feel my granddaughter Natasha loves me when she puts her head against the soft part of my shoulder and I tell her Swedish children's stories. She calls me Moa.) I was only two, chubby with long reddish curly hair. As I got closer to the lily, the bottom seemed to vanish. The water holding the delicate, fragile water lily betrayed me, and I sank to the bottom. My mother ran into the water in her white bathrobe. She saved me.

Today I can only hold her hand, turn her body, comb her hair. We have changed roles, only there is less pleasure than with a child. She is only skin and bones and open wounds from lying down too long. It had begun when she was forty-five, this disease called arthritis. She is seventy-two now. Bones twisted and bent by pain, like the spirit when violated by stronger wills, others as well as one's own, causing, whether we like it or not, ambivalence, panic, inactivity. Pain weakens your antibodies.

My mother had been very beautiful, fragile, with long, silky black hair. She was taught all the things that a well-brought-up girl needed to know in order to please the man. What she didn't know was to take herself, her talent, seriously.

Yet she, too, must have felt the conflict between the loving woman and the creative one. She played the piano until her hands began to swell from bad circulation. She painted until her fingers were crippled and she could no longer hold the brush. She painted yellow houses with black roofs and chimney tops that she saw across the courtyard through the kitchen window while watching the dinner on the stove, or the corner of the living room with the old grandfather clock and the sparse winter sun coming in through the curtains. She could still hear the doorbell when we got home from school or answer the telephone or receive the delivery from the butcher.

Today I cherish those pictures. I love seeing her room in Stockholm on the walls in mine, in New York. At the time, nobody took them seriously. "How nice, Karin," one would say, or "How lovely. Is that the house across the courtyard? How charming." As if she were a child coming home from school. If she offered one to you, there would be an embarrassed look. "My God, what do I do with it? I can't throw it in the paper basket, as I do the children's drawings after they have hung on the wall for a few weeks." Neither could she, for they were the only things that affirmed her talent. Since of no consequence to anybody else, they led back only to herself. She drowned in her own paintings. She left hundreds of watercolors behind her. I found them in the kitchen drawers and cabinets, overflowing the disarranged apartment. Her talent was unused, like an actor without an audience.

Not even my father, in his intimacy with her, understood that she was no different from him. He was not an insensitive man; neither was Sigmund Freud. But she was a woman.

The price seemed high for my mother to pay. But to have lost him might have seemed even higher. I understood her better now. "I don't want to pay a price for our love anymore," I had said to G.T. at the end of the marriage. I didn't know about the girl then. I had to eat up those words, vomit them up, and swallow them again. But I must have wanted it.

G.T. kissed me goodbye on the street where we lived for eighteen years—the writer, the actress, and the three children. Only Brandy was with me. We walked upstairs to the third floor into his study, opposite our bedroom: as in a crummy TV drama where the camera closes in on a close-up of the empty closet, we saw there was nothing left, not a jacket, not a sweater, not a pair of pants—just one pair of dirty underwear, slightly yellowish where his penis used to rest! And I hated him. I wished he had died, that the girl had died, that they had been struck by lightning, swept away by winds, and crushed by falling down trees. I wished that I could have killed them both in an orgy so wild, so insane, that nothing would be left except me, me, me!

5

"Your mother's heart is very strong," the doctor, a woman, told me. "It won't give up." It isn't ready, I thought. I had an image of it, pumping and pumping, until it finally was filled. And only then would it let go, peacefully, I hoped, for her, for me.

It was the day before I had to leave her. I had been there for

three weeks. I was combing her hair. It was still black—not a
streak of gray. I was careful for I could feel her skull through the
teeth of the comb. There was barely skin in between. "Do you
love me, Viveca?" she asked.

"Yes, I love you, mama," I said slowly, for I wanted to mean
every syllable. I wish it had come easier, for she had saved me
from drowning once and during those three weeks sitting by her
bedside I had experienced her compassion again, as I had once long
ago as a child in search of white lilies on dark, still shimmering
waters.

She never came back to me that day. She knew it was of no use
any longer. I was leaving for New York, the children, the grandchildren, work, my house. And she had heard me say, however
fumblingly, "I love you."

My mother left us peacefully in her sleep in the fall, when the
leaves were turning red. She left a note behind her: "I wanted to
be joyful but I couldn't." There was no blame in those words; she
simply meant for me to go on trying.

6

I faced my own death one long, black, sleepless night a few
weeks later. I had received an offer to do a film in Madrid.

I arrived by plane from New York. I felt ill, defeated, and so, so
lonely. I experienced feelings as if my mother were pulling me
toward her into the earth. I was overcome by a desperate sense of
defeat for us both. Hers for lack of work, mine for lack of love.
Both for lack of living. It seemed I was caught in a mad journey. I
couldn't stop.

What gave me life gave me death; what gave me strength gave
me weakness; what gave me joy gave me pain. Love turned into
hate, involvement into indifference, success into failure, excitement
into boredom, goodness into evil, generosity into possessiveness. I
had no control over my life, I felt, as if I were on a roller coaster
of emotions forever pushing itself slowly to the top and therefore
forever thrusting itself down with deathly speed into an endless
abyss of blackness and despair. "I can't make it up once more," I
cried out to myself in my dark, medieval-looking hotel room, in a
strange city, in a faraway land. "I can't. I am too weak. I can't."

I felt defeated like my mother as well as humiliated by those
same feelings, for my life had been and was different from hers.
My life had been and still was full of promises! In my mother's

lifetime there was no sisterhood, there was no analyst to help her understand herself. There was no man in her life who could have understood her, because he wouldn't have known how and she could not have taught him, for she didn't know for sure. She was another generation.

I knew in so many ways that I had no excuses, that I was another generation, that despair had nothing to do with age—fifty, forty, or sixty—or with a man leaving me. There were other men. I knew it had nothing to do with being a woman. I had seen Anais Nin making it brilliantly, using her compassion for womanhood, for the world. I had read and played Colette and felt her complexity sparkle with clarity. I had watched Martha Graham and experienced her philosophy, her wisdom and strength. I had seen Agnes de Mille put on her ballets at a time when her body was totally gone because of the stroke.

I knew that the vitality of life was in the gut and that it blossoms in the most unexpected places, like stepmother violets. I had experienced it over and over again from an early age. I knew it. One part of me knew it.

"You have no excuse. None, Viveca," I screamed at myself in that gold-framed mirror in the bathroom, that black night in the hotel in Madrid. I saw her and I spat at her, that ugly lonely pathetic woman-child-martyr, Viveka with a "k." I spat at her again and again until she faded behind my saliva. I finally stumbled back into my large medieval bed, mumbling to myself, "Grace . . . grace . . . grace . . . grace . . . grace . . . grace . . . grace . . . grace . . . You either die or live: but with grace." I gave myself an ultimatum: three months, the deadline being my fiftieth birthday. I pictured myself with a small gun against my temple, like Cheri in Colette's novel. And I knew that, however theatrical, I meant what I had said. I broke out in a cold sweat and fell into a deep sleep.

I faced it that night. The enemy was not G.T., not my mother, not my father, not my brother, not the outside world. The enemy was me, or one part of me. "How far gone is the disease?" was the question.

❧ II ❧

Birth of a Female

<blockquote>
*"My life has been so very full
from the very start and that is
the sole reason I can laugh at
the humorous side in the most
dangerous moments . . ."*
The Diary of Anne Frank
</blockquote>

I LOVE TO FANTASIZE that on the first day of May, the celebration of spring when the stepmother violets search themselves through the cracks in the rocks by the salted sea in my childhood country, my gorgeous strong father made passionate love to my white-skinned and fragile mother, and the moment his sperm went into her body there was total and joyful communion between them. And so, way up in the north, conceived in the air of celebration, a new human being, a female, came into the world between Christmas and New Year . . . the darkest and coldest time, but also one of giving and hope.

What ingredients went into the making of me? How did they feel that night? How much of my father's *joie de vivre* and my mother's despair went into me? How much of my father's impatience and irony and my mother's tenderness went into me? How much of their love and hate? I often feel as if their struggle between each other is still in me, pulling me apart. I am their third child, the last.

They had been married for five years. What did my mother feel that night? Was it a marital obligation? She often hinted to me that sex was just that. And yet her skin was white and soft and lips full and my father was very sexy. Were they passionate that night? Or was she afraid that night she would not be able to give him of herself totally, fully? Or was it one of those wonderful nights when lovemaking is easy, deep, when we feel we have the right to this pleasure, purer than any I know. Was it a night like that?

The name given me was Elsa Viveka Torstendotter Lindfors. Elsa is the name of my two aunts. Viveka comes from the Latin and means life; Torsten is my father's name; *dotter* means daughter (it is an old Swedish custom). *Lind* is the name of a tree and *fors* means stream . . . Lindfors. I have taken other names and dropped them, but always kept my own.

"Let's drive by the place where I was born. We have time," I was talking to Dalas, my Swedish driver, young, blond, always looking for girls, never finding one, and Doug, my American stage manager, older, grayer, not looking for girls. We had just arrived in Uppsala. I was to perform *I Am a Woman* in two schools that afternoon. "The address is Nedra Slottsgatan 6. It means the street below the castle," I explained to Doug. "Isn't it fabulous that I remember it?"

We had been driving through the medieval part of the town. I love the feeling of an old city, an old place. It gives me a sense of continuity. I learned to walk on those ancient rounded stones. "Uppsala was a very romantic town at the time," I explained to Doug, "the mingling of university life and army life, of students and uniforms . . . the perfect combination. In the spring, on the first day of May, there is an old custom. The students throw their old caps in the river and exchange them for new white ones. In the evening there is a big fire on the top of the hill, by the castle. Everybody goes there and everybody is singing. It's the celebration of the arrival of spring. Maybe I was conceived on such a night."

"There is the castle," I screamed. "And down there is the building where I used to live." It looked much more elegant than I remembered. I thought we were poor! There is a movie house next to it. "That's new! If I lived here I could go to the movies every night," I added. "One part of me always yearns to live in a small, old town."

Doug laughed, "But you live in the biggest city in the world."

"Yes, and I have moved enough times in my life. The first time was from here to Stockholm. I was two!"

My father had an old Ford. My sister and brother were sick all the time. Every time we stopped, the car stopped too. My father would have to go out and wind up the engine. It seemed like a forever trip. Today we drove down in an hour and a half and it was a cold day in February and the roads were slippery.

The Volvo pulled up in front of No. 6. "I'll be back soon," I said to Doug and Dalas. Will I? I might just take off forever and ever. I was happy here!

So was my mother, the young wife of a major, beautiful with

three small children. There were parties, festivities, and the security of the weekly paycheck. There was sisterhood among the wives. They helped each other. There was the park across the street and my brother's school around the corner. Life was pleasant in a small town. Loving, too.

I am walking up the old stone steps to the second floor. I remember my sister only vaguely. Blond, blue-eyed, disapproving of my existence, I felt, in pain about it, surely. She was only a year and a half when I was born. She needed my mother still, for herself only. I was aware of none of that. My brother cried easily, but that was then. They had wanted me to be a boy they told me later. I didn't know it then. I was happy in Uppsala.

"Office for Undeveloped Children" is written on the door where we used to live! I laugh and ring the bell. No one opens. The door is unlocked. I walk in. No one is there. I turn right. I walk into a small room. There is a fireplace in the corner. A man comes in. He looks at me strangely. "I am just looking around," I explain. "I was born here. This used to be my room. I won't stay very long. Do you mind?"

"Not at all." He understood. If he noticed tears on my cheek, he didn't show it. It's very Swedish to understand the need for privacy . . . and darkness.

"A soldier's daughter never cries," my father had said. When I was two going on three I wanted to be brave if only for him. It was easy. I was in love with my father.

I wish I hadn't felt I had to leave him for my lover, the father for my children. I wish I could have moved on gently . . .

He used to take me to the stable; he would let me ride in the ring. One of his underlings would lead the horse. He stood in the middle like a king. Joyful, beautiful, in charge. I was the princess in a white fur coat, long red curly hair, my short legs hugging the saddle, and a wonderful smell of sawdust and horse sweat and leather embalming the air. Everything was safe; anything seemed possible.

When I was ill and my mother wanted to take my temperature, I would scream. I wouldn't let her. I knew she would give up and say "Wait until your father gets home," which was just what I wanted.

He put me on his lap. His pants smelled of horse, sweat, sawdust and of him. His hands were rough from holding the reins. He was a jumper and winner of prizes. He hit the thermometer down, then put it in me, firmly, gently. I didn't mind. I trusted him completely. I was only two. I suppose that's how he made love, too.

My father was quite a bit older than my mother. A man with a dashing, romantic past.

When I was a young student in the Royal Dramatic Theatre School and my father knew I had a boyfriend and therefore would understand him, he showed me a large aluminum box that he kept in his office. As he opened it I saw masses of letters, all from a Russian princess. As a young officer he was sent to Moscow for six months and had fallen in love with her. She was married and had three children. When the revolution came, the princess miraculously escaped the massacre and fled with the children to Paris. The prince was killed. When my father finally heard from her and about her extraordinary tale of survival, he had his own family.

One of the daughters, Anastasia, like the name of the play which was my first success in New York, came to stay with us in Stockholm for three months. I was barely eight and when Anastasia told me that my father and her mother had been in love—the idea was unbelievably exciting—we began to speculate, could Anastasia possibly be their daughter? When did it happen? Where? Anastasia knew more about the secrets of sex than I. She was fourteen, and so we were proven wrong. She could have been my good sister. I loved her. Our friendship lasted until she died at the age of forty in Paris, married to a Russian prince.

It was good of my mother to accept her in the house. Taking in the child of a former mistress of my father, with only one servant in help, and treating her as if she were one of her own, was quite a gesture by my mother.

It's strange that I don't ever remember seeing her do work in the house. She must have. I had such an unreal sense of women's value in those days, yet my world centered around them. I seemed to value the achievement of men much more. Yet I knew so little about it or them.

When I was a young actress I was dark and very unSwedish looking, and if they asked me, "Do you have foreign blood?" I answered "Yes, Russian. My father was in love with a Russian princess before he met my mother. That's how I got my Russian blood. She was in his blood and his is in mine now." I denied my mother's, had for some time.

I took a last look at the trees in the park across the street from the little room where I first lived. "How was it?" Doug asked.

"Terrific," I said. "I dreamed of getting married to an officer, having three children and living in a house with a small white fence, meeting him every evening when he came home in his uniform, smelling of horse and sawdust. I would hug him and kiss him and be a good wife. I didn't fulfill the dream," I said, "but I tried."

Doug laughs. "Boring, boring!" He knows me only as the gypsy. We take off to do what we are supposed to do. Put on a show. We have one more to do before we go back to Stockholm.

The move from Uppsala must have been difficult for my mother. She had married an officer. She now found herself married to a businessman. Sweden was demobilizing. The cavalry, the old A3 in Uppsala, was disbanded. My father was not promoted into the Intelligence Service where he wanted to be . . . where he belonged, for he was brilliant. I heard stories that he told some big shot the truth, probably laughingly, unaware of the enemy's need for revenge. He didn't get the job. He decided to change the course of his life and became an intellectual, a publisher, his own boss. He first took a job in a publishing firm in Stockholm just to learn. Within a few years he started his own firm, Lindfors Bokforlan. It was a courageous move, but risky. Our economy was constantly up and down.

My mother, who had nothing to do with the choice, was totally unused to this kind of unstable existence and was often anxious about money. For my father, the new life in Stockholm seemed to offer an exciting possibility. For my mother there seemed to have been a price involved, in more ways than one. I could hear her cry at night. Years later I understood. My father had begun to take mistresses.

When I was at The Royal Dramatic Theatre School, one woman in the class, a whore, or at least that's what they called her, kept mentioning his name, looking at me funny. I hated her. "He is mine," I wanted to tell her. "Mine and my mother's." How unfair I was in my hate. I had an affair with a married man myself shortly after. But in those days for me women were the heavies and men the heroes, no matter.

It was confusing about my brother, for he no longer was one! For me!

The move must have been turbulent for him too. He seemed to get thinner, his eyes blacker. I never saw him cry any more. With the intense intuition of a child, I sensed his defeat one early evening by the swimming pool in his new school. I gave him up then and there, I think.

We were sitting on long, cold benches. My mother, my father, my sister, and I. My brother was one of the boys standing in black woolen swimming trunks at the end of the pool, shivering . . . it gets cold in Sweden in October, much colder in the big city, it seemed. My brother was seven and a half now. Tonight his lips were blue from cold and from shaking nerves. There were new demands on him in the new school, in the new city, confusing his own demands on himself even more so now. My father's will was strong. He wanted my brother above all to be like him.

The signal went off. The boys went splashing into the water, the crowd screamed. The boys made the first lap to the end of the pool, touched the edge, pushed back. The crowd screamed louder. "Where is my brother? I can't see my brother." There is one boy going in the wrong direction. He hasn't even finished the first lap. That can't be him. Where is my brother? The first boy is in, the winner. That's not my brother. The second one, the third . . . none of them is my brother. The truth becomes clear. It is he, the last boy, behind everybody else! He hasn't even made the first length yet! Now he has. Finally.

He is touching the edge, he is turning back, all the others are already in . . . he is the only one left behind in the enormous blue-green swimming pool. The crowd grows silent . . . it's embarrassing to watch failure. But the tiny, thin, black-haired boy is making it anyhow, stroke by stroke, slowly, slowly. Finally he is making it in after all. Nobody cheers him. Nobody knows how to pay attention to the effort. Nobody sees the courage it takes to stick it out. The courage to admit "I am not very capable but I am making it anyhow."

Where was my father? Why did he not support him? Cheer him? His own son?

I started to cry. I cried and cried bitterly. I couldn't stop. I was crying for him, for myself, for the hope that we had all felt, stupid words, setting standards leading to deadly wars. Who set those standards? Who set those images for men and women to live up to? Not I. I was only five. I had adored him. I didn't dare to any longer.

For me the move to Stockholm had been heaven. My mother's mother (Moa, as I called her, as Natasha and Katrina call me), lived there. She was part of the big city. I wanted to be part of it, too. I was in love with her, had been from the day I wanted to pick her a water lily. She lived around the corner from me. I used to sit in the window in the morning in my room and wait until I heard the church bell ring ten. I would run downstairs by myself —in those days there was no danger—up the street, over the cobblestones, passing the pharmacy on the corner with a golden elk above the entrance, and the stationery store. (I loved the stationery store with its smell of paper. At Christmas, it would be filled with nativity cribs, large ones, small ones, medium-sized ones, colored ones. I bought a new one every year. It was made out of paper; you could pull it apart like an accordion and it magically turned into a stage set. The characters were the baby boy, the Virgin Mary, and Joseph the father.)

I didn't want to pass the prison on the right side. It scared me so I crossed the street and ran up the hill.

I turned another corner by the church and there was my grandmother's house. I ran up the steps, rang the doorbell. The maid opened the door. She always had maids. Her house was kept superbly. She greeted me with open arms. I was in heaven. I wanted to be her friend, her very closest friend. I adored her. She was a beautiful woman, half Jewish, elegant with a streak of coarseness.

My grandmother was very dramatic. She used to tell me of movies she had seen. I listened with goose pimples on my arms. She would sit in front of her dressing table, combing her hair, as she told me the story. She had long dark hair with a few gray streaks in it. Sometimes she would let me comb it. She liked it when I scratched her scalp with my fingernails. And she would do the same to me. It felt wonderful! Sensual! Over her dressing table was a painting of an angel carrying a dead child in her arms to heaven. Sometimes she would tell me the Hans Christian Andersen story about the little match girl who died and was going to heaven to her grandmother where she wanted to be.

My grandmother couldn't have been more than fifty-eight years old when she lived alone like me, only she became a widow, not a divorcée. For her, life with a man was over. Her four children were grown and had moved away. There wasn't even the speculation of finding another man, yet she must have been hungry for love as I am. She used to tell me with great passion about her lover in her youth, a piano teacher. He fell in love with her and asked her father for her hand. He was refused. Her grandfather, a wandering Jew from Germany, had come to Sweden in search of security. Certainly his granddaughter ought to experience it. The price had been high for him. The price was even higher for my grandmother. She married my grandfather, a nouveau riche self-made business man. She treated him like a boring child. A strange, slightly sneaky anger seemed to force itself through the elegant facade.

She died in the psychiatric ward of a hospital, cursing, spitting, furious, angry—this elegant lady—using words none of us dreamed she even knew. I still can't grasp that my grandmother is gone. She still exists in me, and I am glad. One day she will tell me all of her story and I will tell her mine.

Natasha, my grandchild, has long dark hair. It was hot the other day. I cut it off. Now she looks like Anne Frank. I don't give her what my grandmother gave me. I am a working woman, and I often feel as if I am violating myself and my grandchild for not returning the gift once given me. And I don't like that. I am struggling with it.

A couple of months ago, Natasha and Katrina were both sick. That's when the structure falls apart for working mothers like my daughter. Lena called. It was an emergency. The need for a grandmother has not changed, but the grandmother's availability has. Luckily I was not performing so I went, figuring I could do my writing out there as I took care of the children. I didn't get anything done. Sick children need you. By the end of the day I was exhausted and couldn't get into the writing. I identified with the grandchildren as I did with my own. I am perfectly aware that I love them passionately and idiotically, and that there is nothing to be done about it. I even like it that way, only I don't want to feel pulled in two directions. It shouldn't be necessary for a woman of my generation.

Fredrika Bremer, a contemporary of my grandmother's, wrote in a letter to the man she loved, the man who asked her to marry him, whom she turned down: "If I were to marry you, I would have to accept it as a full-time commitment. To take care of your house, to bear your children. But I have already made a full-time commitment to become a writer, to be a writer. And I can't change, it is too late." She didn't see it possible to combine the two.

"We don't have to be freaks any longer," Betty Friedan said the other day at a conference. She is right. So when the children were better, and knowing Lena was on her way out to the Island, I decided to leave, no matter. Natasha was unhappy about my going and tortured me. I understood but didn't budge. "That's the whole point, Viveca," I said to myself. "To learn to say no to grandchildren, dogs, and lovers, old ones and new ones, and not feel pressured. Even if they do pressure you. And it doesn't make you a freak!"

It worked. Suddenly she switched, having been crouched over a second earlier. Her whole body went through a chemical change as if a surge of life was poured into her. She lifted her arms like a brilliant ballet dancer. "I send you love, Moa, I send you love," she sang. "She knows not to destroy life!" I thought happily to myself and started the car. Natasha danced around it. Katrina, the younger one, only three going on four, picked up on it and together they fluttered like butterflies toward the gate. I laughed, relieved, as I caught up with them by the end of the driveway. Natasha had pulled her pants down. She was peeing standing up, as I used to do when I was five. I laughed, too, as I slowly drove down the main road. Suddenly I saw them in the mirror dancing down the side path, and, over the sound of the engine, I heard them sing, "We send you love, Moa, we send you love."

I had a dream that night. I was growing a mustache. A woman came up to me, a working woman, an independent woman. "I have a housekeeper now," she said to me, "for my child." She was comforting me as if to say you can be a woman and work and bring up a child or a grandchild.

Would I have understood if my grandmother had taken a lover? Would I have been able to share her with him? She was all mine, I felt.

Natasha was angry with me the other day. I didn't defend her against H.T., my lover after G.T. left. She had put flowers in my cottage on Long Island and a mattress on the floor, taking for granted that she would sleep with me as she often does, although she did suspect that with H.T. things might not be quite so simple. "I am going to sleep here," she said firmly as we entered. H.T. took offense. "If you are going to sleep here, I won't," he said. Suddenly I had two five-year-olds in front of me, fighting about who would sleep with me. Oh God, will it never end? Each time a new man moved into the family, I would be confronted with those possessive struggles between him and the children. And now, it is happening with the grandchildren! I tried to explain to Natasha, "Since I have invited him to come and stay with me, I must ask him," I said.

I did. "Would you mind? It will be so nice, the three of us together."

"I'll drive home, then," he said, red in the face. He then stalked

41

out of the room. Natasha was crying. But he didn't leave. Two hours later, the two of them took a long walk in the woods together.

It is not easy to begin a new relationship at this point in life. "I am fifty-four and you are sixty-one," I said to him as we were driving back to New York. "If you take me on, you end up taking on fifty-four years of past life: children, grandchildren, friends, a dog, and former men, too. I will try to do the same with you."

I am sitting at the dark brown oak dining room table with its eight, straight, high-backed chairs, that once was a wedding present from my grandmother to my mother, and now is standing here in my daughter's cottage on Long Island. The painting of my mother is hanging above me. She is sitting elegantly on a piano bench wearing a low-cut blue velvet dress. Her hair is cut short and chic. Her hands are resting delicately. The artist made them slim and white instead of swollen with blue veins. There are white lilies on the side. A bourgeois painting by a bourgeois painter who only saw a bourgeois woman. She looked sad without understanding why, for she seemed to have what every woman wants. On the opposite side of the room hangs the painting of my grandmother. It is a dark painting. She wears a high-collared dress. Her hair is piled high. She holds a pair of gloves in her hand. She too looks sad, but yearning, and less confused. Two generations of women. Natasha and Katrina, a fifth generation, are playing on the floor. They are both naked. It's a warm day. I am third, writing about us all.

I realize I know so much more about my mother's side of the family than my father's and almost nothing about the men.

I have vague images of my mother's father. He was white-haired, quiet, kind, and distant. He died of cancer of the stomach, like Strindberg. In the arms of a woman, my grandmother at home, like Strindberg. When I came to visit toward the end, before he died, my grandmother would hush me. One day she told me to go in and say goodbye to him. I saw him lying with lit candles around him. I felt no identification with his suffering. I don't remember ever touching him or being touched by him.

My father's father died of a heart attack before I was born. He was a famous surgeon, a gynecologist. He was well known; his discoveries are written up in medical books. (Would he have approved of my hysterectomy?) One of my cousins told me that my grandmother wrote his speeches for him.

42

Gerda, my father's mother, was slight and brittle; she often laughed ironically, like my father. It frightened me the way she handled my mother's darkness. She dismissed it as something ridiculous.

In spite of this I sensed that my father's mother was one of the few fulfilled women I knew from my childhood. She was alive and curious about life. She spoke French fluently and traveled alone to Paris, even lived there for several months. She led a rich and intellectually invigorating life. I was jealous of my sister who spent more time with her. I felt Gerda preferred her to me. Perhaps she was balancing things since my mother's mother openly preferred me. Moa made no bones of her favoritism and although I loved her I suffered from the exclusion from the more intellectual part of my family. I was too stupid to be with them, I thought. The feeling stayed with me.

I was only five when I began first grade, and was taken out of school because I was "too little to do my homework," my mother explained. I *am* too dumb, I thought. I was sitting on the toilet. I have such a clear memory of the moment.

I became ill that fall. I got an infection of the bladder. I needed to pee all the time like a baby. When I did, it hurt. I was put to bed and stayed there for weeks, for months. My sister was in school until the late afternoon. I was alone for hours. I learned to love it.

My room was facing the street. I loved the squeaking sound of streetcars turning the corner below my window. My bed was all white and had dowels. I could look through them as through a prison window, except that I could fly away any time I wanted to. Imagination became my best friend. I would wrap a white handkerchief around my finger and carry out endless conversations with it or him or her or them or, even better, with my fantasy lover, Karl XII. It didn't matter that he had been dead for two centuries. He was dark and mysterious, lonely and a warrior. While my father was in the army in Uppsala, they made a film about Karl XII. They used my farther's regiment in the battle scenes, and my father played one of the generals. It was the one and only time my father was an actor. He is even listed in the Swedish film dictionary for it. I had succeeded in getting a black pom-pom from my father's helmet in the film. I put it in a tiny wooden box together with a picture of a painting of my secret lover. It became my shrine. I was very happy in my room, even if I was sick.

I still love to spend all day in my bed. Fantasizing. I don't even have to get sick to give myself the luxury. This morning I saw a tiny pale moon between the bare tree trunks. It was early and the sky was pale blue. I was alone but I didn't feel lonely.

When I was five, my brother's room was across the hall, as was the maid's room. They kept changing. My mother was a child-woman. How could she possibly give others orders? I remember one maid in particular. She took care of me while I was ill. She was blond, healthy looking in a beautiful way and, as it turned out, pregnant. As she told me, I felt thick and warm and full of feeling. The father of the baby was a man of God, a priest. He had made her with child and then sent her away. He didn't want to marry her. I was the only one who knew. Later when her stomach got too large to hide her condition, my parents sent her away. I never saw her again.

My mother got pregnant, too, that spring, but her baby was stillborn. It was lying outside the womb, never let inside. Did my mother not want it? Had she hoped for time finally for herself? To paint or play the piano or just be more of a woman for her man? She was still exquisitely beautiful. She and my father had gone away for a holiday before the new baby would take up all her time.

I was in the country with my grandmother. The call came in the morning. The pain had hit her in the middle of the night as the train rushed through the landscape toward the south. The pain became unbearable. My father had to pull the emergency brake. The train stopped at the first nearby station. She was rushed to a small hospital and operated on immediately, but the baby was dead. It was a boy and I would remain forever the third child, the odd one without a partner, the little one, for my mother could no longer have another child.

I knew my father had wanted a boy, had wanted me to be a boy, too. My sister had become a tomboy more and more. I didn't want to be like her. I wanted to be a real boy to please my father. A better son than my brother? Finally, my father gave in. I was sitting in his lap, dressed in my brother's pants. "When you are ten years old, I will fly you up to God," he said, "and I will ask God to change you into a boy."

I barely remember my sister. She must have frightened me. Was it that she was the stronger? She was so much faster, tying her shoelaces, running, going to school, anything. I felt I could never catch up.

I remember one particular Christmas Day party. We always went to my father's sister's house that night. They were well-to-do. Fresh pineapple, a rare delicacy in those days, was served as dessert. My sister and my older cousin disappeared into the bathroom. Finally I was allowed in. I was the guinea pig. They put pencils up my behind. It was sexy and marvelous, hateful and ugly, filled with hidden secrets. Strange. My mother would call, "Girls, what are you doing in there?"

They would answer in little girls' voices, sweetly, "Just peeing, mummy." They would look at me and say, "Don't you dare open your mouth."

I admired them for lying, for controlling, for getting what they wanted. I felt utterly dependent on them, as if I were controlled through intimacy, through some unbearably strong blood tie that I wanted to break but didn't dare. Not until years later, when I became stronger. "Fuck them! Who needs them," I thought then. "I have an emotional logic and they don't. I am an artist. They are not." I dismissed them. It was my way out of a dilemma.

It was my mother's family that involved me in emotions, in inner life, in darkness, in the movement of my body and the expression of myself through it. It was my father's family that used thoughts, intellectual ideas, words.

Like my mother and my grandmother and her mother and so on and so forth, I thought I had to make a choice. Either Or.

My grandfather's funeral was the first and last family funeral I ever attended. It felt special to be in mourning. The whole week after his death I wore a black armband on my coat. The day of the funeral I was dressed in black. I wasn't sad. I barely knew him. It was a solemn day, a day carved out of the year. There was time to feel, to cry over life past and present. I sensed the pain without identifying with the grownups. After the funeral, in my parents' apartment, the women removed their veils. I could see their swollen eyes. The men were clearing their voices as if they had colds.

That same afternoon, after a few glasses of wine, the arguments began. Harsh words never to be forgotten between my father and my Uncle Fred, married to my mother's sister Elsa, whom I adored. She and my mother cried bitter tears. It was all about money. It seemed ridiculous, for Uncle Fred was extremely wealthy. There was nothing the women could do. It seemed even more ridiculous since it was their father who had died. That was the last time the two men spoke to each other for the rest of their lives. It made it hard for the two sisters. Despite this, they remained friends forever.

"Don't fight about the furniture," my mother used to tell me. It was useless. After her death, my sister and I fought over a silver spoon. How ridiculous. "Keep the spoon," I said. I couldn't cope. Couldn't cope forty years ago, either.

It was my mother who understood something about me, perhaps because she never dared ask for it herself. It was my mother who took me to Jeanna.

She first wanted to enter me in the ballet school at the opera. We sat on the cold stone steps of the old building and waited for the office to open. Perhaps she had made a mistake about the time. Perhaps she was just impatient. Perhaps she was a spoiled, fragile woman who easily gave up. Perhaps she did not want for me the strict discipline that the classical ballet demands, and perhaps she wanted for me something else, a freer form. She suddenly pulled me away and took me to a young, modern dance teacher instead, to Jeanna. I remember it as if it were yesterday.

I stood in my new black leotard in the simple dressing room with benches. A drawn curtain separated me from the studio. I can see it still, clearly, in front of me, as if in a film or in a dream, or in my past life, which is becoming more and more real. I see a large, empty space, where the possibility of happenings is endless. The sheer white curtains are gently moving, dancing, playing hide and seek with the pale September sun on the shiny birch floor. There are bars along the walls. There are mirrors too. I can see myself clearly, with no possibility of hiding. At the far end of the room a door suddenly opens. She entered, dressed in a mauve leotard, a skirt tied around her voluptuous body, her coarse black hair freely falling around her beautiful strong Jewish face. With her is a man, her lover, tall, blond, dressed in uniform. I didn't hear what they said, but she was laughing as she kissed him goodbye. Then she moved toward me.

It was Jeanna who taught me to dance, to put my fantasies into forms, to turn my dreams into actions.

A year later, I changed the spelling of my name from Viveka with a "k" to Viveca with a "c." I took my life in my own hands. I created an image of a woman different from my mother, different from any woman I had known. I wanted to be a dancer. I wanted to be an artist. I wanted to be joyful with a man. I wanted to be like Jeanna.

46

2

*"I have made up my mind now to
lead a different life from other
girls and later different from
ordinary housewifes."*
The Diary of Anne Frank

"A little girl nine years old, eyes glittering and blue, a mouth so red and turned up nose with freckles, her walk a dance on toes, she smiles and plays all day, embracing life with joy, and Viveca is her name, little girl, rich will be your lot, if you forever keep the magic gift, to love what is great and good, to do the right thing whether in large or small." My father wrote me a poem on my birthday.

There was an unmistakable clarity about me now. It didn't matter to him or to me any longer whether I was a boy or a girl. I just was. We both knew it.

But Viveca with a c was still fragile. The wind easily blew her away. The flame easily burned her to nothing, it seemed.

My grandfather, the white-haired, kindly gentleman, nouveau riche, looked down upon by my father's family, the self-made man whom I barely knew, finally had an effect on my life. With the money he left behind, my mother bought a large rambling wooden house in Lidingo, one of the suburbs outside of Stockholm. It was her last chance to get to the kind of bareness needed for an artist. She was free now. We were no longer babies. The time was finally her own. But she chose once more to get involved in "woman's work." Moving and changing is time-consuming. Yet this time it was her money, her house, her move, her choice.

The price was high, higher than the last time. The atmosphere in the suburbs was not stimulating her already weakened desire to be an artist. The price was high for me, too, this time.

I was given everything a teenage child is supposed to want. A house in the country, trees, garden, flowers in the summer, and ski slopes in the winter. Eventually a bicycle, a red one. Fresh air. Rooms with terraces. Almost my own bathroom. Eventually my own bathroom. A dog, totally my own. I didn't want any of it except, maybe, the dog.

I wanted the city where everything was possible, everything within reach. The city where the streetcars woke me in the morn-

47

ing, suggesting trips to faraway places and yet not too far; where the court musicians sang their tragic tales, making themselves less tragic; with the stationery store next door and the pharmacy with the golden elk over the entrance in the corner; with the foreign school and its quiet nuns affirming the spirit, the boundless imagination, and the graveyard reminding me of death, of a limit.

I wanted the city where I could run to my grandmother's all by myself, without arrangements; where the street lights would gently go on in the afternoon and barely noticeably tell me night was arriving, and, when blackness came, burn strongly and compassionately.

I wanted the city with the park across the street from where we lived, where the rustling of the leaves was mingled with human voices, human-made sounds where I would walk on Sunday mornings with my parents, meeting other families, seeing us in them. My mother held my left hand, my father my right. It was just the three of us.

I wanted the city where Jeanna lived, the only woman I had seen who was happy, the only woman I had ever met whom I wanted to be like, wanted to be near. I needed her as I needed myself. I needed to dance in her studio with the flowing curtains and the music filling the air, letting me fly, letting me leave myself behind and yet not.

It was all gone now. I cried and cried and cried. Nobody understood why. Neither did I. I couldn't say: I want to dance; I can give of myself through dance, only through dance, not through you . . . or you . . . or you . . . or you or you or you. I can't! I can't live your kind of life. I can't!

I couldn't say it, only cry.

Finally my parents realized something was missing in my life and arranged for me to go to Jeanna on Thursdays after school. The ride into town was complicated with trains and buses and, to want to be a dancer as I did, once a week is not enough. Dance is a way of life.

There was another girl. Her name was Viveka, too, spelt with a 'k', a strange coincidence, for it is an unusual name even in Sweden. She lived around the corner. She danced every day. Her body was brilliant. I forced my body too hard, wanting to get to her level, and I injured my hip. I went to the doctor. "Don't dance," he said, "for a year. Don't dance." That's when I gave up.

I hated myself for it. I felt somehow that I lacked the courage of my conviction. Like my mother.

I ran smack into her, that awkward, lost, withdrawn, ungenerous girl, thirty years later, when the Volvo station wagon with me, Doug, Dalas, props, and theatrical paraphernalia for the *Woman* show turned the corner of the building that used to be my school in Lidingo. I ran smack into her, that sullen, defeated little girl with uncombed reddish-brown hair, longing to get out of the classroom, out of herself, not knowing why, as I do today.

I had no idea that it was in my old school I was to perform that morning. I didn't even know where I was. Things had changed. There were new buildings, new roads. "I don't even recognize the bridge," I said to Dalas and Doug as we crossed over it from Stockholm. "I used to be afraid I would be caught in the train tracks when I bicycled across it. I don't see them anymore."

"It's a new bridge," Dalas explained. "Look down to the right, that's where the old one is. It's only used by people who walk."

I also walked it when I had been to the movies. It saved me twenty-five öre. If I had seen Ginger Rogers and Fred Astaire, I would tapdance across it. I was in love with the American movies, with American movie stars. I had begun to dream of becoming one myself.

There was a filmmaking couple, Mr. and Mrs. Svanstrom, living around the corner from where we lived. One day I wrote a note and tied it to the collar of their dog, an old, fat dachshund. "Hello. I want to be in the movies. I am ten going on eleven. I have freckles and red hair. I live around the corner." Maybe the message was lost. I never heard from them.

My first film role as an aspiring actress was as a maid in the film *Crazy Family*, produced by the Svanstroms. I told them the story. We laughed.

I was telling Doug and Dalas all about it when the car turned the corner and I recognized the building. I screamed, "It's my old school. God, it *is* my old school."

The school hadn't changed at all. There was the courtyard with the gravel where I could park the bicycle or put my skis up against the wall in the winter. It took me an hour to ski to school. I loved the feeling of the skis sliding over the snow, my body moving as in dance. Snip, a black mongrel like Brandy, patiently waited for me underneath my classroom window. Snip followed me around. I could cope with his love. It made no demands on me that I couldn't fulfill, unlike my mother's. Her needs overwhelmed me in the country. The hugging, the clutching, as if I were a security blanket against her anxieties. And I didn't *want* to love her anymore. I was angry with her. She never took my side. And she hadn't understood—after all—how much I needed to dance. And in the country there was no escape.

The summer had been so different. The summer had been the beginning of tasting that exquisite feeling of belonging to the world, not just the family.

To make the move easier for my mother, Bjarne was sent to Germany to learn the language and I to my Aunt Elsa's and Uncle Fred's in the Stockholm fjords. Only Marga stayed home. She had to have a tonsil operation and needed to be taken care of, perhaps given the attention she never got as a baby. She was only a year and a half when I arrived on the scene.

In the beginning I was homesick. I had never lived this kind of life. They owned a brilliantly beautiful country estate, a castle. It scared me, this life of luxury, servants, food, fruits and candies always standing around in delicate glass bowls available for anybody, the tennis courts, the sloping green lawns, the flowers. I couldn't appreciate it. I slept alone for the first time in my life. My two cousins slept in the nursery. I was the oldest this time. It was all quite scary, but I got over it.

My aunt was, and is, a generous and joyful woman. She had that special quality of saying yes to life, of always seeing the positive side of the moment. It is astonishing that two sisters can be so different in their attitudes toward life. For my mother, the scales always tipped toward the side of pain. It's not meant as a judgment, and I know today that, had she been able to use it for her painting or playing the piano, it might have equalized itself.

My aunt was pregnant that summer with her third child, her belly like a football, growing larger each day. I can still feel the palm of my hand against her expanded stomach, sensing the movement of the baby, the wonder of it all. I would touch it carefully, as if I might hurt it. I didn't know then of the power of a woman's body, but I sensed it.

She was a wonderful mother. One day, years later, I asked her —the children were grown up by now—"Elsa," I said, "how did you do it? How did you bring them up so beautifully?"

She laughed at me. "Bring them up? Viveca, darling," she said, "I wouldn't have known how. I just loved them. That's all."

She loved me too that summer. She made no difference between me and her own children, the way my mother had with Anastasia.

I fell in love with my Uncle Fred. I sat for hours in his lap, listening to him, adoring every word he said. He took me into his confidence, shared thoughts and ideas with me. Nobody had ever done that before. I was special to him and he to me. His passion turned on mine and it wouldn't have mattered to me what he said. At the age of ten, I easily could have become a Nazi, for my uncle was one. He was obsessed with the idea of the Master Race, the purity of the Vikings. He was an important member of the party in Sweden. He seemed to have forgotten that his wife's mother was Jewish, that his children had her blood in their veins, as I had.

(I did not know myself that I was part Jewish until I was past twenty-five, when I fell in love again, this time with a Jew.)

I came home that summer to the new house in Lidingo feeling very special about myself. I lost it quickly. During dinner I started to tell about my wonderful summer. It was perhaps not the best time. Family meals were an institution in our home and always tense to begin with. We had to stand behind the straight, tall, dark chairs and wait for my father. I finally could see over them. When he arrived, we sat down, my father at the head of the table, my mother at the other end, my sister on one side, my brother and I on the opposite side. When everyone had finished eating, we would get up, kiss my father's hand first—a rough beautiful hand. Then I would have to kiss my mother's hand. It was swollen from the frostbite she had gotten as a young girl. Sometimes it was bluish, sometimes very white. It felt physically uncomfortable for me. Yet, often when I work on the stage I think of their hands and I am in touch with my basic feelings in no time.

That evening, my first meal in the new house in Lidingo, I began to tell them about my Uncle Fred, about his political beliefs, now also mine. My sister, still sick after a tonsilitis operation—she wore a scarf around her neck—started to cry. Indignantly she told me how cruel the Nazis were toward the Jews, how wrong I was. Her compassion seemed way out of proportion. I still didn't know what a Jew was. I only knew about the purity of the "Master Race" and that my uncle was one of them, that he was passionately involved and committed, that he adored me and I him, that we had given each other pleasure, and so I didn't believe a word of what my sister said. I was about to answer her back when my father spoke up and agreed with her.

It was devastating. Suddenly everything became worthless. I didn't say a word nor did I ask for an explanation. "What's the use?" I thought, feeling defeated. I had tried to be part of life, of the world, for the first time. "Wrong choice again, Viveca. Wrong choice."

My father was ambitious about educating us, but unaware of a lack of moral consistency and its imprint. Like many other Swedish parents, he sent his son, my brother, to Germany to learn the language, but was not worried about the confusing atmosphere in the Nazi home where Bjarne was staying. Hitler was now in power, although the war had not yet begun. Bjarne was only fourteen. When he brought Wilhelm, a Nazi *Jugeng*, back with him to spend equal time in a Swedish family, he was allowed to speak about his political beliefs, when Uncle Fred and I were dismissed for ours. It made me angry.

The feeling in me erased the real issue. If there was anything I should have understood or learned that day at Lidingo, I didn't. On the contrary, I decided, "I'm not smart enough for politics. It is not my territory." Children are easily formed.

I have often wondered how it affected Bjarne to be exposed to the "justified" violence of the Nazis that summer when we moved to Lidingo. How could he continue to trust my father who spoke about doing the right thing "whether in small or large"? And if he couldn't trust him, how could he trust himself? He couldn't. Bjarne finally chose to commit violence, but, unlike the Nazis, against himself rather than against others.

So did my Uncle Fred. He shot himself a few years after that summer, after the war was over. By then he had moved away from my aunt, the most loving woman I have ever known, and the four children. He chose to live with another woman. He died in the hospital. He had cancer and someone had smuggled a gun into his room.

I saw a photograph of my father and my brother in an old album among the papers sent me after my mother's death. My brother is four, maybe five years old, breathtakingly beautiful, like a fairy tale prince. He is holding on to my father's hand with both his hands. He is laughing. He is happy. Neither my father nor Bjarne knew how to keep their love alive. The photograph tells its own truth. The promise is here in black and white.

Dear God, let me hold onto it always!

Ten years ago in the first therapy group with Madame—I was forty-five—I met Arthur, a Jew. He was short, stocky, ugly, past fifty, gray-haired. He had escaped from Austria having grown up under fear of the Nazis. He owned a small jewelry store in New Jersey. Time and time again he was robbed by Puerto Ricans and each time he found it impossible to report them to the police.

"I feel too guilty," he said. "You are forgetting they are the minority *and* the criminal, as well. Not like you. Stand up for your rights." The group tried, exhausted after years of trying, but he couldn't. He couldn't separate using power from misusing power. The image was too deeply imprinted in him.

One evening, a woman in the group whom he liked, perhaps even loved, burst out at him. "I hate you. I have been wanting to tell you I hate you." Her voice was low and deep. It was difficult for her to say it. It was her way of getting rid of the Arthurs in her. It was her way toward health. But not his. He could not take more hate, for he could not hate himself.

"My heart," he said as he moved his hand toward it. He smiled an embarrassed smile.

"Come on, Arthur, face it, don't cop out, it's just an excuse." The group had no pity. Nobody believed him, although we knew he had had two attacks before.

"No, no," he said, confused by the argument but convinced by the pain. "It hurts here." He pointed again toward his chest.

Being Swedish or a mother or an actress, or finally on the road to health, I heard someone else's scream over my own. "I don't think he is well," I said. I opened his shirt and made him lie down. By now I was angry with the rest of the group, for, no matter what, you must accept someone else's truth as he tells it to you. "Call the hospital," I said. Madame went to the phone. The others sat there, still not wanting to believe for reasons of their own. Afraid to feel compassion for the victim, perhaps. Afraid it would make them victims. I must have finally learned something!

I put his head in my lap, rocked him gently, but the pain grew steadily worse. The ambulance came. They carried him down. I went with him. The last time I saw him he was stretched out on the hospital bed. He looked like a spider with wires coming out of his body trying to connect him with life. He smiled at me. "I love you," he said.

"I love you, Arthur," I answered.

The next morning when I called the hospital, he was dead.

The group went to his funeral. It was a hot spring day. We drove to New Jersey where he lived, where his sister lived, too. The temple was filled with people. For a moment, it surprised me. I had thought of him as isolated and alone, but then, of course, that was no real contradiction, for what he needed was a deeper intimacy. He had tried it fumblingly with us. We were his only lead to himself but he couldn't break through the wall to his own sense of worth. Power over his own life turned to violence. No matter. History had set too deep a mark in him.

It was a hot, smoggy afternoon. I hated the mediocrity of the funeral, the machines sinking the coffin down into the earth, instead of human hands, the fabricated grass laid down on top, instead of real earth already familiar with death, and seeds of grass planted, taking their own time to grow. I hated the denial of a simple ritual—allowing nature to play its own given role. I hope that my children, when that day comes, will take my ashes and scatter them into the sea and then drink a toast of champagne—the very best—to the continuation of their lives and choose to spend the rest of the day in Pegasus' world. Hopefully, they will hug each other or touch in some way, unafraid of intimacy.

The group didn't talk much on the way out or on the way back, but it felt right to be there, all of us together. The people in the temple were intrigued by us, so distinctly different from them. They knew Arthur had died among us. If they felt we were the killers, they didn't let us know.

The woman who told him "I hate you," changed her profession from a teacher and is today a psychiatrist dealing with disturbed children. She was given a second chance, as I had been. We were lucky. Our journeys were not yet completed, as Arthur's was, as my brother felt his was.

The summer when I was ten going on eleven, when we moved into the big wooden rambling house in Lidingo and I had everything a teenager is supposed to want, my sister became my tormentor. I could not free myself from her any longer.

My sister was the only one who was happy in the country. Of the three of us she was the only one who had stayed with my mother that summer, who had been part of the move, who felt at home. Lidingo became her territory.

She was a tomboy. She played kickball with the boys. She was one of their buddies. She stood in the net! She jumped from the highest ski slopes. Her courage was extraordinary. For the first time I felt threatened by her. She seemed so much more intelligent, sensitive, so much more decent and pure, confusing since none of those virtues ever seemed directed toward me. She never took my side as she had for the Jews, I thought. Neither did my mother, especially not in front of my father. How could I ever trust either of them!

Another stupid incident happened that first year in Lidingo, another effort to be part of a group, not to be special or the little one, to belong! We were playing on the tennis court, my sister and I, with a group of new neighbors, maybe friends. Much was at stake. One girl in the group was a bitch and a bore and drove us all mad. I took charge and picked up a racket and hit her over the head, not too hard, but hard enough so that she ran home to her mother, our new neighbor, screaming. Hurrah! She was gone! Everybody was cheering me, including my sister. The mother called my mother, of course. Shocked, she questioned me.

"Yes. I did hit her," I said, "she deserved it. Everybody knows it."

"Wait until Daddy comes home," she answered, seemingly disinterested in my side of the story and unable to teach me how to be in charge of a situation. "Go to your room," she said.

"Ask Marga," I said, but Marga was gone. She was playing with the rest of the group.

When my father came home in the evening, he called me into the library. My mother was sitting next to him, smiling her embarrassed smile. "Pull down your pants," he said. He didn't ask me why I had done it. He simply took my mother's word and attitude. The game of punishing instead of showing new ways of living continued. I had seen him do it to my brother. I never believed he would do it to me.

"Here, lie down," he said.

The tension in one's body when one knows one is going to be hurt is incredible. My teeth were chattering. I tried to hold them together. I lay across his knees, and, with his hand, strong and hard—he was still a rider—he beat me. "You don't hit anyone with a tennis racket," he said.

He was right about not hitting anybody over the head with a tennis racket. But he was wrong about not listening to me, not understanding the importance of what was happening to me. Did he not know me? Just as I was walking out, my pants hanging down, not crying (a soldier's daughter never cries), did he say, "Why did you do it?"

Now he wanted to know! I didn't answer. I kept walking out, mumbling to myself, "I don't trust you any longer! I didn't think you were ever going to do this to me! Not you! I hate you! You take advantage of your power! I hate you! From now on I will hate you!" I went to my room and sat in the window that whole evening. I sat there the whole next day, watching the group play without me. Nobody seemed to care. The world was now on the opposite side.

The anger about it all came months later. I threw a stone the size of a baby's head at my brother. I missed, but I meant to kill him. I took it out on him and he had nothing to do with it or the move, the injustice, and he, too, must have been deeply angry.

The competition between my sister and myself became worse. I avoided seeking any of her battlefields in school, in studies, in sports.

My sister was an intellectual. She read everything. Our house was filled with books; my father, being a publisher, talked and read books. Not me. I never read a single book. My sister is dumb, I maintained. In spite of all that reading she knows nothing about life. I do. I will. And for a long time I only read what I needed for my work.

Sometimes I wonder if I chose to become an actress only because it was a safe area, an area where she was not. Competition became a driving ambition. When I gave it up forty years later on the analyst's couch, I was in a panic as if I had been robbed of my main motivation. Not true. I had only used it as a confusing substitute. No more! Let my life be bare!

It was my sensuality that put me into the sunshine and out of the shade when I was twelve going on thirteen, changing from a girl into a woman—not into a boy as my father had promised years before. I thought he had wanted that more than anything but I was wrong. He seemed delighted in discovering my female charms. So was I. And when Alaric, a boy who lived around the corner and was one grade ahead of me, told me, one cold, snowy night on top of a hill, that I had stars in my eyes, I forgot that I had wanted to be a boy, about the struggle with my sister and the loss of dancing. I began to want again!

Margaretha was way behind me suddenly. I was much prettier, too, and we both knew it.

At parties at our house the older men all paid attention to me. The three of us would help serve—my brother in black pants and a white shirt with a black bow tie, my sister and I in black dresses with white aprons and little white caps like the ones the maids wore. My brother would serve the wine, my sister the main course, and I would tramp after her with the sauce or the lingenberries or the cookies for dessert.

At parties everybody was in a festive and totally different mood. My father would give speeches written as poems. There was a poet in him although he chose to be a publisher, publishing others' works. My mother, after a glass of sherry, would become flirtatious and lively.

At the parties were artists, intellectuals, and friends from the

Uppsala time, and when the guests left we were still allowed to be up and help them on with their coats. I got more tips than the other two and I knew why. I liked it, although I wasn't sure I had earned it.

My brother, like my father, was proud of my newly discovered sex appeal. He showed me off to his friends in a loving way, also like my father.

It was my brother who taught me to foxtrot, to waltz, to tango. He wanted me at the dance he and Marga were giving that following weekend. "Come on," he said. "Loosen the arm. The arm should be loose." He was rough. He enjoyed being the controller, the authority, the teacher. I was scared but I wanted to please him. I wanted to do well. I needed it. I wanted to be at the party! I charmed and I smiled and I seduced. He put his arm around me tight, but saw to it that my body didn't touch his or his mine.

I discovered why during the party, dancing with one of his friends. I could feel the penis dangling against my crotch. I felt funny and kept holding myself away, as with my brother. When we turned off the lights, he pressed me against him. It wasn't funny anymore. It was nice. I felt warm.

I had borrowed my mother's dress. It was black and white and sexy. I was a success. My sister was not. Her buddies were still her buddies but they all wanted to dance with me.

I finally felt strong enough now to fight her and I knew where it would really hurt. She was a Girl Scout, a devout one, a leader. I had been a Girl Scout, too, but soon realized I loathed every moment of it and I refused to go. I finally knew what I wanted and didn't want. Yes, I was getting stronger. "I hate you, I hate you," I screamed as I threw the Girl Scout Manual, her bible, at her. I had been waiting for this moment of revenge. I hurled it across the room. It hit the wall and fell into pieces like snowflakes falling over her. She cried; I laughed.

Our parents built a wall, splitting the room up in two, but it didn't help. There was too much history between us now. The game would have to continue.

"There are different ways of learning, of achieving what it is you want to achieve," I thought to myself forty years later, sitting on the stage in the auditorium in my old school in Lidingo. I looked out into the house. "Not much has changed," I thought. "All the walls are painted bright yellow today instead of gray as they were then, but all colors are beautiful." The crowd was noisy and lively and I began to see Bjarne in the boys and myself and my sister in the girls. I saw us in the teachers, too. I started to laugh, close to tears, and began the performance by telling the audience what it meant for me to be there that day, that I was finally able to use the place, that it finally had become mine, too, for I was part of it now.

It was a brilliant morning. It became a brilliant afternoon, too. For the extraordinary coincidence was that I was to perform *Woman* that same afternoon in my sister's school where she is a professor of German and English, where she has worked for twenty-five years, where she is loved and appreciated by students and parents, where she has created a life for herself.

I had just freed myself from a partnership with another woman. It had been a painful process, as if she were the sister I had always wanted and never found. I had only known this woman for three years, but had come to love her. She was wonderful when I was in pain after G.T. left. I could call her any time of the night. She would listen and believe me. Eventually, we decided to go into business together. As I grew stronger and I insisted that we deal with each other on an equal level, I felt as if I had become a threat to her, that she perhaps preferred me to be the weaker. Things became unbearable. We finally split and it was painful, for I had loved her like my sister.

I don't know if Marga ever acknowledged that she wanted to be the stronger; I know I did—as well as the weaker. I will continue to meet her in other women and shake inside until I am completely over the spasm of competition.

Doug, Dalas, and I arrived in the Volvo at my sister's high school, where she is principal, right after lunch that same day.

It was early spring, still chilly, but the apple trees were beginning to bloom. "I am going for a walk," I said to Dalas as I put my black canvas bag on the stage. I traveled lightly for the school shows. I use only a few props, a wig, a shawl, and the mask, of course. No costumes. It all has to happen during a class period, fifty-five minutes. I do a few scenes and poems from the show in English but then explain and do the dialogue in Swedish. The boys spoke more than the girls in Sweden. The opposite is true here in the U.S.A.

As I returned to the building, I saw my sister pass through the crowd going up the steps. I hadn't seen her since our fight about the silver spoon a few weeks after my mother's funeral. Marga had started to shout at me with such conviction, as if deadly injustice had been done to her, that I didn't know how to handle it.

I knew I didn't want to throw a book at her any longer. I couldn't stand hate anymore. Didn't believe in releasing it, either. I *did* begin to shake, as I had when G. T. left, as if I deserved the punishment. That was two years ago. This morning I wanted to face and cope with her differently. I didn't want to depend upon revenge, upon being the stronger, or the weaker. Must find another way!

But I wasn't ready. I let her disappear. She seemed harried. Perhaps she too was tense. There had been much in the papers. The show is personally connected to my life and I talk openly about our past. It must have been strange for her to read about it, different, perhaps, from her memories, her impressions. I didn't mention her too often. If someone had asked me about her, I might have said that I had wanted to finish our relationship many times but never could, and probably never would.

I continued backstage to check the technical part with Dalas and prepare for the performance. The stage was open. No curtains. The audience began to fill up the house and was watching me with some curiosity. Showtime was coming closer when I saw Margaretha coming down the aisle.

My God, she walks just like my father. Her body is just like my father's, flashes through my mind. I study her this time. Her hair is lighter. She was always a blond, but now there is white mingled in. She has gotten heavy. She is wearing a light blue dress. I never liked the way she dressed. I never liked the way she combed her hair. She was awkward. It used to irritate me. Did I need her image to affirm my own? Do I still?

She is walking very slowly. She hasn't discovered me yet. She is coming closer. I suddenly see someone bringing her a wheelchair. Why? She was walking fine half an hour ago. I am suspicious. Come on, Viveca! Be generous! Maybe she is in pain! You know about a weak back! What other similarities are between us and why is it so terrible to face them?

The first time I saw myself on film, I saw my sister in myself. I recognized the sullenness, the need for withdrawal, even the control. I panicked. I am familiar with that woman in me now. I don't like her always, but I do take her seriously.

I walk up the aisle to greet my sister. After all, she asked me to perform in her school. I can't go on the stage without having said hello to her. It's simple.

We hug each other, and yet we don't. I am moved, but I don't want to cry. She introduces me to her colleagues.

"What can I do to help?" she asks me.

"Nothing," I say. "Everything is fine. I love your auditorium. It's light and modern."

"Yes, we are proud of it," she says. And then again, "Can't I do anything to help?" She is telling me in a nice way that this is her place, and I sense a flash of the old spasm.

Oh God! Am I still allergic to her taking care of me? For years I was haunted by a fantasy about the two of us. My worldly shallow life collapsed and I had come home to her begging for shelter. The sinful sister returning to the good one, the pure one. "No, no," I say to her. "I am fine." I wanted to break the pattern. All patterns.

I go back on the stage. The lights dim down.

"Pegasus comes on speedy wings./Inviting you to follow into the world of creativity." Lines from another poem that my father wrote to me go through my head.

The audience became one enormous human being that morning, my sister, myself. I invited her, all of her, to join me in Pegasus' world. She does. They all do. Only she is one with more "inside information."

During the dialogue one of the students asks me, "How can you go so quickly from laughter to tears and vice versa?"

"It was easy," I answered. "My sister is in the audience. There has been an ocean between us in more ways than one: an ocean of emotions, unspoken sentences, happening, never talked about. I used it all for the work this afternoon."

> To follow Pegasus on his proud journey
> Towards his high goals, courage is needed.
> Life is not a lazy nirvana.
> Life is hot as fire, cold as steel.

This was the rest of the poem our father had written. We both knew what he meant now.

Under the umbrella of art, all walls seemed to crumble. Perhaps she, too, felt it.

Just as I was about to say goodbye, a young man jumped up on the stage. He was about sixteen, blond, tall, graceful, and gallant. He kicked his heels, bowed, and handed me a bouquet of flowers. I laughed and felt a flow of strength coming over me, like strong, wild water.

"He reminded me of Father," I said to Marga as we walked to my car.

"Yes," she said and looked at me quickly with her light blue eyes as if she also was afraid of starting to cry.

3

"When did you decide you wanted to be an actress? I mean, how old were you?" my granddaughter Natasha asked me. She was about four or five. We were riding in the car to go swimming. I have had many intimate conversations with children in cars.

She had looked at a painting of my mother's that morning. "Viv," as she sometimes calls me, "She was an artist, your mother." And then she set about copying it. She was frustrated when she didn't have the exact color crayon. Maybe Natasha will be an artist, too. She draws brilliantly, I thought to myself as I tried to answer as carefully as I could.

"I was six when my mother took me to dance class," I said, surprised by the question. "I knew somehow I wanted to be an artist already then. I felt good when I danced. I didn't know how to say it, but I knew. When I was about thirteen, I said it aloud for the first time—I want to be an actress."

"Were you married then?" she asked. That question surprised me at first but I answered seriously.

"No."

"When did you marry?" she asked.

"When I was eighteen I married John's father."

"Why are you still not married to him?"

Here we go again, I said to myself. I am going to have to explain to my grandchild all about my various marriages.

"I was kind of careless in my choice," I said. "I didn't ask myself, 'Can he be a father to my children?' I didn't think it through." I was too busy becoming an actress. But then I didn't ask myself about being a mother, either. I simply took it for granted. But I didn't say that to her.

She was very quiet. Then she said, "My daddy will always stay married to my mommy."

Natasha, at the age of five, wanted to combine it all—work, love and commitment.

It was my father who introduced me to words, who taught me the beauty of words. Together we read poetry.

I was thirteen when I entered a poetry reading contest and I came in second!

My father had moved my sister and me to a new school in town for girls to expose us to "femininity and grace" as he said. My sister was more of a tomboy than ever before and I was still in a fog about myself, except for boys.

It was my last school. I had two years before graduation and I never really felt at home. But it was the best school that I had been to and it gave me my chance.

I had worked on the poem together with my father, who was quite a talented actor, filled with bravura and a "larger than life quality." Had my father made it his career he would have become a popular leading man, probably a great actor, and would have been allowed to be a more sensitive man.

Kristoffer, my youngest son, is the only one of my children who looks like him, has his temperament, his hands, his chin. The other day, he caught me crying. He put his arms around me, didn't say anything, just held me. He is a sensitive man and a fine actor.

The poem that my father and I had chosen, by Gustave Froding, a poet from Dalarne, was joyful. I read it with a certain bravura, a certain quality larger than life. I knew I made a hit and I should have won first prize, but the girl who read a sensitive, serious poem and was plain-looking did. That's why, I thought, being young, attractive, and arrogant. It didn't matter for I got a part in the school play the next season.

My part was that of a businessman. I wore a gray suit, I smoked a cigar and put a pillow under the jacket. My father, the major who used to be tall and thin, riding wild horses, jumping over hurdles in his blue gold-braided uniform, was now a businessman in a gray flannel suit, sitting behind a desk, smoking cigars, and making deals over long lunches. He had gotten heavier. It was easy to portray him. I studied him with the objectivity of a daughter. I saw his tricks, his charms, his weaknesses. I sensed a change in him and it suited my purposes.

I must have done well, for Olaf Winnerstand, a fine actor at the Royal Dramatic Theatre, said about me after the performance, "that Lindfors girl has talent." It went click in me. He is dead now and I never told him how much it meant to me. But a few days afterwards I made up my mind.

Three of us—Greta, Ingrid, and myself—were on an island, the same island where Strindberg's *Dance of Death* takes place. It is a military island and Ingrid's father, a general, was stationed there. We were spending a weekend together. In the middle of the night we were fantasizing in whispers about the future. "I am going to

Karin Dymling; my mother's engagement photograph

Viveka, 1923

My father, my sister Marga, and my brother Bjarne. Bredsjo, 1921

Blood Wedding *by Garcia Lorca. I found myself going beyond boundaries I had never even imagined.*

My first film. Swimming naked through Stockholm—In Paradise, *Luxfilm, 1941*

Before leaving Sweden in 1941 (PHOTO: SVENSK BILDREPOTAGE)

Georg Rydeberg and I in If I Marry a Minister, Luxfilm, *1941: "Does he really mean 'I love you'
when he says it in front of the camera?"*

Folke Rogard and I, 1946

Harry Hasso and I, Lidingo church, 1941

John, Lena, and I, Christmas, 1945 (PHOTO: KARL G. KRISTOFFERSON)

First day on the lot—with Joan Crawford and Curt Bernhardt—"I want to give a party for you," Crawford said.
(PHOTO: LLOYD MACLEAN, WARNER BROS.)

First day on the lot—Gary Cooper, tall and lanky, and with a smile as though he had a secret to share. (PHOTO: LLOYD MACLEAN, WARNER BROS.)

Arrival in the City of Angels! Where were the tough guys with the cigars in their mouths? (PHOTO: FLOYD MCCARTHY, WARNER BROS.)

"Wet your lips, Viveca!"
(PHOTO: BERT SIX, WARNER BROS.)

Ronald Reagan and I. Who would have known he was to become President?
(PHOTO: EUGENE ROBERT RICHEE, WARNER BROS.)

Errol Flynn and I. "To drink or not to drink?"—that was the question! (PHOTO: WARNER BROS.)

marry an officer," or "I want two children," or "I want three." I said nothing.

When it was my turn, barely audible, not knowing what it would mean, but sensing an overpowering desire, I said it: "I want to be an actress."

A long silence followed. I could hear the waves beating against the stone wall of the medieval castle where we were sleeping. The reaction finally came. "How interesting, an actress." It didn't matter to me what they said or thought. The moment had been total. Life was as crystal clear as the silvery moon on the black sky that shone through the windows.

In that room that night there was just me and those words. From that day my life formed itself mercilessly toward a new goal aside from being a female.

I don't remember my first kiss as clearly as I wish I could. Perhaps I didn't keep a journal. In those days I only wanted to feel, not to write, not to think. Only feel. Oh yes. Images come back, slowly, the touch of his lips against mine, of a Nordic summer night, a dark shiny lake, a canoe, of stillness in the air, of gentle sounds of the paddle, of tiny fluttering waves caressing the thin bent wood, so thin my bare thighs shivered from the touch. Oh yes, he had red hair and came from a small town. And oh, yes, it was just the two of us and I felt no doubts and I asked no questions. Oh yes.

I was spending the summer at a priest's home in the middle of Sweden. I was thirteen and it was a common practice among the bourgeoisie to send their children to be confirmed, to learn the Bible, God's words, around that age. We rarely spoke about God at home, nor did we go to church except on Christmas Day at six in the morning, with burning torches in our hands as we walked or skied to church, or went by sleigh if we were away in the country. I did pray every night. The last line of the prayer—"The one God loves will be happy"—was confusing. I could never figure out if it meant that I had to love God or He me. But perhaps it meant both. Otherwise, we were not a religious family. It was the thing to do.

There were eighteen of us. At the end of the eight weeks a ceremony took place at the church. We were all dressed in white, boys and girls. I don't remember any of the priest's words, only the kiss. My first kiss.

It was the awakening of my slumbering female sex, of total

giving and receiving, followed by a question. A slightly fearful one. "How does one get pregnant?"

She was an older girl who shared a cottage with me. "I can't tell you." She was embarrassed. "My mother gave me a book. Why don't you ask your mother to do the same."

When I got back home, I did ask my mother for the book.

"I want to discuss it with your father," she said.

"Oh God! Here she goes again!" I thought.

I had begun to hate the vagueness in her, the embarrassed smile that appeared whenever she withdrew from her responsibilities as a woman, as my mother, even in such a simple thing as explaining to me about the body, mine and hers.

We met after dinner in my father's library, a small dark room with books and silver prizes won from his victories as a rider. She, too, had been a rider but she gave it up when she got pregnant.

My father sat in his big leather chair smoking a cigar. My mother sat next to him in a small chair, smiling. She knew something was wrong, that this moment should have been shared between us, two females.

My father began cheerfully to tell about the seed finding its way inside the woman and miraculously a baby would happen. I didn't dare ask what seed and from where. Like my mother, I was overwhelmed by the presence of a man, by the contradiction of his words and my own feelings that I had experienced in the canoe on the black shiny lake with the stillness in the air and the touch of lips against mine.

Eventually, I learned by doing.

I was fifteen. So was he. His name was Stefan. It was the following summer, on the coast of Sweden, way out on a sun-warmed cliff, with the salt water spraying us gently, making our skin taste of the sea. I was filled with generosity and giving. So was he. It was the first time for us both.

The next day Stefan, the idiot, the dummy, the ignorant, uninformed, conditioned, despairing, pathetic, confused male, said to me: "I will never marry a girl I have slept with." I didn't say anything. Maybe I even smiled. We never saw each other after that.

Stefan died at the age of forty-two of a sickness called "old man's sickness." The body turns ninety-five years, in spite of the birth certificate stating it is only forty-two years old.

Perhaps it was his silent scream, never let out. I lost myself with you. I don't know if I want to. I am afraid. I am afraid.

Oh, Stefan! I wanted you only in order to stay myself. Just like you.

It took me months to react. I didn't even allow myself pain as if it hadn't mattered that my virginity was gone and for what? And to whom?

It finally hit me. I had gone to see a film about a schoolgirl whose lover rejected her. She walked out into the lake slowly. The camera stayed on her as she walked and walked and walked, until the bottom seemed to vanish from under her. She didn't care to breathe any longer, just a few bubbles came to the surfaces.

That night I cried over me and Stefan, as I had cried for my brother at the swimming pool, as I had cried the year I left Jeanna, as I was to cry after G.T. left.

In the fall I entered the Royal Dramatic Theatre School. Among two hundred applicants, they accepted twelve. I was one of them. Perhaps it was lucky for me about Stefan. I was more ambitious when free. On the stage I could be a loving woman, a mother, a wife, or a mistress, without being stuck, even a mistress with a child. I could be a businessman like my father, or an officer like my brother. I could be a teacher like my sister. I could be a nurse, falling in love with the doctor or a wounded officer. I could be a rejected or abandoned woman. I could be a failure, and yet be a success. I could live out all my dreams. My nightmares, too. It was in my hands.

My parents had put me through five schools. I had learned not to depend upon their opinions.

The auditions were scheduled for the end of August. The school, and the stage where they took place, were on the top floor of the building. The stage was all the way over to the left and the school all the way over to the right. The third row balcony was in-between. There was a long corridor through which the applicants wandered back and forth. I wasn't nervous or frightened. I only felt excited.

I had spent a year preparing for the audition. I had taken a job in my father's publishing firm as a receptionist in order to finance my studies with Karin Alexandersson, a heavyset, unattractive, unemployed actress: a good teacher, supportive, enthusiastic, and practical—a rare combination. She helped me choose the three scenes required for the audition: *Monique*, a monologue about a young girl in love; *Herr Bengtson's Wife*, a passionate and wild creature in the play by the same name, by August Strindberg; and

Dorrine in *Tartuffe*, the funny, earthy lady who puts everything straight. Three scenes showing the various me's. I am this and I am that. I am different and yet the same.

The studio stage was small and intimate. An older student stood in the wings and read the lines from the other characters. The jury sat out front. Once in a while I caught a glimpse of them, the directors from the theater, some board members, other actresses, and, of course, the head of the theater, Pauline Brunius. She was the first woman to hold that position. Yet it didn't seem peculiar at the time, 1939, that the theater was headed by a female. Brunius had been an actress and had run her own touring company. She was Sweden's answer to Sarah Bernhardt and Eleanore Duse. Today I realize how impressive it was not only that she was chosen, but that she was committed thoroughly to her position, and with grace and conviction. Like Jeanna, she was a strong, active, attractive woman, another image for me.

I was wearing a black crêpe de chine dress that I had made myself. I knew for sure I was sexy now. After Stefan's cop-out, I had met an Italian lieutenant whose ship was visiting Stockholm. He was crazy about me and proposed to me. He said he couldn't make love to me until he married me. I was beginning to learn about men.

The first audition went fine. I was asked to come back for a second. The second went fine. I was asked to come back for the third. I began to believe it was happening. There were twenty of us left. It was getting unbearably exciting. After the audition, we were asked to meet at the stage door entrance a few hours later. I had made friends with a girl; her name was Miriam. We stood together, holding hands. The head of the school, Dr. Torslow, arrived and started to read the names of the lucky ones. He read three names beginning with "L." It flashed through my head that there can't be one more with "L." There was. I never loved the sound of my name more. I felt Miriam's hand withdraw from mine. Her name had not been called out. She left quietly. There was nothing to say or do.

My own feelings sat like an enormous, gorgeous clump inside of me. Eva, the girl with the fairy princess look, who had gone to the same girl's school as I, whose name also had been called out, walked with me out of the beautiful building with the golden cupolas and marble pillars that was to be our home for the next five years. We walked politely, like two well-brought-up Swedish girls, down toward the water, in front of the theater. Politely we said goodbye to each other. Eva went to the right and I to the left, toward my father's office.

I started to run along the waterfront. I ran all the way to the building and all the five flights up. I burst into my father's office, tears streaming down my face. He thought I had been rejected.

"No, no, no, I am accepted. I am accepted. I am accepted," I cried out.

I never went to sleep that night. The advanced students threw a party for us at a restaurant overlooking the river. We ate. We drank champagne. We danced. And I kissed Bengt, a new comrade in luck, on the terrace, with the late August moon looking down on us approvingly. I had borrowed my father's car and drove everybody home.

As I crossed the bridge, seeing the sun rise like a luscious orange behind the dark green pine trees, my life seemed more promising than I had ever imagined.

The day I entered the Royal Dramatic Theatre School was the beginning of a life so intense, so glorious it affected me forever. The theater has never lost its magic. I am drawn to it like a dope fiend to dope, only it offers me the purest of spring waters. It takes me into labyrinths of unending discoveries about life, human beings, myself. It is where I want to live. It is where I want to die.

❧ III ❧

Birth of an Actress

*"In school I was always cold,
except in the art room. There
I felt warm. My body just warmed
itself in that room . . ."*
                    LOUISE NEVELSON

SCHOOL BEGAN the day after the party. It was a three-year course as a student plus two as an actress with a small salary. There was no fee involved. It was supported by the state. The school had the right to drop you if you did not live up to expectations.

Classes ran six days a week from nine in the morning till twelve at night. There was a class in theater history and a voice class with Karin. There was fencing for the male students and ballet for the females. Witzansky, our ballet master, a turbulent Russian, feeling alienated and unused in Sweden, was a great teacher and always in love with one of us. There was a session in performing poetry, but scene study did not begin until second year. An old lady, Anna Norrie, a musical star, taught us "stage presence."

"Walk as if you swallowed a stick," she said, "and go out and live, girls." I don't know what she told the boys.

It's hard to pinpoint exactly what I did learn during those three plus two years. I know they were of enormous importance to me. To begin with, I discovered my capacity for work. I, who had been sleepwalking my way through school, unable to listen, to learn, couldn't wait to get up in the morning to go to the theater. I loved the discipline of the classes, the total twelve-hour-a-day commitment becoming an actress. Motivation is everything!

Comparing my training in Sweden to that of the young American actor who gets his mostly in college, the advantage was that I got my training *for* the theater *in* the theater. To be part of, to exist in the building where theater actually happens from nine in the morning till twelve at night, to experience what goes into the making of a performance, to breathe in the air of sweat, of tension, of physical as well as mental struggle, air filled with conflict between wills and egos, but also air that seems finally to bring everything together into a play, a performance, belonging to us all, made me slowly and organically grasp the nature of the work.

We were allowed to sit in on rehearsals, in the third row balcony and during the second year we were used as extras. Watching hours of often boring, tedious rehearsals, rehearsals of fumbling and mumbling, seemingly leading to nothing, and then, weeks later, suddenly experiencing a clarity bursting forth in the performance molding logic and emotion into one, was invaluable. I became aware of the thin line between telling a story and illuminating humanity, between a good actor and a great one. I became aware of what is called "inspiration," the most complex part of our craft. There is no other way to grasp the untouchable, to understand what cannot be understood except to witness it, affirming the magic, the reaching for the utmost.

At the age of sixteen, I took it all for granted. At the age of fifty-six I understand it was three-fourths of my training. Without this experience at the Royal Dramatic Theatre, I might not have been able to wake up from another slumbering period in my life—the five years in Hollywood.

The Royal Dramatic Theatre continues to represent a beautiful image. Every time I arrive in Stockholm from abroad, I ask the taxi driver, on my way to the hotel, to pass by the white marble building with the golden cupolas by the waterside. I did again the day I got in from the airport with the *Woman* show. "Let me get out, I'll walk to the hotel," I said to Doug.

I went in through the backstage door where Mrs. Anderson sat when I was a young student. She was still there. I hugged her and cried a few tears. She didn't. "I am going up to sit on the shelf for galoshes," I said. She laughed. When I was a student we were not allowed into the greenroom but we were allowed to sit on the shelf outside and since all the big actors passed by us it didn't matter too much. In those days I believed in flirtation and so did everybody else. I sneaked up and it seemed nobody noticed or recognized me. I sat down very quietly on the shelf for a few moments. A young girl, obviously a student, walked by me. "Are you allowed to go into the Green Room nowadays?" I said.

"Sure," she said, "We are all equal nowadays!"

"In my day we only got this far!" I said. "But it didn't matter. We sort of mingled anyhow."

She laughed. She understood. "Are you Viveca L . . . ?"

69

"Yes, come and see my show."

"Maybe," she said and disappeared up the steps.

"To her I am an old hag," I thought to myself. "I am over thirty-five."

The 1937 class at the Royal Dramatic Theatre School was a wild, turbulent group. Fourteen students were accepted. Of the five men, two are dead. Bengt started to drink and died in his forties. Eric was killed in a plane crash. The others—Anders, John, and Ahsel—are still functioning full time in the theater. Of the nine women, only three are still in the profession. The others got side-tracked by love and marriage. One of them was Eva, the fairy princess from my class in the girl's school. She, like me, became quickly famous but her career got lost. She married first a director, then a famous Norwegian actor. She moved to Norway and had two sons. One died. She was ill a lot. Today she lives alone, but still is brilliantly beautiful.

"What are you doing with your time?" I asked her the other day. We had a reunion meeting. Her hair was almost as white as mine.

"I love to travel," she said. "I'm having a wonderful time. Only I wish I could find a lover." But she laughed when she said it.

Guje had a careless beauty, à la Carole Lombard. She was talented and different. It showed that she had lived many years in America with her father, Victor Sjöström, the famous silent motion picture director, also actor, who contributed to making *Wild Strawberries* one of Ingmar Bergman's most human films.

Guje was way ahead of us all as a woman, we felt. She had numerous love affairs. She wrote them down in a black notebook. In detail. She never wore underpants and it's cold in Sweden! I was impressed and didn't see then that her obsession with men, sex, and love diminished her energy for work. She later got in and out of several marriages and had several children. Today she lives alone. She was imaginative and daring, but she turned her life into a play instead of the play into a mirror of her life. It must have been painful. I wish she would write another black notebook about it all.

No doubt, the males in the 1937 class of the Royal Dramatic Theatre school took their work more seriously than we did.

Several of them were into Stanislavski and it sounded too intellectual for our female brains. It took me years to realize that Stanislavski was for me, too, and that emotion does not exclude

70

logic. I learned that in New York, years later, with Lee Strasberg at the Actor's Studio. And today, in my brochure for workshops is written: "I have no other tools but myself, my body, my voice, my soul, my inner self. I must exercise them every day in order to grow. That is my commitment." My inner self was perhaps the last to be dealt with in the Royal Dramatic Theatre. But there is a time for everything.

The first three months at the school were filled with the excitement of a new life. After the New Year I met Hans, a young doctor of medicine who wrote poetry and loved art and now me. He was my first steady lover. We made love any place available—in doorways, in cold empty summer villas, on kitchen tables, and, as a last resort, in his room. We both lived at home, I in Lidingo, he in town with his mother, a widow, a strange lonely and bored dark lady about my age today. She lived through Hans. It bothered her when we made love.

"Hans," she would call out, "are you there?"

We would lie still for a moment, his penis resting inside my vagina, and then Hans would call back, "Yes, I am here with Viveca."

Silence would follow, for she had no way of dealing with the mad flush of confusing emotions that must have come over her, fears of losing Hans, envy, generosity, perhaps even moments of courageous wishes, "I too must live and love or I will shrink, fade. I don't want to. Oh dear God, help." Hans and I couldn't have cared less, for we were one with the secret of life. Nothing stopped us—having my period, fear of pregnancy, his mother, nor my father.

Hans's mother, like my grandmother, felt unwanted, unneeded. They were taken care of by income left by the husband. Necessity did not force them into seeking life. On their own, they had no knowledge of how to do it. Hans's mother couldn't have been more than fifty-five at that time. As I am now.

There is no substitute for the special deep exchange that exists between men and women. "I wanted to give it to you so much," H.T. says, when he comes inside of me. I am 54, he is 61. It has nothing to do with age. When it is good, it is good, only when it is not so good it is less painful. Each time I reconfirm my own biological sex through the total giving and receiving. I need that. I always will.

I had to tell my father about Hans when we went away to ski

together. The astounding thing was that he asked Hans, not me, as if I were a child, not responsible, to come up to his office to speak to him, "man to man." Hans promised my father not to touch me, instead of telling him we had touched already. They both protected the myth. I was stunned. My father, who used to be proud of me when his friends liked me—*why* wasn't he proud of me now? Being a woman to its fullest. Why those kind of games? My father was not a liar, nor was Hans. I accepted it only because I had accepted that a man's word was the one and only that counted, not mine. How did I feel about it? That I could do the same thing! It was the beginning of hypocrisy between me and Hans, the loss of innocence.

My brother, Bjarne, was another surprise. "Open up or I will break down the door," he screamed. "Open up." He had sensed that Hans was with me. It was one weekend when we were alone in the house, our parents away. It was divine for me. Hans and I could be together all through the night, even have breakfast.

In the middle of the night, my brother came home. He started to bang on the door. He was wild. I was more furious than scared. Who the hell did he think he was? I didn't open the door. I didn't need him for anything anymore. I had replaced him long ago, I thought.

That Hans and Bjarne came to share such similar fates is infuriating, for they were both brilliant intense men.

When I was home this time, doing *Woman*, I met a young man after a performance. "I am a friend of Hans's. Do you remember him?" he said.

"Of course," I said. "He was my first lover."

That's when he told me Hans had married. A rich woman. But found himself getting more and more depressed. Torn perhaps between being a poet or doctor? Not able to make a choice or take a stand when it really mattered, rarely having experienced that muscle of will. However, being a medical student, and trusting the science, he had himself committed. They tried shock treatment. Something snapped in his head. The brain went. He became a vegetable. Still is, today.

Bjarne, too, wanted to be a doctor. He, too, wrote poetry. But he is no longer alive. The intensity of his despairing will won out over the wires.

And Anders, his son, is today a brilliant young doctor.

After the first year at the Royal Dramatic Theatre School, the students were allowed to take outside work during the summer. I was determined to get a job. The idea of not working now when I had discovered I was able to, even taking joy in it, seemed ridiculous. I also wanted to earn some money to rent a room and live in town, finally, again. And on my own.

In Sweden almost every town or village has a "Folketspark" (a park for the people, with a theater, visited by touring groups). These parks are open during the summer and are very popular. I went down to the casting office every Friday afternoon in black silk stockings and high-heeled shoes and sat until finally a Mr. Peterson took me seriously. Perhaps he just got tired of seeing me. He offered me the juvenile lead in three productions out of four, in a fifth-class touring company. I didn't care that it was a shabby group, that the pay was low and the plays mediocre. I was to be on the stage almost every night in front of an audience for four months!

The tour began the end of May, two weeks before the school term was over. I got permission to leave early and began to rehearse. The producer was the director and played the lead in the four plays. One afternoon I was told that his wife was to visit rehearsals. A *he* arrived, not a *she*. I was dumbfounded. Gerda, an older actress in the company, explained to me about homosexuality. I was 17!

After a week of touring, I had to return for a day to Stockholm to be part of the student performance of the work we had done during the year. It was an important day. Not only was the jury there again to see what progress we had made but also directors from other theaters and from the industry, all looking for unknown stars to be discovered—hopefully me, I thought. But something happened to me the night before.

We were playing way up in the north of Sweden and I had to take a train to Stockholm after the performance. I was exhausted and knew I had a long night ahead of me. I tried to go to sleep. I did, in spite of the uncomfortable hard wooden bench. The conductor came for my ticket. Sleepily I gave it to him. He started to ask me questions: What was I doing? How come I was up so late? Where was I going? I told him I was anxious about the performance in the morning. "Let me put you in a sleeping compartment," he said kindly. Gratefully I picked up my one and only piece of luggage and tramped after him. He kissed me goodnight on the cheek and closed the door. The kiss confused me.

Did I have to pay for my bed? I started to get undressed. I had a funny feeling that he had locked the door. Was it my fantasy playing tricks on me? No, dammit, I was right. I couldn't open it.

73

It was locked. I pulled it. I pushed it. No use. I began to scream. Nobody came. I screamed again. Nobody came. I pulled the emergency brake. Nothing happened.

My God, I am kidnapped. I am trapped. I started to cry. This crazy mad conductor. He is going to rape me, I will never make the performance, I am kidnapped. I've got to get out. I screamed. Nobody heard me. Nobody came. Finally, the train stopped at a station. It was the middle of the night and pitch black. There was nobody around. I tried to pull down the window. It was locked, too. In a panic I took my shoe and banged my heel against the glass. It shattered into a million pieces. I threw the hatbox out and followed it myself through the splinter window. It was a miracle that I didn't kill myself. As I ran down the station, blood running down my arms, my face, my legs, I saw the conductor coming toward me.

"What's the matter, child?" he said.

"You locked me in," I stammered. I could barely speak.

"Poor sweet child," he mumbled. He took me by the hand to the sleeping compartment. Without explanation he opened it simply by pulling it to the side, like all doors on all trains (and I had taken many trains in my life). I had been blinded by fears.

The conductor gave me some bandages and washed off my wounds. "Poor child," he kept mumbling. By now I certainly was one, and he was a gentle sweet old man who simply wanted to help me get some sleep.

Hans met me early in the morning when I got off the train at the station in Stockholm. As I began to explain the bandages, he began to smile, embarrassed. A feeling as if I were lying came over me, as if I had been part of a sex orgy. I began to smile too!

I went through the performance in a numb state. I had chosen to do a scene from *Elizabeth the Queen* by Maxwell Anderson. Elizabeth is an ugly but intelligent woman. I did want to prove that I, an actress *and* beautiful, could be intelligent. I failed. I was emotional, but not intelligent. Something took over that I seemed to have no control over, something I would run into over and over again until Lee Strasberg years later confronted me about it. "I want to see you," he said. He meant all of me, even the me that was afraid of not being accepted for being intelligent, the four-year-old.

The night had been too confusing, as had the meeting with Hans. What had he smiled at? What had I smiled at? Unreality had crept in and nothing had reaffirmed the real me. Life in life and life on stage go hand in hand.

I got on the train in the evening to join the rest of the company way up north, depressed and unmotivated. But it passed quickly. I had a matinee the next day. I could go at it again. I was a working actress!

In order to save money, I bought a tent. I put it near the theater and used the dressing room to wash up in the morning. The bus driver left the lights on until I got the tent up. To begin with, the nights were cold, but once I crawled down in my sleeping bag, I felt fine.

When the weather got milder, Gerda, the older actress, camped out, too. She had a Bunsen burner and made the morning coffee. We saved some of the Danish pastries left over from the evening. We ate only one meal a day. If we were invited out for supper after the theater, we starved until then and made up for it. The result was good. At the end of four months I had saved money and was thinner.

Hans and I barely saw each other over the summer. I was an actress on the road and he was a medical intern in a hospital in Stockholm. I experienced that summer, for the first time, the life of a twentieth-century actor and the dangers, traveling alone, not like the gypsies or the Golden Coach actors who traveled with lovers, husbands, and family.

One night two friends of Gerda's, traveling salesmen, invited us for supper in their rooms after the performance. One of them suggested we go into the bedroom.

He was ugly! I didn't like him! I didn't want him! I had never met him before. Did I feel I had to pay for my supper? I turned my character of a young serious actress making a living for the first time in her life into that of a whore. How mediocre did the play have to be? There wasn't even a pimp around to take care of me. I had no way of understanding myself.

I sat in the bus with the landscape passing by me for days, crying, as if something valuable was lost between me and Hans, wondering why I had been so careless, what the play was about this time.

A week later I developed a vaginal infection. I carried it around for weeks. When I got back to Stockholm I went to my mother's gynecologist; I had never been to one before. He took one look inside my vagina and made no bones about his disgust. I dismissed it. "He belongs to my mother's generation. He can go and screw himself—I am an actress. I have to live. How else do I mirror life on the stage?"

I arrived at my first class in my second year of the Royal Dramatic Theatre School in late August, dressed in black stockings, looking pale and gaunt. I felt more independent, more defiant. I felt more sinful but also more disillusioned. I didn't mind. I had met the audience, too. I had earned my own money. It all affirmed Viveca with a c.

I rented a maid's room in town, around the corner from the theater. I was on my own. I didn't have to account to anybody. There was only a slight fear about not becoming the woman I wanted to be, a woman devoted to her man. I stayed with Hans for a while longer. For I wanted to have it all, and why not?

The work in school became more intense. I never left the theater. I was there day and night. Within a few weeks I got my first real break.

I was the first student in the group to be given a major part in a play. A well established actress went on tour and I was given her role: a schoolgirl, a mean little bitch, who had witnessed her teacher commit murder and confronts her. I rehearsed with the stage manager and Anna Lindhal, who played the teacher of the title role *Anne Sophie Hedvig*. The director, Alf Sjöberg, a vital, creative, attractive man, came to watch a runthrough. He didn't stop me once. After the scene was over he leaped up on the stage and, with a generosity and joy that is so typical of people in the theater, he threw his arms around me and said, "You are going to be a great actress, Viveca." I was stunned.

Within ten minutes I found myself running down the street, this time to a phone booth to call, not Hans, but Eric, his best friend, a rich and not terribly good painter and my to-be lover.

He had conveniently financed a trip to Paris for Hans "to buy some paintings." It was an opportunity for Hans, a poor medical student. I suspected it was done in order to seduce me, but did nothing to stop it. Also, it turned me on that Eric was crazy about me. He had his own studio, he was rich, and, perhaps even more important, I was a success now and free to live a flamboyant life. The moment was perfect.

We celebrated that night in his gorgeous white empty studio, empty except for paints and a few canvases lying around. We drank wine to gorgeous yearning sensuous music. I took my clothes off and began to dance for him, candlelight throwing the flickering shadows of my naked body on the wall. We ended up, of course, making love.

Making love to Eric was different—less vulnerable, less pure, less committed. He, too, was an artist. I was less needed. When Hans came back from Paris, it was obvious what had happened. Still, he said nothing. Neither did I. True, one doesn't own another person. But one certainly has the right to say, "I love you. I don't want to lose you. It kills me to see you with somebody else." Hans couldn't.

The truth, however, had put the pin in the pink balloon, no longer even pink, and, although my affair with Eric was a fleeting one, it did end my relationship with Hans.

Anne Sophie Hedvig was good for me. People began to talk about me. When spring arrived, I didn't have to sit in Mr. Peterson's office in order to get a summer tour. Olov Molander, a brilliant Swedish theater director, mostly known for his Strindberg productions, saw me perform and cast me as the girl in the mauve lamé dress, the girl torn between the safe love of the boyfriend next door and the wild love of the gangster in *The Gentle People*, a play by Irwin Shaw.

Molander not only directed the play but also acted one of the two old men. Victor Sjöström, Guje's father, played the other, superbly. It was his comeback after ten years of retirement after his Hollywood years.

Sjöström, Stiller, and Hanson, three famous Swedes, had created history in silent films and made Sweden famous, as Bergman was to do years later through talking pictures.

They left in triumph accompanied by their women, two wives and Stiller's girlfriend, a young actress right out of the Royal Dramatic Theatre School whose name was Greta Gustafson. None of the three men made it in Hollywood, U.S.A., when the talking pictures took over the industry. The actress did. Her name was Greta Garbo. Though it might have seemed like an accident of fate, their return to their native land must have been a bitter act of defeat. Stiller died shortly after. Sjöström went into retirement at the age of forty-five. Whether this was through his sense of failure or whether Sweden is too tough on her returning sons and daughers I do not know. Talking pictures may well have seemed like a step down to begin with. Hanson was the only one who immediately claimed back his position as Sweden's leading actor.

Sjöström lived quietly, isolated in Stockholm together with his two daughters and his beautiful Russian actress wife. I came to know her during the tour. In my eyes she seemed old and tragic. Most wives did. "Victor is so good to me," she used to say. Yet she was the one who had put her career second and followed him

77

wherever he went. Still did. Only perhaps not so willingly any-more. Why should I? she might have asked herself.

Her career up to now had seemed intimately connected to his. When he went down, she went with him. Yet now when he was on his way up again it was too late for her. She was way past thirty-five. Besides, she was a foreigner with an accent. Not ac-ceptable for an actress in Sweden. Yet a situation unacceptable for her, the actress she was, still full of talent and lust to work.

After *Gentle People* Sjöström never stopped working. He be-came the director of the Swedish Film Industry in addition to act-ing leads. His knowledge and talent were fully put to use. Hers weren't. If they felt any envy toward Garbo, or any bitterness about Hollywood, I never heard it or sensed it.

The tour was a major break for me, too. It was my first encoun-ter with great theatrical geniuses. Molander was the first director who inspired me. I didn't know then how rare they are. He made me aware of things within me that I had no idea existed.

Years later when I went to America he wrote me a letter telling me how deeply he felt about my talent. I was astounded. I had sensed it during the tour, but hadn't trusted it. I knew he had wanted me as a woman and, although I worshiped him as a direc-tor, he scared me as a man. He was much older than I, strange, moody and, above all, brilliant. Ordinarily I would have gone to bed with him to overcome the fear, to feel equal. Becoming an actress had released any sexual taboos for me, but I was badly pre-pared for the next step, making a choice about the man I wanted to love. I knew of no other way to deal with Molander's advances than to withdraw totally. It was my loss, for I could have learned more from him as a friend, as a teacher. He was a deep and tre-mendous artist.

Maybe I finally revolted against an attitude that had begun to scare me: "You don't marry an actress, you fuck her." I had ex-perienced a streak of cruelty in men that I did not know how to handle.

"You don't know how to love a man," Adolphson, a popular ac-tor, a male sex symbol in Swedish films, had said to me after a night of love. I knew he didn't mean it sexually!

I got back at him a few years later. By now I had become the number one box office star in Swedish films and Adolphson was my leading man. The name of the film was *Maria*. My name was ahead of his.

We filmed during the night. He was working during the day and

78

I was performing the bride in *Blood Wedding* by Garcia Lorca. I had just given birth to Lena and after the performance I nursed her in the dressing room. One night I was exhausted and took my time. Messages were delivered. "Adolphson wants you to hurry up." I was too tired to care. I thought.

As I entered the studio he made *one* remark about the "star" being late and I saw red. My arm lifted. Bang! I was as astounded as everybody else. The headlines in the morning read VIVECA SLAPS ADOLPHSON. "You don't know how to love a man," he had said. I was a soldier's daughter.

Today I understand his frustration, even his vulnerability. I was another "little girl" who might have become stronger than he. He had done several films with Ingrid Bergman who by now, like Garbo, had become a star in Hollywood when he was only known in Sweden.

It was no longer an accident that Swedish actresses were continually achieving world fame through films while male actors were not. Difficult for most men not to take personally, especially a he-man like Adolphson, even if he understood the unfairness of the situation. It didn't apply only to Swedish actors. Very few foreign male stars have been allowed to make an important contribution to American films. The American male producer has had little interest in them. Why expose the American woman to someone different from himself? That would be too dangerous, certainly too generous. Much nicer to import gorgeous ladies from Europe, teaching her American sister to watch out or her man would leave her. Charles Boyer was one of the exceptions that proved the rule. He even got Irene Dunne when most foreign male actors usually got second leads, the man who doesn't make it with "her."

I don't know if Adolphson understood this, or Victor Sjöström, who was a wise man, or Rydeberg, who became my first big love and was a brilliant actor. Even if they had, it might not have helped, for fame is fame.

I certainly didn't understand it at the time nor did I in my wildest dreams believe that I could be a threat to any man or be as powerful as he. The idea was as far-fetched as touching the moon on a cold winter night. But it happened whether I knew it or not, whether I could cope with it or not, for by now my career had its own life and the rhythm was fast.

It wasn't the part of the girl in the lamé dress and my work with Molander that put me on the front page. It was Diane, the girl in the bathing suit in *French Without Tears* by Terence Rattigan or, as translated from the Swedish, *Diana Goes Hunting*, that did it. Hampe Faustman, a senior student, had taken an option on the play. It was my first experience in taking initiative and raising money. I accompanied Hampe dressed in my one pair of black silk stockings, making sure when I sat down that my skirt was pulled high over the knee. I didn't resent my role at all as the passive participant, the sexy actress listening to the men talking about money. In fact I enjoyed it. But that was then.

We got the money together and rented a small theater for the summer. Toslov, the head of the school, directed and the rest of the cast came from the school. We opened as soon as the term was over. The timing was perfect: Stockholm was ready for the idea of young unknown actors taking their lives in their own hands. Opening night was an occasion. Everybody came. The next morning the headlines read DIANA MAKES SUCCESS. Within a few weeks I was on the cover of every magazine. I became a star overnight. I was ready to meet the king—George I!

2

I fell in love with Georg Rydeberg over the footlights. He was playing *Duo* by Geraldy in a small theater downtown, an intense French play about jealousy, possessiveness, love, and commitment! He was dark and gorgeous in a gypsylike way. I had run into him in the corridors backstage of the Royal Dramatic Theatre already during the fall when he was playing the romantic tragic Prince of Habsburg in *Mayerling* by Maxwell Anderson. He would look at me in his own very special sensual way as he passed me sitting on the ledge of rubber boots outside the Green Room. Although I had established myself as a promising starlet I was still only a student and we were not allowed to mingle with the actors. I returned the look but nothing really happened until a month or two later, the night I saw him playing *Duo*.

After the performance I went for a glass of wine with two boyfriends at a cafe next door. They were both in love with me. I liked that! In those days I never bothered with girlfriends. Men were my friends as well as lovers. Rydeberg entered with his leading lady and the husband, also the director of the theater. It was rumored that Rydeberg was having an affair with her, but then it was rumored that he was having affairs with most of his leading ladies. I couldn't have cared less. I went right up to his table and introduced myself. I ignored her completely. (I might not had she been good in the part.) He rose and looked at me with his tiny black eyes and for a moment only he and I existed. I caught my breath and managed to tell him how sensational he had been on the stage that night. It was clear that I felt that way about him offstage, too. He got the message. When I left the restaurant the doorman asked me for my phone number ("on behalf of Mr. Rydeberg," he explained discreetly). Within one hour my phone rang in my apartment and in ten minutes he was with me in bed. Our bodies were made for each other.

Our love affair was forbidden, delicious, passionate, and romantic. I would wait for him by the bridge below the castle at the blue hour, the early evening, when the lights were beginning to shimmer in the water but it was still dark enough so that nobody would recognize him. Except for me. I could spot him from far away coming toward me by his walk, the way he held his head, the way he carried himself, and by the feeling that shot through me when he suddenly stood beside me, barely touching me.

I was all his, wanted to be all his, didn't mind being all his. I was one with him, and I would do anything to be with him. I traveled on lousy trains to spend weekends with him if he was on tour. I would wait for him in the hotel room after the performance where he had arranged for supper. His favorite brandy was Rémy Martin. For years afterwards, I would order it. Just the aroma was enough to bring back a flood of sensual memories of him.

Sometimes he would surprise me waiting outside the stage entrance if I was playing, or outside the school on the other side of the building, and he knew that whenever he came to my apartment I was ready to love him—any time of night, any time of day. He was my first real love. I loved him for his work, for his soul, for his body, for loving me, and, above all and more than anything, I loved him for the feeling I had for him. It was heaven.

"Yearning is My Heritage," was his favorite poem. What would happen when the yearning was fulfilled? I never asked myself or him. We never discussed seriously how we were to continue our lives. It was understood. At least to me. We loved each other and that was that. I was only seventeen or eighteen. For him it was more complicated. He was older than I, more experienced, and married, second time around. He rarely talked about his wife. She didn't seem very important to him. I was wrong about that. She certainly didn't seem very important to me. Any woman over thirty-five, especially if she were not an actress, was an old hag! I was wrong about that, too. Naturally he would go for me, young,

81

wild, and exciting. My ego was "out of whack" as they say. I forgot that I, too, would be over thirty-five one day. He did talk about the children. He clearly loved them. He often cried when he mentioned them, as if he knew he would cause them pain. In those days it was unheard of that a man would get the children in a divorce. I was insensitive to his dilemma. It wasn't until later when I had children myself that I understood him. I never would be able to give up a child for the love of anybody else so why would Rydeberg?

Rydeberg's childhood was sad and lonely. His father was a sea captain and rarely home. Whenever he was there he beat him up, Rydeberg writes in his autobiography. Perhaps now he wanted to be a better father than his had been to him. But the image was missing. He grew up with his sister and his mother, whom he always referred to as his "angel."

Rydeberg was a combination of bourgeoisie and bohemia. On the one hand he wanted to be a husband and father. On the other he was stuck in the matinee idol symbol, the Don Juan, the wine, women, and song image. He was a sensual man with conflicting needs, and his relationship to women was strongly influenced by the rules of the time he lived in. You marry the angel, the mother of your children, and you fuck the mistress, the whore.

I was the latter in spite of the fact that I came from a respected family. It didn't show much on me, and he didn't like that.

He used to look at my fingernails and scold me if they were dirty, and he hated for me to wear black stockings. I wanted to get away from my bourgeois past. I wanted to be daring and free, dangerous and sexy, both as a woman and as an artist. It didn't interfere with my commitment to him. I had no desire for anyone else and felt absolutely clean in my love. When he said, "No one will ever marry you. You have slept with too many men," I laughed. In a million years I could never have come up to the amount of women he had slept with. Obviously he didn't look at it in the same way and I shouldn't have laughed.

I had a small apartment by now, my first all by myself.

There was a bed and a few pieces of furniture. I couldn't have cared less what it looked like.

Rydeberg lived in a beautiful home with antique furniture, in a most elegant and respected part of Stockholm. He might have worried that I wasn't a homemaker, nor an equal partner on the stage. I was only a student, although a promising one. On the other hand, if I were to become famous that might cause problems. I wasn't aware of it at the time; I hadn't been with Adolphson, either. I only knew that both of them had love affairs with actresses but never married them, and, at the time when Rydeberg and I broke up, a film career like Garbo's and Bergman's was clearly around the corner for me.

As a woman I was "hot" too. I did flirt a lot. I might have used it to taunt him, to make him aware that there were other possibilities besides him. In love and war everything is allowed, was the rule of the time. Fairness and logic were unknown terms between lovers.

"It was you who left me," he said years later. I was astounded. Did I give him a feeling there was someone else? Did he really believe that, or was it more convenient for him to think so? On the other hand, misunderstandings between lovers go way beyond imagination.

I never forgot an interview that I saw with Rydeberg on TV not too long ago. It was shown right before a film, *Appassionata*, that he and I had made twenty-five years earlier. The questions came offstage. The camera never left his face for a moment. "What about love?"

He didn't answer right away. "I could never find the middle ground, it was either hate or love." It was very moving, for he was about sixty, and I knew he had tried numerous times. He could be utterly naked in front of an audience, but it is more difficult face to face. I know about that.

The irony is that Rydeberg married four times. He left them all and lives alone today. Was the price of intimacy too high for him, too? Did he, too, find it difficult to be both an artist and also loving? Our journeys are similar, yet different, for love seemed never to sidetrack him in his work. It did me.

There was the opening night of *The Corn is Green*. I played the girl, a bitch again, a marvelous one. As in *Anne Sophie Hedvig*. It was a big opportunity.

We had made love all afternoon. I took a hot bath and he drove me to the theater and kissed me good luck. The dressing room was filled with flowers. He had treated me royally. Why did I begin to feel dull? What was there to complain about? That he was going to be sitting out front with his wife, the blond angel, the no-longer actress? That he wouldn't come back after the show because he was taking her to a party, not me? Take her home, not me? Or was it that I had no right to complain about any of it since I had known the setup to begin with? I was the mistress, not the wife.

The anger was scary. It was too close to the truth. I pushed it down. I couldn't even use it for the part. Not even the fantasy, the role-playing was safe because he would see me on the stage as I was, an angry bitch! No, no!

I got duller and duller. I had no guts, no vitality. It took me years to use my fury on stage, and not that night. The love affair interfered.

I read in an interview with Rydeberg that he always takes half an hour of total silence by himself before a performance. There is a photograph of his dead son in his dressing room. It takes time and commitment to get to the bareness. He knew it. I had to learn to take my work equally seriously.

"You shouldn't have had a hot bath," he said when I told him about my frustration the next day.

It was the first time I knew I was angry with him. "Why didn't you tell me yesterday? You should have helped me become a great actress! And don't sit with her on my opening night! I am not that sophisticated. I love you! It gets me all mixed up!" But I couldn't tell him.

One night, vivid in my memory too long afterwards, toward the end of the affair, we were invited to spend the weekend with some friends of his outside of Stockholm. He brought me along, quite officially. Maybe it was his way to begin breaking up the marriage. Perhaps that scared him.

He was strange that night. He drank too much red wine. He ate too much. The hostess kept frying him eggs, one after another, laughingly. I began to feel disgusted with the whole evening. What was I doing in this strange house? Maybe I just felt excluded, but since I didn't understand that, by the time we got into bed I only felt scared and alienated. What was I doing in this strange bed with a man that seemed like a stranger? Except that he wanted me intimately over and over again.

His body was hot and sweaty and he didn't care that I wasn't with him. And so I didn't care if he had an orgasm or not, and that scared me more than anything. I had no idea how to say, "Georg, I'm not with you. It scares me," and that might have brought me back to him. But perhaps I knew intuitively that he wouldn't put up with me on those terms, that he wouldn't understand, or wouldn't want to. Maybe what I wanted was a comrade, too, not only a lover.

It was the first time a cool wind blew between us, although ever so lightly. Maybe it was that night that provoked me into

84

further confrontations. I needed to know now more than ever for sure whether he would accept me as I was, for better or for worse, as someone to be taken seriously, or I would never be able to take him seriously and give him what he wanted. And I couldn't bear that, for my own sake. For to hold back love was the worst, the absolute worst. And I'm not sure I don't feel that way still today.

I put it badly to Rydeberg.

"It's me or her," I blurted out. It's not easy to be warm and clear when you are eighteen and afraid of the consequences, maybe even knowing what they would be. Rydeberg and I had run into each other accidentally outside the theater. I had my bicycle. He was on his way home from rehearsals. He barely answered but his eyes got smaller and blacker. He was furious. It was a brief, too brief, meeting. I hadn't imagined that at all. It was unbearable. We didn't see each other the next couple of days. It was even more unbearable. I couldn't stand being alone in the apartment. He didn't call me once. I fled to Lidingo for the weekend.

When I came back on Monday morning I was ready to take him back under any circumstances, only to feel his body against mine, his arms around me. As with G.T., twenty years later, I had forgotten all about "loving in a new way." I opened the door of my apartment. There was a letter on the floor with his familiar handwriting. I opened it, shivering. A key inside it—the key I had given him to come to me any time of day, any time of night!

I don't remember a word from the letter, only that my whole body screamed. Noooooooo. My knees got weak. I sat down on the bed, hugging myself, trying to soothe myself, at the same time hating myself for having said what I had said, regretting every word.

I went straight back home, again to my mother. I stayed in the room under the roof. She brought me tea as if I were a child and she soothed me as if I were a child. But she couldn't help me as a woman against a growing sense of defeat about love. Perhaps that's why I lied to her years later that day on her deathbed when she asked me whether G.T. and I were divorcing—for I didn't want to feel like a victim anymore. Not again, not ever. And I knew I would easily fall into it with her as I had done when Rydeberg left me, and when I cried and cried and cried as my mother had done before me, as hers had done before her and hers before her.

I must have been deaf, dumb, and blind. Rydeberg had met another lady, rich and high in society, ready to take care of him even more so than the wife. Certainly more than I ever could have or would have wanted to. He divorced his wife now, in no time.

It ought to have been clear to me that to him I was just a girl, a starlet, a mistress . . . only a bit more than a whore.

It seems love is a more complex emotion for women than for men, perhaps not only because men have been splitting their interests between love and work successfully, or at least rightfully, for quite some time. But also perhaps for a natural organic reason. A man is intimate with a woman from the second he exists. He goes from her womb to her breast. He never leaves her. Never changes "tracks."

I remember Kristoffer. He was four, maybe five. He had crawled down in the bed with me, in his pajamas covering him from top to toe. He was lying on top of me. I was resting before going to the theater. "I love you, I love you, I love you, Mommy," he said. Suddenly he stood up, put his hand on his penis, looked at me with his big brown eyes. "It's getting so big," he said.

I don't know what made me say it, but I did. "It's because you love me."

Women, at the age of twelve or thirteen, because of an organic change in their bodies, begin to seek new territories of intimacy. Instead of warm breasts there is a flat chest. Instead of coarse, curly hair, there is a penis, sometimes dangling loose, sometimes pointing, wanting something from her. At least so she feels. But everything is unfamiliar, different. It takes us twelve years to catch up to the comfort he quite naturally feels.

It is common that women run home to their mothers in the beginning of a marriage or a male relationship, as I did, more so than for men. Why not? It is threatening, this new "thing." And it takes an emotional involvement to accept the change, to believe in it. Perhaps always for women.

A week after Rydeberg left me, I was offered a screen test for UFA in Berlin. It was the year 1939. Hitler was in power. The war had begun. I felt no moral objection at possibly working for the Nazis, nor any fear that it was dangerous. Nothing bothered me. I just wanted to be famous, be a star, forget Rydeberg, and find another man, and, if there were to be a split between us, I would be the one to leave.

I was in a numb state when I got on the plane to Berlin and checked in at the Eden Hotel. It was my first experience of seeing soldiers without arms and legs. My romantic image of war was shattered in a few hours. I couldn't even avoid becoming aware of a responsibility that had nothing to do with my nationality. The first night I spent with the assistant director, a tiny, thin, and tensed young man, and a Finnish woman, the secretary of the producer, we walked through the dark streets of Berlin. In muffled voices we talked about the political situation when suddenly he pulled me aside. "The intellectuals are going to get him," he whispered. "One day soon they are going to get the bastard."

Years later in New York I was doing a dramatization of *Letters From Stalingrad*. The letters were written by German soldiers in the SS from the front, after having been told this would be their last chance to write home.

Hardy Kruger, a German actor, brought in a passionate, beautiful speech against Hitler written by a young student, the leader of an organizataion called the Red Rose. It led to an unsuccessful and bloody student revolt. Everybody was killed or put in jail or never heard from again. Was the intense young man one of them? I saw him in front of me each night, whispering in a half-lit street in Berlin, as I heard the speech on stage.

The other day, I was part of a memorial for Otto Frank, Anne Frank's father. Jack Gilford read Mr. Frank's description of the last train journey to Auschwitz with his family. He was then separated and it was years later before he knew what had happened to Anne. He finally found two sisters who told him about the death of Anne. Typhoid in the Belsen Bergen camp. "I cannot find words to describe how I felt," he writes.

At the time when Anne was writing her glorious diary, at the time she died of typhoid in Belsen Bergen camp, I was flirting with a possible career in film made by her killers. Was I still suffering from feeling incapable of any political opinion or stand?

Thinking about it all today I am horrified about how long my lack of awareness lasted, how afraid I was to have an opinion.

I was sixteen, maybe eighteen, when I met Raoul Wallenberg. He was twenty-five or twenty-six, dark, intense, and, as I thought, Jewish. We had been dancing that night. He took me up to his grandfather's office to show me some documents about the anti-Semitic situation in Germany. He talked to me almost in a whisper, as if it were dangerous also in Sweden. He was passionate about it as Uncle Fred had been about the Nazis. "Watch out," I thought to myself, "he is just out to seduce me; in a way, isn't that what Uncle Fred did too?" He had become my convenient explanation of that situation when I was ten, almost becoming a Nazi. "This time

I will be more careful." I thought to myself. It blinded me to the extraordinary quality of Raoul. He knew right from wrong in a way I didn't, for he was obviously already then an extraordinary human being, sensitive, tremendous in his imagination and his love for humanity.

At some time after our dancing night, Raoul was sent to Budapest on the behalf of the Swedish government. Without consideration for his own safety, he saved the lives of over 20,000 Jews and assisted indirectly in saving perhaps 100,000 more. He proved to the world that the impossible was possible, except for saving his own life. He disappeared one day in Budapest in 1945 and was put "under Soviet protection." Nobody has heard from him since, but he continues to spread his message of love of right from wrong.

At a meeting not long ago to arouse interest to pressure the Russians for an explanation, for some proof about his disappearance thirty years ago, a Hungarian woman stood up and told us how she had been saved by Raoul. You could see that she was deeply upset to bring all this to the surface again after so many years. Her voice got deep and strong. She talked slower and slower. It was very moving.

She ended her story, "It was a month ago that I was asked to come here and speak. I have had trouble sleeping ever since. I had no idea until now about Raoul's tragic destiny. All this time I thought he lived happily in Sweden. That he who saved so many lives, my life, should not be saved himself is an unbearable thought."

Listening to her, I realized again how many years it took me before I dared to have a social opinion, a must for everybody, including the artist. It took years of exposure to justice and injustice to understand the importance of knowing right from wrong and taking a stand for it. It took years of involvement with Jewish men, years of analysis, for it seems that unless we understand the violations once done to us, they will sidetrack us forever.

Years later when I became aware of my responsibilities, the growing guilt finally forced me into analysis. I finally became sensitive to the pain of the "weaker," possibly the "stronger." It is strange how life goes around in circles and we cannot move on to a new one until the last is completed.

At the end of that week with UFA, after Rydeberg left me and I was nineteen going on twenty, I went back to Stockholm and neutrality. I had at least realized there was more to the world than the love of a man.

Again, I was lucky. I didn't have to make a choice about UFA. My career was suddenly happening all around me in Sweden. The theater exercised its option to use me for the next two years as an actress, and Luxfilm came through with an offer for a film, not a large part, but a part. It was the beginning of a tremendously successful working relationship between me and them.

I don't remember much from the movie except that I swam naked through the fjords with the camerawagon following me from behind. And in front! I didn't think much of it, although it was unusual even in those days to appear nude in a film. My father was furious about it. I didn't understand him at all. The director was a man of distinction and, as far as I was concerned, since I was an actress I would have to do whatever I was asked. (I was somewhat more obedient than I am nowadays!)

Nudity was no doubt looked upon as something more natural in Sweden than in the U.S.A. During the summer as a child I would run around naked up to the age of ten or twelve. A bathing suit was a luxury.

When Lena and John came to California from Sweden, aged two and three, neither I nor Nana thought anything of their running around on the beach in their natural beauty. I was astounded when someone pointed out to me that I ought to get them bathing suits. "Why?" I asked. "There may be people around them with dirty ideas," was the answer.

I have nothing against nudity in film or on the stage or in life if it is called for. If it is used for the sake of sensation, I dislike it. I don't think it was. Unfortunately, the film was no good and maybe that had something to do with it. It was probably the worst fiasco I've ever been part of. It ran for one performance. Nudity or not, it gave me my break.

If I Marry a Minister was the second production planned by Luxfilm. It was based on a bestseller written by a woman, a schoolteacher. It was her love story with the minister in a community way up in the north of Sweden. She had a child with him but he did not want to marry her. He was already married to God, he said.

The book was a sensation when published. Every actress in Scandinavia wanted the role. I got it! I walked down the main street in Stockholm with the thick blue manuscript demonstratively under my arm. I wanted everyone to know!

Ironically, Rydeberg was cast as the minister. Obviously our love scenes were loaded. In no time, through the film, we became the number one romantic love couple on the screen, *now* when our love affair was all over with. I was still in love with him and never knew whether he meant that he loved me or not when he said so in front of the camera. I didn't ask him, either, and at night he went home to the new wife and I to Harry Hasso, the man behind the camera who wanted to marry me. His wife, Signe, had left him for Hollywood, U.S.A., and he was alone with their son, Henry. Harry was looking, no doubt, for a new wife. It turned out to be me.

Stockholm is a small town. Suddenly everybody wanted to get married, as if in a delayed reaction. To whom seemed of less importance. Eric, my former rich lover, had started to woo Rydeberg's wife and married her. Rydeberg had his rich, although not very attractive but quite intelligent, lady. And I did marry the cameraman.

Were we all afraid to once more miss the magic moment, afraid to be left out in the cold, clinging to the heat generated by the Lindfors/Rydeberg love affair? Maybe! It seemed to have promised everything.

3

"Tell me about Rydeberg," Kristoffer, my actor son, suddenly asked me the other day. I was running a bath. Kris was sitting on the toilet seat, the way I used to do when he was little and he took his bath. "Sit with me, Mommy," he used to say. Today he is tall and beautiful and no longer a little boy. He is wearing nothing as usual, since he, too, was brought up in the Swedish way. I was laughing when he asked me because Rydeberg is the one man in my life whom Kris always liked to identify with. Kris never lived with his real father and perhaps like all my children is searching for a father image.

"I love acting," Kristoffer said as I crawled into the bathtub. "When I act is the time I am really happy." Oh God, I thought. He, too! "Tell me about Rydeberg."

"Well, he was very much like you, beautiful and sensual. It might have been easier for him if he had been born thirty years later, like you, and been allowed to fall in love without the pressure of having to get married and the responsibility of taking care of the woman, the children. It wasn't that he complained to me. But that was the impression I got. He had his chance with me but missed out. I just didn't fit into his image of a wife. And I was as stuck with my conditions as he was with his. 'It's a tragedy that we didn't get married,' he said to me twenty-five years later. We no doubt could have made brilliant theater and brilliant children together. His son, by the way, is called Kristoffer, too," I said, laughing.

"Was he a brilliant actor? I mean, how brilliant? Like Brando?" Kris asked me.

"Yes, brilliant like Brando."

"And like Laurence Olivier?"

"Yes, like Laurence Olivier. And like Olivier and Brando and you, he is beautiful and sensual. And, like them and you, he had a strange kind of mannerism, a kind of nasal way of speaking, which he either dropped or maybe it just didn't seem to matter any longer once he became more himself. Hm."

"What do you mean like me? I don't have any mannerisms."

"Well, most actors do. We hide ourselves behind comfortable masks. It takes time to dare to give them up."

"Please, Mother. I don't need a lecture," Kristoffer sighed. "Rydeberg was lucky. He didn't have to cope with television series or staying pure, being in the theater."

I thought about it for a while. "I think the challenge was the same then, but different. He was a matinee idol. Women were crazy about him, swooning over him. He could easily have fallen into a lazy pattern, but, like Olivier, he didn't. He knew instinctively, anyhow, what would make him develop as an actor. He went for the big stuff and moved on and left the sex symbol image behind. It was perhaps lucky for him that he was not popular in films. God knows why he wasn't. His looks were too foreign for the Swedes at that time, too far from the Hollywood he-man image. We were all mesmerized by Hollywood! Anyhow, he became a better and better actor, drawing from those marvelous parts he played. I saw him do *King John* and *Virginia Woolf* in one season. I'll never forget it."

Virginia Woolf was a woman's play on Broadway. It was totally his in Stockholm. I was struck by the intelligence of the performance, combined with a powerful emotion. He gave you a sense of unlimited humanity, of total belonging to the moment. His youngest son died in a bicycle accident. When he talked about the dead child in the play, it was deathly quiet in the house. It was an utterly naked moment. "He is obviously a Method actor," I thought. I hadn't seen him for at least ten years, maybe more, and at the time I was very involved with the Actor's Studio.

I had a drink with him after the performance and I was dying to talk about his work. He looked at me as if I were crazy. "What is there to talk about?" he said. And he went on asking me

whether I wanted red wine or white, fish or meat. And I understood that was as far as we would ever get. It is not that he is not
intelligent. He simply doesn't want to use it in life, only for his
work.

"Did you have an affair with him when you were home this
time?" Kris asked.

"No, not this time," I said, hesitating, not sure whether I should
tell him about our maybe second-chance meeting. I don't always
know whether I am influencing my children by telling them about
my own life. But then, Kris is not a child anymore, and he wants
to know.

"It was that spring when everything was so difficult between me
and Daddy." (Kris lived with G.T. from the age of three months
on and called him Daddy.) "I didn't know that G.T. had the girl
in Berlin, only that things were dry between us. I needed to know
that I could feel again, as a woman with a man. Perhaps I was
afraid of getting old. Anyhow, I had never been able to forget
Rydeberg. It had ended so abruptly I felt it was never finished between us. So why not, I thought."

Kris was quiet. I continued. "It was brief, our meeting, but we
did make peace with the fact that we might never be a couple in
the real sense and that was good."

"Would it have made any difference if you had known about
the girl and Daddy?" Kris asked.

"No," I said after a struggle with the better half of myself. It
was tempting to say yes, but not fair, nor true. "One thing really
doesn't have to do with the other. More important, I think, was
that we both acknowledged that it might just never be finished
between us, not really. Maybe it never is between people who once
have committed fully to each other. That was good too. Don't
you think?"

"Maybe," Kris said. "I remember once meeting him in Stockholm. I was twelve or thirteen. We were having dinner, except for
Daddy, naturally," he laughed. "I kept wondering about this
strange guy looking at my mother as if she were his woman."

"Yes," I answered. "He always acted as if twenty-five years,
husbands, wives, living in different countries didn't matter."

He kissed me in the doorway to the small apartment I still kept
in Stockholm and twenty-five years vanished out into the cold
winter air. His lips touched mine, withdrew, touched again and
again. The kiss was serious, yet filled with joy, even humor. It was

sensual as well as tender. We were two opposites and yet the same. I knew that very second why I had never been able to forget him.

The next day he took me to a party, friends of his. I felt Rydeberg's presence all through the evening and when we looked at each other over the dinner table, or across the room, everybody else vanished.

Around midnight, Jussi Bjorling's son sang lieder about Sweden and love. I was sitting alone on a bench, listening. In the middle of a song, Rydeberg got up very quietly and walked over to me. He sat down next to me, barely touching me, and I knew there was no way not to explore our love once more. That night I went up to his apartment.

It was a tiny, two-room apartment, very quiet. I didn't ask any questions about his wife. I knew she lived in Spain most of the time. Nor did he ask about G.T. He lit some candles and poured me some sherry. I can't describe the feeling, only that it was hard to breathe. He took me by the hand and led me into his bedroom. It was a small dark room overlooking the courtyard. It reminded me of the room behind the kitchen on Karlavagen when I was five and I learned about the maid's baby and the father, the priest so like the story in the film Rydeberg and I did together, ages ago.

There was a large Spanish bed in dark wood. Next to it was a tiny one, painted white, with dowels, a child's bed. "I sleep here," he said. "It's too lonely over there," and he pointed to the large bed.

That's where we made love that night. It was very different, our lovemaking, from when we were young. It didn't matter. "My soul is meeting yours," he said. I found myself crying. I must have wanted him for so long.

"The tragedy is that you and I never married," he said a few days later, sitting in my apartment by the telephone. He had his coat on, ready to leave, but not wanting to. The truth is that we didn't get married. Not then and not now.

I realized that week that I was more committed to my marriage with G.T. than I had known. I wasn't even able to stay all through the nights with Rydeberg in his apartment, afraid that G.T. would call me from Berlin and wonder where I was. Did G.T. worry in a similar way? What strange games we played with each other. I was obviously not ready to let go of my marriage. I wrote in my diary that week in Stockholm, "Can I find the kind of peace between me and G.T. that I feel now? I want to, still."

By the end of the week I went to meet G.T. in London and Rydeberg left for Spain to spend time with his wife. I took him to the airport. He had a special way of crying as if he had nothing to do with the tears running down his face, like a child.

When I got back to the apartment and found a bunch of red roses from him, I, too, started to cry, as if the old wound about letting love disappear from my life without resistance opened up finally.

Rydeberg and were rooted in different countries, different people, and it was too late for both of us at that time to live up to the effort of an upheaval. The journey was another one.

Six months later, when G.T. left me for Uschi, I could fight for what was mine. "I love you. I don't want to let you go," I cried out at last.

Maybe that is all that matters—that one can get to one's own truth. What I needed to find out that week with Rydeberg was that feelings never die in spite of wounding words or even time.

The day before we both took off in different directions, I had to see my mother in the old people's home. Rydeberg came along.

He sat in the garden and worked on the introduction to his autobiography while I was with her.

We stayed in the garden for a while afterwards. It was one of those heavenly Swedish summer days when the sky is so blue and the air so filled with nature's aromas it almost makes you drunk. The grass was so gently green, the flowers in intense, luscious bloom, the whole earth so superbly and quietly celebrating spring, affirming life completely. It was almost impossible to accept the ugliness of death. "I can't stand her suffering. It's inhuman," I said. "I hope I don't have to go like her. I don't want to lie year in and year out and wait for death. Will you come and help me over to the other side? I will do the same for you." He didn't say anything but he took my hand in both of his.

The pact between us, whether lived up to or not, signified the importance of our bond, however crooked our journey had been.

❧ IV ❧

Weddings and Babies

*"And then he comes and he asks me
to marry him . . . He tells me that
my present, unmarried position
was not one for a nice woman . . ."*
GEORGE BERNARD SHAW
Lina in Misalliance

THE FIRST WEDDING took place in a church. The actress was wearing a slinky black velvet dress. It was sexy, too. The man she married was the cameraman and German-born, and, more important, became the father to her firstborn, a son. It was winter and snow lay on the ground. Her stepson, aged six, carried a bouquet of spring flowers in his hand. The woman's name now became Mrs. Harry Hasso.

The second marriage took place in an office. Under the proper blue linen dress stirred another child, one of her own sex. The father was the lawyer who successfully divorced her from the cameraman. He now became the second husband. Her stepson had gone to his real mother, but her own baby boy was at home playing in the garden. She wished he had been at the wedding, holding the lilies of the valley in his tiny hand. Both he and the woman changed their names to Rogard.

The third marriage took place at the American Embassy in Paris. The bride wore a baby pink suit with white pearls embroidered on the lapels. The man she married was an American film director. He became the father of her third and last child. But not for some time. Her son and daughter were with the lawyer in the country. She missed them. It was early summer and the chestnut trees were in bloom on the Champs Elysées. She didn't want to blame anyone. The woman's name became Mrs. Don Siegel now. Siegel means "seal" in English. Don was her age and they both loved making films.

The fourth marriage took place on the beach. She held her last baby boy in her arms. Her daughter, Lena, whose father was the Swedish lawyer, was there. She carried a snake in her hand at the luncheon. The woman used to have nightmares about snakes crawling under her bed when she carried her in her womb. Did Lena remember that? John, her older son, whose father was the German, was away in camp and today she wonders how she could have made that mistake, as if she dared not involve him in more changes. The Hungarian became his fourth and last father and her fourth and last husband. She never had a child with him. The marriage lasted longer than any of the others, but not long enough. Their bare feet made imprints in the sand, and the loosely hanging sheet around her body was the color of the sun-hazed waves. She hoped for the best. She wanted a lover only. They all took on the name Tabori. George was a writer. They both loved the theater.

The four marriages had one thing in common. The woman vanished when she had to promise to love the man "until death do us part." She wasn't sure she could but she wasn't good at lying openly. Only the actress and the child were left and the latter was always crying. After some thirty years, her name was back to what it had been for some time—Lindfors, and Viveca with a c.

2

I shouldn't have married Harry. I said I would one late night. It was almost morning. We were in the kitchen eating Swedish pancakes. We might have made love before, I can't remember. It didn't seem important as it had been with Rydeberg. Harry had just told me, after I had promised never to tell anyone, that he was Jesus Christ who had returned to earth. Right after that statement he asked me to marry him. I don't know if it was his theatrical brilliance, which he ought to have used for his work instead of on a silly, confused girl like me, or if I needed a god. Since all men were godlike in my eyes, he must be one, too. Therefore, he was telling the truth, as all gods are supposed to do.

Perhaps it was because of Henry, only six years old, who was lost and needed a mother. His real one, Signe Hasso, also an actress, had gone to Hollywood. The war had begun and communication with the U.S.A. seemed worse than ever. Things were pretty drastic. Not even the checks arrived to pay for the groceries. Or perhaps Signe, the ex-wife and Henry's mother, had gotten tired of Harry not getting off his ass and earning his own living for himself and his son. I felt that way myself within a year. There were excuses, of course, for Harry's not working in Sweden. He was German and it was difficult to get a working permit. Swedes were less friendly toward foreigners in those days. However, necessity knows no law, and my film was the first one he had done in some time.

It didn't help, either, that the maid who had taken care of them was pregnant and wanted to go home to her husband and give birth to her baby in peace. I just couldn't stand seeing Henry being left all to himself. Who was to take care of him, but me?

There were other reasons in my favor. Harry, like no other man I had ever met, seemed to take my career seriously. He wanted to help me become a star. I thought I needed help. He seemed to know how. He had been successful with his first wife. She had a contract with Hollywood now.

Then, in the end, of course, I was needed. Which I needed.

Because of all those reasons, and they seemed to multiply, now when the real reason was missing, I succumbed to the pressure from within and without and said, "Yes, I will," that night in the kitchen.

Oh yes, one part of me did!

Although the youngest of three, I was the first of my mother's children to get married. When she heard I was wearing the sexy black velvet dress for the wedding, she refused to go. She didn't understand. How could she? I was hard and said I didn't care. I had forgotten how she had understood me a few months before when I was crying in the room under the roof. I had tried to explain to her that it was the only good-looking dress I had. I was slightly fat and liked the way I looked in it. I still had no money and, with the grocery bills and everything else, I couldn't afford another one. It was a theatrical dress, too, and as I wandered up the aisle on my father's arm I wanted to be true to the image of an eccentric actress!

It paid off. The church was filled with photographers. As I wandered back down the aisle on Harry's arm, the flashes were going like mad. My mother had changed her mind, of course, but it wasn't until I saw her crying, sitting on the church bench, that I started to cry.

In the evening, Harry, Henry, his son and now my stepson, and I went home to the sixteenth-century carriage house in Drottingholm, near the castle where the Swedish kings used to spend the summers, and still do, and where Harry lived with Henry. The park was endlessly large and filled with ancient and enormous trees. I would take long walks under them on Sundays. They gave me a sense of safety and protection against myself, telling me not to worry and that life would straighten itself out eventually, even love. I believed it then. I was only twenty-one.

At the time of the marriage, we had just finished the film, *If I Marry a Minister*. Everyone involved sensed we had a hit on our hands. It was a simple, straightforward film, poetic in its own naive way. The filmmaker, Ivar Johnson, was better than everyone gave him credit for. We worked long hours and on Saturdays, too. I had moved in with Henry and Harry already during the fall and I had to get up at 5:30 AM in order to catch two bus rides, often in ten degrees below zero weather. I had to be in make-up at 7:00, and on the set at 8:00. I was never home until 8:00 at night. I thought nothing of it. I liked it and liked that I liked it. I was a working person.

The film was shot on location and in an old stable that had been turned into a film studio. There were few airplanes in those days and little need for soundproof walls. I had a simple but friendly dressing room and Marianne, my hairdresser, took care of all my needs. She helped me dress, make-up, brought my lunch, et cetera, and it was even possible to become friends.

It was Henry, my stepson, who awakened my sense of mother-hood. Before becoming with child myself, I became his mother. Henry was tall for his age, thin, with dark eyes like John's, my own son.

He was intelligent. I don't mean smart, for he was too vulner-able or too human for that. I didn't know what his real mother was like, and if he missed her he never said so. Perhaps he was afraid of admitting it, afraid of hurting me. I didn't know how to help him talk about it, either. I liked being responsible for him, but wasn't quite ready for the new role. Motherhood is not something you learn overnight. There are few shortcuts and I was only twenty that fall when I moved into the house and Henry started school.

I took him there the first day, but didn't understand that I ought to help him with his homework until his teacher called me one day and told me I should. It hadn't even occurred to me. But then, my mother never helped me and how would I find the time to do that now that I was a working actress?

The situation was, no doubt, difficult for Henry. His mother was in a faraway land. There was a war going on. The communication between the two of them, through letters and telephone calls, be-came more and more infrequent, nor was Harry an ideal father. He was a violent man, whether I wanted to face it or not and I didn't want to. The first time I saw him chase Henry all over the house, furious with him for God knows what, eventually catching up with him, framing him like a rat in a corner, beating him up, slapping him with his bare hands, I was stunned and paralyzed. I had never experienced open violence.

I gave myself ridiculous excuses about not interfering. "He's not my child, I have no right, he's not my child." I still have nightmares about not being able to defend myself or find the way to defend myself, or somebody like Henry; about not having the guts to fight back when it really matters. And what if it were me, and nobody came to my rescue?

I didn't have to deal with the situation with Henry for too long. Henry's mother sent for him a few months after the wedding. She was doing well in Hollywood. There was a ship sailing from Gothenberg to New York. It carried a neutral flag. This was 1941 and, although America had not yet entered the war, it was a question of days, maybe hours, and the white-flagged Swedish ship was the last safe chance to make it across the ocean to the U.S.A. People from all over Europe came to get on it.

We went to Gothenberg to see Henry off. He was to travel with the Swedish ambassador and his family. I took him down to the cabin and helped him unpack. I began to feel strange and uncomfortable—with life, with myself, with giving up Henry.

I talked with the governess who was to take care of him and the ambassador's children. I tried to explain to her about a rash Henry had and how it was to be taken care of. She was insensitive about it, I thought. I had this unbearable identification with Henry, as I had later with my own children, as I have now with my grandchildren. I was suddenly aware of not being Henry's mother for much longer, having to turn him over to other women, strangers, and I didn't like it.

Suddenly I became aware that I wasn't ready to say goodbye at all. I didn't express it. Neither did Henry. Politely we went back up on the deck to look for Harry. He stood by the railing looking out over the ocean toward where Henry's future lay, way off in the distance, but a future without his father. Would he ever see his son again? There was a war going on. Nobody knew when it would be over or when they would see each other again. The pull to leave with Henry, to join Signe, to be a family again, must have been killing. I knew he had loved her very much. Still did, perhaps. Could he have expressed it to me, those feelings? I might just have played some stupid game: "You love her more than me!"

I was too young, too inexperienced to understand about blood ties, about roots in each other, about respecting them in spite of separations and other relationships.

I had enough sense to leave Harry and Henry alone and was the first to say goodbye. Henry looked at me with his dark eyes. We hugged each other awkwardly, again as if we had no right to the pain. As if we did only what was expected between a stepmother and a stepson. Besides, what was the sense of emotions? He knew he had to go. He knew I had to go. I knew he had to go. I knew I had to go. I had no claim on him at all, and if I discovered in that moment that I loved him more than I had meant to, I didn't allow myself to share it.

Henry didn't cry or even say, "Do you have to leave me?" as John did years later and as Natasha would. He knew no one would pay attention to it. He knew it then, there, and forever. But what do reason and logic have to do with the right to express one's feelings? Damn it.

I walked away. I waited for Harry by the gangplank.

He came a few minutes later, cursing and spitting in fury, as he always did when he was in pain and defeated. He didn't fight to keep Henry. He couldn't, or didn't know how. He knew it, Henry knew it, I knew it. I would take a child away from him too, barely within a year's time. I, too, felt that John, our child, was only mine, and that I would not give him up to Harry or any other father who wouldn't fight for him.

There is an Indian saying: "He who uses the land owns it." It begins with yourself. At the time I was married to Harry, Harry did not belong to Harry. He had never belonged to anyone, so his child never belonged to him. I heard John say the other day, "I will never let anybody else bring up my child. I and Susan will do it together." It is possible to break the pattern. The sins of the fathers do not have to be inherited, nor the sins of the mothers.

Henry arrived safely in the U.S.A., surviving dangerous mine-filled waters, unfriendly enemy planes. Fourteen years later, not a child anymore but a grown-up, supposedly an independent man, he bumped ever so lightly into a telephone pole with his car—I was told—and his heart stopped. No one else got hurt, not even the car. Only Henry's heart gave up.

Signe called me: "Viveca, can I come over?" We knew each other only through Henry. We had seen each other on rare occasions when she brought Henry over for a visit. Otherwise we were strangers.

"Oh my God, of course! Do come." It was late in the afternoon. She was pale and thin. She wasn't crying. I didn't either. We talked about Henry. Had she grasped his death? Can one?

She was appearing in a play on Broadway and wanted to go on stage that night. I went with her to the theater. I sat with her in the dressing room. I caught the moment when for a second her eyes met the truth in her own. She couldn't avoid it. She was putting on her eyelashes, making up for the show. She was an actress.

In that flash of a second she saw the unbearable image: "a woman who has lost a child, a woman whose child was gone forever." Oh God! The panic! She looked away quickly. She took a breath, like a newborn baby when the navel string is just cut off, not yet used to breathing, not knowing why, doing it only in order not to die. She faced his death, the death of her own flesh and blood, that very moment and survived.

That she had come to me that day made me wonder if Henry talked about me. Even loved me. We had known each other for only ten months when he was six going on seven, but I had become part of his emotional horizon, which gave him the right to love me as well—if not as much—as his real mother. Children of my own, love and work and distances, too, made it difficult for me to nourish the tie between us. Or so it seemed. For a child, and Henry was one, perhaps it was not possible to accept those sophisticated reasons, even lies, we grownups figure out to protect ourselves against emotional responsibilites.

I see it all clearly today. For better or for worse.

Henry died at the age of twenty-one, a child of two actresses. Two actresses in the twentieth century, wanting to be, trying to be, women as well as artists. Not freaks, not goddesses. Women living with men and children.

A few weeks after my stepson Henry had left for the U.S.A., Harry and I left for Rome, Italy. My career as an international film star began.

If I Married a Minister had opened right after Christmas. It was a tremendous success and so was I. I became a film star overnight. They wrote about my cheekbones, my sensuality, and a mysterious, photogenic quality à la Garbo. I wasn't sure that it all was happening to me, but I decided not to ask too many questions and sailed along with the wind of fame. It blew all the way down to Italy, and two producers came to Stockholm to discuss a three-picture deal for me in Italy. The Italian industry under Mussolini's regime was trying to move beyond its own national boundaries and become a European Hollywood. To sign a Swedish actress was by now a guaranteed success formula. Ingrid Bergman was the second Swedish actress to become enormously popular. This was before Ingmar Bergman proved that Swedish films as well as their actresses could become world-famous. It's unfortunate that Lux Film and I didn't have the vision. Through the partnership we brought each other money and success, and when I went to America the company faded. Nygrin, the head of Lux, took on a subordinate position representing Fox Films in Stockholm, and I didn't achieve anywhere near the position at Warner Brothers that I had had with Lux Film in Sweden.

It was Harry who took me to Folke Rogard, *the* lawyer in Stockholm for dealing with film and film stars. He had negotiated the contract for Signe with Hollywood. He now negotiated mine with the Italians. Eventually he became my husband, Lena's father, and John's stepfather. Oh yes!

This was 1942. That I ought not to have worked for the fascists did not occur to me, nor to Harry who was very apolitical in spite of being born a German, nor to Folke, a politically aware man who had negotiated many deals with the Nazis, representing rich Jews, buying freedom for them and their relatives. If he tried to make me aware, I didn't listen. Not unusual for Swedes at that time.

Harry and I were not the only ones going to work for the fascists. Sven Nykvist, the cameraman who works with Bergman, a superb artist who paints with his camera, was another Swede who went. Thirty years later, in my house on 95th Street, Sven and I met again. "I am still ashamed that I worked for the fascists," he said. "It's amazing but I totally lacked political conscience." He was doing a film for Bergman about that particular period. "So did I," I said.

So did the entire country, it seemed. The line between neutrality and passivity is a thin and dangerous one. Safety was bought with our neighbor's blood. Mysterious trains were seen passing through in the middle of the night, carrying German troops on their way to occupy Norway.

We closed our eyes and acted as if we knew nothing about it. It was not for us, anyhow, but for the leaders to make those decisions. I reacted the same way.

Even later, when I knew what I knew, I continued to sell myself. "I am an actress, a woman. It isn't my department." It would be years before I understood how it undermines you, this noncommital attitude, both as an artist and as a woman. You cannot take a stand on the stage if you do not take a stand in life and vice versa. But at the age of twenty-one I certainly wasn't ready. I signed a three-picture deal with the Italians.

Harry seemed overjoyed to leave Sweden. Surely it wasn't an easy place to be a foreigner there in those days. The question was, would he be any happier in Italy and would they understand his talent better. His contract called for cameraman and director, but it soon became clear that the Italian producers had little interest in him. Besides, he was a German and Germans were not popular in Italy, no matter how much Mussolini screamed about loyalty to the brother country Germany.

Of course I understood none of that and was excited for us both. Nor was I aware of my roots or being held back by them.

We boarded the plane in Stockholm one early April morning. It was still cold. There was still snow on the ground. It had been an endlessly long, bitter winter.

I couldn't believe my eyes when, a few hours later, I looked down through the window and saw green olive trees, lush woods covering the seven hills of Rome. I thought I had arrived in Paradise. In a way I had.

3

Rome 1942 was, in spite of the war, in spite of Mussolini, an extraordinary city. During the nine months I lived there, although living conditions changed drastically, Rome remained Rome, a holy city. We were never bombed. It became a rare place for the battle-fatigued to rest, to find distraction, even safety.

The Germans had invaded the city in more ways than one. They took over hotels, pensions, apartments, villas, beaches. At night, with the street lights turned low in order to save electricity, and the watermelon stands providing the gray image of the ancient city with a few passionate spots, one could hear German spoken as much as Italian. It was a splendid time for the whores. The only way to get some eggs or milk or coffee was to know a German or a whore. I preferred the whores, and, when they saw I was pregnant, they went out of their way.

I had begun to feel tired and nauseous during the filming in Rome. I thought it was the change of climate, but it persisted and I went to the doctor. It was an early morning in the beginning of June when I wandered up one of the seven hills in Rome where

the clinic "for women only" lay imbedded in green. The nuns
moved softly and gently in their white uniforms, their faces
washed white like masks. The doctor mumbled in Italian, but I did
understand the word "bambino." He wanted to make a test. "What
for?" I wondered. I had never gotten pregnant before, not even
with Rydeberg, whom I was wild about.

So why now, with Harry? Not that I had used contraceptives.
I didn't know about them in those days. Perhaps I was more
bourgeois than I had known. Wanting to "give the man a child"
as a good wife should?

"Come back for the results Friday morning," the nurse said in
broken English. I did.

Again the doctor told me in Italian. Again I recognized the word
"bambino." But it was not until I looked into the eyes of the nun,
filled with warmth, that I grasped that I was with child.

I felt an intense surge of happiness, as if a miracle had happened. I danced down the hillside, singing to the trees, to the sky.
"A human being is inside of me! Inside my body is a child! My
child! I will, never, never, never, never be alone anymore." I accepted it without question, without a doubt, without fear. It never
occurred to me either that there was a choice, and if there had
been, I would not have known how to make it. Never did. I have
never regretted being a mother. I have loved and love that part of
my life. My difficulty in combining motherhood with being an actress was, by far, outweighed by the pleasure and the richness
the children have brought my life.

It didn't occur to me either that it might cause problems as far
as completing the contracts with the Italians.

I had finished my first film and was to begin my second film in
November. It was called *La Donna Picato*, the sinful woman.
Lucky for me, it barely showed that I was pregnant. It wouldn't
have fitted in with the image! However, by the end of the film I
was wearing big coats and shawls, and Hans Heinrich, the director,
lovingly and most tenderly covered me in close-ups. Pregnancy
had not stopped me from working nor from falling in love. Nor
did it stop Heinrich from falling in love with me.

To be in love in the middle of the violence and chaos seemed
the only possible way to stay human.

Heinrich was a German Jew, a refugee. He had escaped from the
Nazis and worked under a pseudonym in Rome. It was still possible. The Italians didn't really care as long as he was a good
director, and he was. There were many Jews like him existing in

Rome. They were safe, as long as the pressure was not unbearable. But then, nobody was really safe.

Harry had become more and more impossible to live with. What had become apparent was that he was along for the ride only as the husband. Still, he was given opportunities. But, although he was gifted and talented, he did not have the stamina nor the commitment it takes to carry work through to its fullest, as Heinrich did, in spite of the circumstances. Nobody had taught Harry. Defeat was in his blood.

He became more and more depressed, lying in the hotel room with the curtains drawn. When I came home from work he would be unpleasant, hating the world, himself, and me. I had no way of coping with his depression, and perhaps insensitivity was my only defense.

Heinrich was married. She was a German actress and slightly older than he. She was an Aryan. She had escaped with him. Her loyalty was one hundred percent. They were comrades from way back, working together in the German theater.

None of that stopped us from being in love, but only spiritually! Whether I was hypocritical or just old-fashioned, or afraid to commit, afraid it would lead to a confrontation which I wasn't ready to cope with, I don't know, but I never did let him inside of me. It didn't seem to matter. We had a marvelous time anyhow. We would make up for it one day!

We had lunch in my dressing room, and after work we stopped for a glass of wine on the Via Venito. Hans told me about what happened in Germany to him, to his people, to the Jews. Slowly I began to get a glimpse into the horror of the crimes that were going on. I had begun to grasp the destructiveness of my Uncle Fred's beliefs, and how lucky I was that, at the age of ten, sitting in his lap, loving him, I did not become a Nazi myself. I had gotten by by the skin of my teeth.

We spent Christmas together, all of us, Hans, his wife, Harry, I, Sven Nykvist, and another Swedish cameraman also under contract in Italy. Sven knew about our love affair. "I used to bring you letters from Hans; don't you remember?" he said to me thirty years later in New York. I had forgotten. "Where is Hans now?" I asked him. "In Germany. He is running his own theater."

We had fantasized, Heinrich and I, that he might come to Sweden after the baby was born. But, like Brecht and Weigel, Heinrich and his wife returned to their country, their language, and their own people, in spite of the violence and hate that had driven them away from there a few years earlier.

My baby's birth was estimated for February. Times were progressively chaotic, and the tension in the city of Rome grew. The bombing in the south of Italy was brutal. The American and the British armies were getting closer, but nobody knew what would happen next. The fascist government was in a state of collapse. Mussolini and Hitler were at the end of their ropes and, like wounded animals, were becoming even more dangerous and more hysterical than before. Life was at stake. I was anxious to get home as soon as possible.

Hans did everything to finish my work in the film, and one beautiful sunny morning in late January I took off for Sweden, for safety, for neutrality, leaving the seven hills of Rome and the two men in love with me behind, using my pregnancy as a shield against facing the future with either one of them. An old female trick.

I stopped in Berlin to visit some friends. Berlin 1943 was tense and depressing. Both the city and the people seemed exhausted. They were bombed day and night. I was lucky. During the evening and the night I spent there, I could hear the rumble, but at a safe distance. I had worked with Gustav Diesel, a wonderful actor, and I had met his wife, a German opera singer, in Rome. There was no such thing as a taxi, so I took the bus to their house. For the first and last time in my life I saw a Jew with a yellow star around his arm. He was a tiny man. He stood in the back of the bus, for he wasn't allowed to sit down with the rest of us. There were signs of acknowledgment by people passing him. The guilt showed itself in various ways. Some preferred not to notice him at all. Others pushed him around, as if needing to affirm he *was* inferior, an enemy, a human being standing in their way. Some appeared deeply apologetic, depressed, victimized, with thin smiles on their lips, as if they were saying, "I am suffering too, with you," not daring to show too much sympathy, to save their own skins. Was I so different? I ask myself. I remember a sense of deep rage. True, there was nothing I could do at that particular moment, just like the rest of the passengers. Only I could get out and they couldn't.

Whether my friends that I was having dinner with could or couldn't was unclear, above all, for psychological reasons perhaps. I felt the tension and understood their dilemma without words. We avoided talking about politics carefully all evening, and I will never know the answer because a few months later Gustav died.

He was a mountain climber. He had slipped, it was said. Perhaps he could not find within himself the hope he needed to leave his country and start a new life somewhere else. His wife died of cancer a year later. I don't know what happned to the two children.

At the airport the following morning, I got into a fight with the customs officer. He wore an SS uniform. It was enough for me to hate him, because of Heinrich, because of the Jew with the yellow star around his arm, and because of Gustav, my friend.

I was emotionally involved and therefore no longer safe—Swede or not.

Suddenly, in the middle of the argument with the officer, I realized the danger. Nothing would stop this Nazi from arresting me—not the Swedish embassy, not my neutral passport. I could simply disappear then and there. I quickly got very polite. "I must find more effective ways to fight," I mumbled to myself. "How? Where?" were the questions. It would be years until I found the answer or, better, the courage of conviction.

Ironically enough, the films that were to make me famous within the next couple of years, box office star number one, the Marilyn Monroe of Sweden—I couldn't walk the streets without being mobbed—were written by two German Jewish refugees who found safety in Sweden. They astonishingly enough worked under pseudonyms, like Hans in Italy, like my friends in the U.S.A. during the McCarthy period. I never met them, nor did I know anything about them. Who would have believed that this was happening in a safe and neutral country like Sweden? We, too, had chosen the sickness of silence in the face of injustice.

Circles, circles . . .

John, my firstborn, who that day in Berlin was swimming safely inside my womb, showed me twenty-five years later what I so totally had lacked at his age.

His wife called, one early morning. It was 1972.

"I am worried! John is still at Columbia. I have been listening to the radio. The night was bloody between the police and the students. I can't even get him on the phone."

"I will pick you up in ten minutes," I said. I met her at the corner of West End where they lived. We drove up to the gate. There was a mob there. We parked the car a few blocks away. We walked up. "I am a Swedish journalist," I said to the guard. He believed me. I am an actress and I didn't have to work for the accent. Getting inside the camp we faced a dreadful sight. Groups of students with bloody bandages were sleeping on the lawns, huddled together. Broken windows. A strange kind of intense exhaustion in the air. We asked everyone, "Have you seen my son? Have you seen my husband?" He was one of the organizers and therefore well known. We went on looking.

"Have you seen John Tabori?"

"Yes," someone answered me, his eyes bloodshot and his arm in a sling. "I saw him earlier in the morning. Up at the library."

"Was he all right?" I asked, my stomach trembling.

"When I saw him he looked all right." As we found the library building, we saw John come down the steps, drawn, tired looking. We hugged. "I'm fine," he said.

Completely at peace with himself, knowing he had done what he had to do. I felt tears in my eyes, but remembered Brecht's words: "Don't get moved. Get moving."

"Thank God. What can I do?"

"Go up to the radio station and speak about what you see. They don't report on it correctly in the papers. Tell the parents that they've got to be on our side. Tell them the truth."

I went up to the radio station. Everybody was exhausted. They had been there for twenty-four to thirty hours. They let me get in front of the microphone. "I am Viveca Lindfors, a mother," I said. "I must tell you what's going on. I am speaking to you, the parents and citizens of New York." I spoke excitedly, intensely involved, about what I had seen, about the injustice, about the cruelty, about the brutality. I spoke up.

It was helpful being married to G.T., a man of social conscience. He provided me with knowledge. Without it, passion vanishes and fear takes over. I had already experienced my own rage during the McCarthy period, but was constantly haunted by questions like "Will I be able to stand up under pressure? What if I am called to Washington before the Un-American Committee?" I was lucky. I was never put to the test. Then came the war against Vietnam and I found myself deeply involved in the peace movement. This time I had no choice. I surely didn't want my own sons to die in a senseless war. It made things very clear.

I read poetry whenever I was asked. One day at Columbia University, in the middle of a performance, I discovered a major network camera in front of me. My knees began to shake. "I'm on record now," passed through my mind, but I continued. We were not as alone as those who were blacklisted during the McCarthy period, nor as the Jew in the Berlin bus. It was not life and death for us. Again I was lucky. But that event and many others became significant to me in the sense, "If I do not exercise this muscle of taking a stand, how will I be able to when it really matters?" The Brecht actor talks about having a point of view, social or political. I agree. If I can't take a stand in life, how can I do it on the stage? And vice versa. It makes you a better actor.

But that day in Berlin, thirty-two years ago, when for the first and last time in my life I saw a Jew with a yellow star around his arm, with my unborn son, a future politician, still tied to my navel, was a beginning of an awareness in the right direction. But it was an emotional one only, and soon success, warm and seductive, embraced me, lulling me back into the seemingly comfortable atmosphere of neutrality. As did Folke, my lawyer, my friend!

Stepping off the plane from Berlin, 1943, I found him waiting for me at the airport with a three-year contract, ready to be signed with Lux Film, negotiated by him.

The first film was to be made the moment I stood on my feet after the baby was born. We were a team now, Folke, me, and Lux Film. We knew it and they knew it. It paid off brilliantly.

Folke took care of me in more ways than one. When the landlord turned me down as a lessee for an apartment, because I was an actress, Folke handled it. He took me to the theater and out for dinner. He loved my pregnancy and worried about me. I was flattered by his attention. He was an important man, and although I had a suspicion that he might be in love with me, he didn't demand anything or talk about it. Since I liked him for his warmth and his taking care of me like a father, I didn't bring it up, either.

Awaiting my baby, life was suddenly safe and soft again. Heinrich and his battle for survival in Rome seemed less and less real, less and less mine as time passed. It is hard to face today, but there it is.

Then there was Harry. I knew he would show up one day from Rome. He did, a few weeks before the baby was born.

I knew clearly I didn't want him as my husband, nor as the father of my child—and rightly or wrongly, I felt the child was mine, only mine—but I didn't know how to go about confronting him. Whenever the subject of divorce was approached, he got wild. No doubt Harry was in a vulnerable position. As a German subject, he depended upon his marriage to me for his visa in Sweden. Life in Germany was a horror and no place to return to. "If you leave me, I'll kill you *and* the baby." I didn't really believe him. Until the night at the Grand Hotel, where we stayed while waiting for the apartment to be ready. I tried to talk to him about us, also about Hans, to tell him that I wanted to be free. I didn't want to carry the secret by myself any longer. That was the mistake, wanting to be straight with him.

He started to beat me. I screamed, but no one came to my rescue, no one heard me. I was sitting on the bed, leaning over. All I could think of was trying to protect my football-like belly, my unborn child. I was petrified. I felt stuck, like a rat framed in the corner. I had seen Henry, his six-year-old son, stuck. It was a horrendous experience, being alone with a man, knowing he wanted to kill me because he loved me. Horrendous, also, to be punished for wanting to talk about feelings, clear or unclear—feelings that interfered with our relationship. For that he beat me. He thought he had that right, like the Nazi with the Jew.

Suddenly he stopped. Perhaps I had promised by then to write to Heinrich, for I was ready to do anything to save myself and my baby. I was ready to say, "I don't love you anymore. Get lost. I love my husband Harry. Get lost. Don't come to Sweden. Don't write to me. Disappear. Get lost."

Perhaps he saw my eye bloodshot, puffy, beginning to swell. After all, I was a film star. My looks were my fortune. He told me to get dressed, dragged me downstairs, got me to a taxi, and off we went to the hospital. I mumbled something to the doctor about an accident in a cab. I was lucky again. The eye was OK, just bloodshot and turning black and blue. I could hide it behind black glasses and nobody could possibly believe that a pregnant woman had been beaten, certainly not a film star, certainly not Viveca Lindfors. Neither could I. It became unreal.

I didn't say to the doctor, safe in his examination room, "Call the police. My husband beat me up." I joined a long row of women, mesmerized in their feeling that to be with child *and* to be in love with another man was sinful—no matter—and has been since way back in time!

However, something clicked in me that night. No matter what I promised, and, oh yes, I did send a letter to Hans telling him I no longer loved him, that the affair, which had never been an affair, was over; oh yes, that much Harry accomplished; and I did tell Harry that I loved him, but that was a lie, for along with the end of the "affair" the marriage was over, too.

How stupid, how utterly unimaginative to believe that you can love out of fear, that you can love holding anything back.

For me it was only a question of time now. I wanted to give birth to my child in peace. I knew I couldn't cope with another scene. I bought strength with time. A week later I gave birth to a son. John was born March 18, 1943.

I was afraid as we drove to the hospital in the early morning. Harry was with me, but not farther than through the registration office. In those days fathers were not allowed to be part of the birth of their child. I was relieved, for I wanted to be alone, away from him. I finally would be, for ten days. Pain or no pain.

Giving birth to John was my experience, only mine and his. It was a long labor, and when they brought John into my room washed and dressed in swaddling clothes, he looked like a tiny tired old man. The experience of trying to get himself out of me could not have been an easy one. As he was lying there next to me on the pillow, I knew we loved each other enormously, always would. I knew, too, finally, I could be a mother and an actress. I did not have to make a choice, either/or, as my mother thought she had to. Like many women, her generation thought they had to.

"The pain is beyond imagination," my mother had told me. I knew nothing else about childbirth. But since I knew that she felt more pain about her life than I ever wanted to or thought necessary, I experienced a wild, godlike power in my body that was glorious and astonishing, and it made me forget in no time whatever the pain was.

I tried to sell Susan, John's wife, about it when she was giving birth to Nicholas Jan, their firstborn. Afterwards she said, "It has to be experienced to be believed."

It was an exciting event for me. I was waiting in the Father's Room with Kris, who had shown up straight from the airport from California. Once in a while we went to the hallway, trying to find out what was going on. Suddenly John appeared out of the delivery room. He looked like some enormous robot dressed in green surgical clothes with a mask over his face. I could barely tell it was him except for the gesture that something terrific had happened. He was jumping up and down like a monkey. "It's a boy," said Kristoffer. I didn't hear because I was hard of hearing at that time!

"A boy! How is Susan?" We gestured back and forth.

"Terrific!" They wheeled her out an hour later. I saw her.

"Couldn't have done it without your son," she said, putting her thin, pale hand in mine. She added, "I couldn't have gone through it without John in the delivery room."

I thought, "Good for her and him." I never did experience that, and I know it is a loss.

Nursing became another glorious experience. I was totally unaware of its value. "I am a film star," I had said to the doctor after I returned from Italy to Sweden. "I am going into production right after the birth of my child and I cannot nurse."

He barely looked up from his desk where he was writing a prescription, but I, determined not to be sidetracked from becoming a working woman, continued, "It's quite common, doctor, outside of Sweden, to give the child a bottle. It's perfectly safe."

He faintly looked up at me with his tiny blue eyes. "There's a law in Sweden, Miss Lindfors," he said. "Women must nurse their children for six weeks after birth. Usually, by that time, they do not want to give up the experience."

He was absolutely right!

I nursed John for seven months. I loved it. After a few days nothing would have stopped me from doing it, and nursing didn't stop me, either, from making two films at the same time. Nor did it hurt my sex symbol image with the audience. On the contrary, my popularity grew. A baby at a woman's breast is a sensual image.

I once remember a man leaning over and sucking from the free breast of his woman, who was nursing their child on the other. It was a glorious picture. It must have been a glorious experience for the three of them.

Having a baby, even nursing it, was no problem for me whatsoever, nor an interference in my work. I was lucky to have found a most sensational nurse, Klara, cheerful, firm, and superbly competent.

At six in the morning she would emerge with John all cleaned up, screaming for his breakfast. I fed him half asleep in my warm bed. I had plenty of milk and one breast was sufficient, and as Klara served me freshly made coffee in the bright, shiny, beautiful nursery, an electric breast pump emptied my other breast (a not uncommon practice for working mothers in Sweden). John was lying there, laughing, gurgling, watching it all. I kissed him good-bye and bicycled to the studio. At ten she served him my valuable milk from a bottle, and at lunchtime a chauffeur-driven car brought me home and together John and I had lunch. At five in the afternoon, Klara would bring him to the studio in his carriage. If the weather was bad, the chauffeured car was available again.

True, I was a special case, a film star, and most women would not get the service I was given. It was in everybody's interest to protect my energy and my looks, and money was of no matter.

I don't know if this schedule would work in Hollywood where distances are much farther, making life more complicated, and where an actress is a money-making proposition and not a baby-making one. But *it's possible!* It is a question of attitude, of accepting children as part of life, as a plus, not a minus.

From the hospital John and I moved into my new apartment. It was glorious. So was my career. My child was beautiful and healthy and well cared for. Everything was going my way, but— the father! Harry! I knew I could no longer put off what had to be done. *How* was the question.

I had only one trump card in my hand. Without my signature on his visitor's visa, Harry would not be allowed to stay in Sweden. I decided to refuse to sign. It was a dirty trick. But in those days I believed that in love and war everything is allowed, and there was a war between us now. He had set the rules. I played the card accordingly, I told myself, for I was still petrified of him after the night in the Grand Hotel.

I fled to the country with John and Klara to my parents' summer house, a small cottage located in a military zone where no foreigners were allowed, a lucky coincidence, and I let Folke handle the confrontation with Harry, the unsigned visa, the divorce papers. Only one thing he could not protect me from was my presence at the divorce hearing in Stockholm. Harry's presence was not needed. I did not have to confront him, but he was still around in Stockholm that day.

With John in my arms, I drove through the city to the courthouse, pressed against the back seat, hidden behind black glass, petrified of being caught. I saw Harry in every corner, coming out of every doorway with a gun in his hand, ready to kill me and my baby. It was all in my fantasy and the day passed safely according to schedule. In the evening we returned to the cottage with the birds singing and the green trees embracing us both.

Harry left a few days later for Germany. Neither I nor John have seen him since.

Today I wonder what it felt like for John to have that face disappear suddenly, the face of the first man he saw, the voice of the first man he heard, the presence of the first man he sensed while in the womb. For Harry, in spite of his violent temper, his depressions, had moments of tenderness, however rare. He used to put his head on my stomach trying to hear the heartbeat of the baby, talking to it through my skin. I suddenly remembered it all one day thirty years later when John was a grown man himself.

I was on my way into my study when he stopped me. "Can I see a picture of my father, my real father, Harry?" he asked me.

"You mean I never showed you a picture of him? I can't believe myself," I said.

"Well," John said with a laugh, for he has a sense of humor about it all by now, "you always wanted to give me what seemed to be a better reality. I understood that. But now, since 'they' didn't work out so well and it is all behind us, I might as well have a look at the real father. I don't even know what he looks like."

John has been through three fathers since Harry left, G.T. being the fourth and last. He was certainly right in his request. Perhaps the most painful split for John was when he was four and I left Folke, his stepfather. He knew him well. Loved him. He never could switch that love to anybody else. He didn't talk about it, for no one would or could listen, just like Henry. John was eight when I left Don and, at 15, after I had been married to G.T. for six years, he had a nervous breakdown. It was his way of saying, "I can't take any more fathers. I don't want to."

It's ironic, for I always felt I must find the perfect father for John. Yet I never asked him what he thought was perfect. One afternoon after his breakdown, he came home from the psychiatrist; his eyes were shining. "I have to be my own father," he said. It was his solution until he became one himself.

"I will find the pictures and mail them to you," I said.

"Is he alive?" John asked me. "Do you know where he is?"

"I think in Sweden someplace, but I am not sure. I never kept contact with him." I felt heavy but I continued. I wasn't going to let the guilt get the better of me. "I will check it with Signe; she had more contact with him than I did. She knows more about him. I will drop her a note." I kept on talking, feeling a need to tell him the truth, at least as far as I knew it, sorting out what would be important for him to know. "I didn't love Harry. I couldn't." I stopped myself. I had a terrible feeling in my stomach. Was it wrong for me to say that? Yet I continued. "He did provide me, however, with a link that was essential for me in order to go on, and you were the best thing that happened in the marriage." I still felt uptight, for perhaps what John needed to hear was that a woman loves the father of her child, no matter what. Again, I felt I couldn't give him what he wanted. I continued, "But I want you to know I wanted you very much. I had no doubts about that. You were loved and cared for, you were my prince, my firstborn," I said with a laugh. I got out of my momentary depression. "I will mail you the pictures if I find them," I repeated. A few hours later I said a halting goodbye, and he was off to Washington.

Had I taken enough time? Had I answered his questions? Had I hugged him enough? I decided to write him a letter and send it down with the pictures.

It was Kristoffer, his younger brother, who found them. I had told him of the conversation. Knowing himself how painful it is to live with ghosts, he started to look for them. He had been only three years old himself when he realized that there was another man existing, a real father other than G.T.

"Is this John's father?" He showed me a picture of Harry holding a baby boy in his arms.

"Yes, that's Harry and John." And I sent it off with a letter.

"Dearest John,

"I want to add to our conversation. Perhaps it's not necessary; perhaps you understand anyhow; perhaps it's just a need of mine. No matter. I wanted you to know that at the moment when you happened, I wanted to believe that Harry and I could love each other. I fooled myself, but it was a brilliant experience for me to be pregnant with you, anyhow. It performed something for me that I had never thought possible. I had almost dismissed the idea but I must have wanted it, for, when I discovered it, I was deliriously happy.

"When Natasha asked me the other day why I hadn't stayed married to Harry and I answered that I was careless and hadn't thought it through—whether he would be a good father or not—before I married him, I should have added, perhaps, and hope I will one day, that at the time I had set very few standards for myself, which is all right as long as one is aware of it and one begins to collect new ones. Life is a long process, sometimes even kind in giving second chances.

"I am enclosing a letter to Signe and I hope she will contact you so that you can find out what you need to know about Harry. The picture is in black and white, but you can still see that Harry had a beautiful face, especially when he was happy, which unfortunately was rare. He was a wounded man, which doesn't excuse him for letting you go forever out of his life, but it explains it, perhaps.

"He was born in Germany in the Schwarzwals where Brecht,

too, lived as a child. His mother was a blond German girl, his father, I was told, an unknown soldier from India. The story is that Indian troops marched through Germany on their way someplace to conquer something. They left their human marks. There was nothing blond about Harry. His eyes were as black as yours and his hair as sparse. He was brilliant, too, but unschooled and too proud to learn. There was no consistency in his work as there had been little consistency in his life. He was brought up by his grandparents because his mother, soon after his birth, married another man. Was she too scared to fight for her motherly rights and keep her son? Patterns repeat themselves. Harry didn't fight for Henry or for you. Perhaps he has finally broken the pattern, for I understand from a Swedish journalist that he married once again, a Swedish woman, and has two children with her. He is still married to her. She is not an actress.

"I send you love and I am only sorry I can't show you the pictures myself and fill in with images and memories that might come to me. Take care.

"Your mother"

I read the letter over, wondering, "Is it out of a need for honesty or is it to soothe my guilt?"

Later when John called and I expressed the feeling, he said, "It's better not to have more pink-colored lies between us." It made me feel good, and I thought, that's why he has become one of my closest friends. I wouldn't have known what to do without him when G.T. left. He was the one of my children who seemed to be able to put aside his own feelings and be honest with me. Fair and yet compassionate. I never minded being told the truth by him. There were no hidden motivations, no guilts, no put-downs, no competition. At the time, I needed it desperately. When I told him how much it meant to me, to be able to talk to him, he answered, "Most men do not know what it is to treat a woman as an equal. I do from having lived with you and Lena."

John's belief in reality is his strength. So opposite from Harry's. John is in politics and has trained himself to accept only what is based on facts. Yet he is creative. The combination makes a scientist.

Maybe John picked up the vibes already in my womb. He was conceived in Rome while Mussolini was fighting for his last gasping breath, and, the day Mussolini was captured, July 1943, was the first time John laughed. He was three and a half months old. It was catching! We all started to laugh, Klara and I and Folke.

Oh yes, Folke, too.

4

After Harry left, for the first time in my life as a woman I lived alone. For the first time in my life I tasted the delicious but dangerous sensation of liking it. What did it mean? Was I a freak or a goddess? "I want to be alone," Garbo had said. She had never married and she didn't have children. That's being a freak. But her love scenes were exquisite and romantic. That is being a goddess.

My aunt, my father's sister, lived alone, too, and she was looked upon as a freak! Strange? She had been married and divorced and had children! She even had a male friend off and on. Of course, nobody saw them in bed together. Still, she was looked upon as a freak. Freak and goddess, is it the same thing, perhaps? Both seem to exclude human relationships on a deeper level. Not living together, not sleeping in the same bed every night. I didn't want that. Or did I?

I might not have known it for sure then, for I had begun to feel a need for space, for bareness, that all artists have, must have. And I didn't know how to combine that, or take it seriously, and yet share the rest of my life with someone else intimately. Yet I knew I needed the sharing. It would be another thirty years until I knew it for sure and could say "I need you."

But, at that point in my life, I was only twenty-one and I had a child, not really "alone, alone," and a career that was immensely promising. In my new film I was in every frame and my name was above the title. I was economically independent, too! I really could have afforded this tingle of pleasure of forming my own life, taking my time, figuring out what I wanted, waiting for the "king," and I knew clearly that Folke was not that. Still I couldn't. It was too scary, as if denying Folke meant denying love altogether. Denying man altogether.

Oh yes, I was only twenty-one. Oh yes, I was hungry for life. Oh yes, I had weakness of will. Oh yes, Folke was offering me a position in society, taking care of me, wooing me, loving me as if I were the last chance in his life. He was getting close to fifty and the heat was on, and, Oh yes, he was stronger and he was a man and he knew what he wanted, and, Oh yes, felt every right in the world to have it. And so I succumbed and I said, Oh yes, I will, and, Oh yes, and it wasn't true. I didn't mean it. Oh yes. And Oh yes, I was with child again, and that was a fact.

I knew exactly how it happened that I got pregnant. It was one of the last fall days, still warm, still light. Harry had been gone for three or four months. Folke and I had had dinner in the country. We drove back to town on a tiny, winding road. I was filled suddenly with a sense of security, safety, freedom, promise, gratitude, as if he and I could drive like this endlessly together, unafraid of anything that might appear around the curve. I moved closer to him. He put his right arm around me. Dark trees were passing by us on the side. "Lillian, I love you," he mumbled. He called me that, as my mother used to. Folke was strangely shy when it came to the act of love. I was attracted to this man, both aggressive and tender, who needed me in spite of his power. I moved closer to him, barely noticeably. He pulled over to the side of the road, turned off the engine, pulled the brakes, put his arm around me. "I love you, Lillian," he repeated as he fumbled for my lips. They were open and full. He went on top of me. I unbuttoned his trousers and he went inside of me. I wore no underpants.

I thought I was safe from getting pregnant because I was still nursing John. To use the pregnancy to make up my mind to marry Folke was the cop-out. I could have had the child, no matter. I didn't see that. It was either/or. Abortion or marriage. I first went to a quack woman. She gave me a shot. I was to come back for a second one in a week if it didn't work. I made the mistake of telling Folke, mistake because I knew my only chance was to make up my mind without him pressuring me. I knew if I told him he would be deliriously happy about having a baby with me and he would be pressuring me. I knew, I knew, I knew.

He was deliriously happy and I never did go back for my second shot. Thank God, for there is Lena today and Natasha and Katrina and so on and so forth and life has to be lived.

If it hadn't been for the feeling of the decision not being mine and the sense of defeat about that, it might have turned out all right. But instead, I think, then and there, I began to nurse the idea. "Okay, I'll give you the child and then leave you," which I did, five years later. Except I didn't give him the child. I never could leave any of my children with their fathers, but then the fathers didn't insist on keeping them either. That was part of the problem of my whole generation. Men and women didn't share parenthood.

Guje, Folke's wife, knew perhaps that my reasons for the marriage were vague. And in her mind even devious. Yes, he was married.

I had, as usual, barely acknowledged her existence except that it flattered my ego. Daddy chose me over Mommy! Ha, ha! I was totally unprepared for her fighting back.

When Folke, filled with incentive about his new future, confronted her with the matter, she insisted on seeing the two of us together, in spite of being ill in the hospital with T.B. and a high fever. Of course she knew nothing of the pregnancy, and if she suspected it she certainly didn't mention it.

Guje had been married before to a brilliant entertainer-writer-producer. He had burnt himself out and died ahead of his time. She had joyfully followed him in the ups and downs of his theatrical career, but had not counted on being left alone and broke at the age of forty. Folke was their lawyer. He was drawn to artists. He was a mathematical genius as a child and his professor had wanted him to continue and become a scientist. But Folke had been caught since childhood in the loveless game of competition and chose to be the judge.

He became a lawyer, a successful one, and married the widow of an artist. It was his third marriage. He must have thought or hoped it would be the last. Something was obviously missing for them both. He began to resent giving her what he thought she had missed before—security, stability, a respectable position—and Guje perhaps missed life in the theater. In any event, she became very ill.

Now, when she faced losing him, the incentive to fight for what was hers flared up. They were both in their late forties. It was late. Too late. He was in love with a young girl, me—the age of his daughter from an earlier marriage.

Today I understand Guje's need to confront me. Thirty years later, I was even willing to pay for an overseas call from Uschi, G.T.'s girl—the age of *my* daughter.

"Person-to-person, collect, to George Tabori," the German-accented operator announced through the black plastic messenger that I pressed against my ear. "Not home," I answered, coldly. "But I am Mrs. Tabori, the wife. Perhaps the lady would like to speak to me." That's when I heard the voice, anxious and childish, above all, anxious. From the other side of the world, the other side of the ocean, I could smell the anxiety as if it were my own. It didn't stop me from using the opportunity. There was nothing sophisticated about my language. It was safe to hate her, not G.T. I wanted *her* to leave, not him.

The operator was too stunned to shut off the connection. Uschi and I became a reality to each other. Finally. It had no effect on my marriage to G.T. It went the way it went. But hate chokes you. And reality is better than fantasy. Anything is better than silence.

Guje's confrontation with me and Folke in the hospital had no influence on her marriage, either. It, too, went the way it went. But I never will forget that cold, early evening in November, with a tiny female growing in my womb.

I wore a tomato-colored coat and a brown hat that I had worn in a film I had just finished. I was filled with a growing discomfort. "Why do I have to be dragged into this? It isn't my business to clear up their mess." I was right. Still I submitted myself to a painful and melodramatic confrontation.

"Do you love him?" Folke's wife asked me. I stood by the door, Folke by the bed. She had already asked him the same question and he had answered quickly and clearly, "Yes, I do." He had no doubts. In that room I was the only sinner of ambivalence. I didn't answer for a while. I was surprised by her courage and directness and found myself torn between admiring her on one hand and hating her for putting me in this spot on the other.

"Do you love him?" She repeated the question. It didn't help much that her face was as white as the sheets of the bed and her voice raspy from fever and fury racing through her body. I felt awful. What did she expect me to do? Admit the truth? Admit my own confusion?

"Do you love him?" She repeated the question for the third time, almost triumphantly, sure of her victory.

Here was my chance to answer maturely, "I don't know, Guje. For Christ's sake, I am pregnant! What do you want me to do? I am with child! Help me." But I couldn't, for I wasn't mature and Guje was a woman in love with her man. Not my mother.

Guje looked at Folke. Folke looked at the floor. I looked out the window. Finally I mumbled that goddamn word, "Yes."

I went along for the ride—his ride. Not knowing, of course, that he, too, for his own reasons, perhaps, did the same. Not yet knowing as I do now at my age, that if one is careless with the truth, hope eventually gives up, as the muscles of the heart, if not exercised, gets sluggish. And it gets scary when the coldness creeps in. At age twenty-two one doesn't understand that for certain, or doesn't want to.

It was very quiet in the hospital room. Ambivalence was hanging thick in the air. Exhausted, Guje lay back on the pillow. She closed her eyes. I could hear her breathe. She had weak lungs. I sneaked out of the room. Folke joined me a few minutes later. And from here on there was less chance for Folke and me to be lovers, or even to be friends, which we had been to begin with. From here on it went downhill for us. Guje died seven years later.

It didn't help matters much that in the film *Appassionata* I was opposite Rydeberg. In my ambivalent state it was easy to fantasize about us again. When he said in front of the camera—and he is a brilliant actor—"I love you, I love you, I won't let you go," I wondered, "Does he mean it or is he acting?" Just as I had during the first film we made together. The best and only delicious part was that in the film the roles were reversed! I, the woman, wanted to leave him, the man! I had scene upon scene telling him that!

Maybe it rubbed off, for when he asked me, spitefully, "Are you really marrying the lawyer?" I answered equally spitefully, "Why not?" The dialogue in my head was even spicier: "You son of a bitch! You are marrying the banker's daughter, Why not I my lawyer!"

And so, at night, I went home to Folke and he to the banker's daughter.

The day after the confrontation with Guje in the hospital, in spite of her illness, in spite of my ambivalence, Folke had started divorce proceedings. He wasted no time. Within a few weeks his furniture mingled with mine in my apartment on Narvevägen that from now on in became his.

We had a chauffeur, cook, maids, and a well-laid-out future. We soon bought a house in the country, and early in the spring I moved out with John and Klara and awaited the birth of my second child.

The combination of pregnancy and comfort was dangerously close to my mother's lifestyle. I got lazy. The white light that I had experienced the first years at the Royal Dramatic Theatre School faded, and depression crept in. I began to dream of snakes under my bed night after night. Petrified and half-awake, I would try to find them in the half-lit Nordic summer night. Klara, the nurse, would wake up, and, although she knew there were none, she helped me pull the beds apart to assure me. And so the summer passed, for there was nature around me and John, my gorgeous baby boy. I rarely felt the new baby in my womb and I couldn't believe my eyes when I looked at myself in the mirror. I had obviously swallowed a football!

That is how I got married, discreetly, in Folke's office, in August, a week or so before Lena was born. Folke and I were in a high-income bracket and could save money on taxes by marrying this late. My parents were the witnesses. My mother didn't cry this time, and no child carried flowers for me. I don't know why John was not in my arms, but Folke adopted him that same day and gave me a diamond ring in the shape of a rose. Within me moved restlessly our unborn child.

Lena was born August 23, 1944.

A mother has a daughter has a mother.

It all came back to me—Lena's birth—watching *her* give birth to her daughter, Natasha.

I was allowed in the hospital room. For more than an hour I watched her, my own flesh and blood. As I did, I experienced again the power in a woman's body. Ugly in its brutal effort and at the same time so heavenly beautiful. It's wild, this total involvement, this total commitment. Only you and your child exist. Just the two of you. And yet it is almost as if you have nothing to do with it, this powerful will to push the child out of you mingled with the powerful will of your child wanting to get out of you. The pain is the least important part of it all. The glory is the important part. Once it is experienced you never forget it.

A mother has a daughter has a mother.

"Where does the baby come out, through this hole or this one?" she asked me, Natasha, five years later. She was sleeping overnight with me, dressed in her nightgown, lying on my large king-size bed. She had pulled her legs up.

"This one," I said, pointing to the tiny, pink slit between her thin legs. "It doesn't hurt too much because the muscles keep getting stronger and more flexible as the baby grows in your stomach."

"It's about this big," she said, measuring a tiny space between her fingers the size of a large bumblebee. She was scared.

"No," I said seriously, "it's about like this," and I moved her fingers slightly apart.

"You are wrong," she insisted, "it's like this." And she moved them back into a space short of in between. I let her believe it, figuring when she gets bigger the image of the baby will get bigger, too, and she will discover the glory of it all, as I did, as Lena did, as women have done for years and years and years. And I proceeded to tell her about her birth and she loved hearing about it.

"I was in the room, my darling. I saw your head with some dark hair coming through the legs of your mommy. It was you."

I see myself in Lena and Lena in Natasha. I see my grandmother in myself and myself in my grandmother.

A daughter has a mother has a daughter.

My pregnancy with Lena was different from that with John, my son. There was less ecstasy and more reality. Did my body know that it was to be a girl, a person of my own sex? Is it in the womb that we begin the separation from an intimacy that can never be fulfilled, physically, an ecstasy that must be saved for the other sex in order to dare to move into each other's bodies? Still, there are other intimacies, and I feel we have a better chance today, mothers and daughters, Lena and I, Natasha and Lena, than I had with my mother, or my mother with hers. There are no shortcuts. The challenge is to be closer to each other in total respect and compassion. And when Lena lashes out at me with the anger of a powerful woman's body and soul as I did, perhaps, with my mother, I can sort out the reasons and know that they have little to do with the moment, but are perhaps related to times way back in her life and mine when I knew less about myself and therefore her.

It was not until two days after her birth that I realized how much she mattered to me, that she was my flesh and blood, that I wanted to fight for her, that I wanted her to live more than anything in the world. I thought she was near death, and all vagueness, all indifference about her, this tiny, baby girl, disappeared.

It was not as serious as I thought. But the intensity of the moment was, and she became real to me. I knew for sure that I loved her.

I had a tremendous amount of milk when I began to feed her. The next day when they brought her in she was crying bitterly and wanted none of my milk. As insane as it sounds, in this private hospital the rule was to keep the baby in the nursery away from the mother. The next time she arrived for her feeding and was still crying, I asked the nurse what was the matter. "Nothing," she answered. "Little babies cry."

"Why is it natural for babies to cry?" I ought to have asked. "Why is a baby different from grownups?" But I didn't know for sure. I was a young mother, so I accepted the nurse's knowledge ahead of mine. When she brought Lena in for the early morning meal—and by now she was blue in the face and could barely breathe—"Get a doctor," I said clearly and definitely. I held her in my arms and rocked her back and forth.

"It's Sunday morning," the dumb nurse answered.

"I don't care," I said. "I want to see a doctor." And I kept rocking her back and forth, wanting nothing more in the world than for her to live.

The doctor came. "It's simply that she has been overfed," he said. "Too much milk. Don't worry. Weigh her carefully after each meal."

"Did you?" I said to the nurse, whom I thought had more knowledge than I. She obviously hadn't. From that moment on I didn't let Lena out of my sight.

When we returned from the hospital to Backa, a young woman from a village in the north of Sweden had moved in and taken Klara's place.

Folke had fired Klara. "She has worked for another man in your life," he explained to me, having no consideration either for the baby or for me. It was perhaps the first time I realized that his need for domination would affect me.

Of course I didn't have to accept his decision. The fact that both Klara and I did was our contribution to the "big daddy and little girl" game. Klara had become like my mother. She took care of me as well as John, and I loved it and her. Yet, in spite of us both being devastated and crying for days, we indulged in an almost enjoyable understanding of Folke's jealousy, affirming the hypocrisy of the game. It takes two to tango.

However, Anna Ostblom, known as Nana, became a tremendous asset to us all. Today at the age of sixty-three she takes care of Lena's children. She has seen lovers and husbands come and go, but she hangs in there, for she is now part of the family.

The silence between me and Folke that had begun in the hospital room with Guje turned out to be the real enemy, for, had we dared admit our doubts, it would have been a way of saying yes to each other and to life. And I know that is what Folke wanted. Me, too. It is just that we thought it meant saying no.

It was twenty-five years later, when nothing seemed at stake between us anymore except for the moment, which really is all that ever matters, that we finally talked to each other and became friends again, the way we had been in the very beginning and the way it ought to have stayed forever. It was a strange coincidence. I had just gotten off the plane from New York. The headlines

stared me in the face as I entered the terminal: APPASSIONATA ON TV
TONIGHT. THE FAMOUS LOVE COUPLE. RYDEBERG AGAINST LINDFORS.
DON'T MISS IT.

It was *Appassionata*, the film I was doing at the time of the confrontation with Guje, at the time when Folke moved in with me in
my new apartment, that brought us together. *Appassionata* had
represented a tremendous opportunity for us all at the time. It was
Lux Films's first effort to produce a high-class film, not just a commercial venture, about a girl getting in and out of bed. It turned
out to be a big commercial success in spite of its artistic aspira-
tions. It was even shown in the U.S.A. where Kay Brown, Ingrid
Bergman's agent, saw me in it and brought me to Hollywood.

I was the star of the film. My name alone made it financially
possible to produce. It was ahead of Rydeberg's. If he was jealous
he never gave any indication of it. It was generous of him, for I
was in no way up to him as far as our craft was concerned. But he
was not considered commercial in the movies. I was.

I saw all this, of course, much clearer twenty-five years later
when the film was shown on TV in Stockholm. Rydeberg was getting first billing *now*. He never left Sweden. His list of great roles
grew. He was and is loved by the people. Also, the Rydeberg/
Lindfors coupling had become such a myth that little pink roses
seem to grow on the grave of our buried love affair. Even the dust
had become pink.

I called a friend who had a TV set. "I am coming over," I said.

"Do you know who else is coming to see it?" Fanny asked me.

"Rydeberg?" I asked.

She laughed. "No, Folke."

We watched the film together. I went home with Folke afterwards and we sat in his apartment and talked until the wee hours
of the morning, the same apartment where we had lived together
for two years, in the same kitchen where Klara, twenty-five years
earlier, used to boil diapers endlessly. It was during the war and
there was no hot water. "I can still feel the smell," I said to Folke
that night. He laughed.

The windows in the kitchen looked out over the courtyard as
they had then, only there were no gypsies, no court musicians
playing anymore. The lobby doors are locked today, and everybody is afraid of robbers as in New York.

That night I learned and understood more about Folke than I had
during the four years we were married. I needed his friendship
again!

Folke told me things about his mother that I never knew. She was one of the first independent, successful businesswomen in Sweden, but her ideas about how to bring up Folke and his younger brother were puzzling. Their hair was long, hanging over their shoulders. It wasn't until Folke was thirteen, after having fought her bitterly, that he cut it himself. She also insisted on providing them with a tutor at home instead of sending them to school.

He sat in the window, he told me, watching the children go to and from school, and made up his mind that he belonged with them, with the world, not only with her. Folke fought her and eventually won. Early in his life he learned to prove that to be the stronger was necessary. The pattern was established. It's not difficult to guess where her need to control came from. For a woman with her intelligence to have gotten where she was, an enormous amount of will power was needed, forcing a kind of insensitivity from her, the kind I had experienced in myself. Folke must have admired her independence and success, for he admired those qualities in me. He liked it that I was self-supporting, and we had fair and equal arrangements in all financial matters. In many ways he wanted to be a modern man. It was only in the face of disagreement that he would revert to old patterns of domination, being the stronger, the controller, as if disagreement were a rejection of him personally and he, like a little boy, couldn't handle the hurt.

"When men imagine a female uprising, they imagine a world in which women rule men the way men have ruled women. Their guilt, which is the guilt of every ruling class, allows them to see no middle ground," Sally Kempton says in *I Am a Woman*. It isn't only between men and women, this game.

That night in the kitchen Folke also told me about his brother. Although he didn't clearly say so, it became obvious that he had been close to him, for it had been a shock to find out that his brother was a common thief and had been put in jail when Folke was a young lawyer, just beginning to make it. Rightly so, he was worried about his reputation. He was living in a hypocritical time and in a small town. Whether the family liked it or not, and his energy was powerful when he wanted something—I knew that by now—Folke insisted on moving them all to an even smaller town far away. He changed his name from Rosenberg to Rogard. "My God," I was thinking, "he too is Jewish. Rosenberg is a Jewish name."

I didn't ask him, because his first wife was Jewish, which made his daughter half-Jewish, and he seemed never to want to mention that. In any event, it was obvious that he cut all ties with his family and I asked him, "How come you never told it to me?" And he didn't answer me, for it probably wasn't too important to him. What had been much more devastating was that when he was a small boy he realized that the marriage between his parents had been loveless and filled with conflicts. Perhaps nothing else after that mattered. He told me about it that night.

"There was an uncle living in the house, obviously my mother's lover. And my father had mistresses. Who started the dance?" Folke shrugged his shoulders. "I only knew my mother's anger. One day she sent me, I was eleven, maybe ten, to look for my father. She gave me an address on a piece of paper. I held it in my hand. It was late at night and I wandered through the dimly lit and quiet streets of Stockholm, Stockholm at the beginning of the twentieth century. It was very quiet and I must have been a pitiful sight—tall, awkward, with long hair and short pants. Then!" Folke laughed. He was quite heavy now.

"I found the shabby apartment building. I remember well I wandered up gray, stone steps and finally found the name I was looking for engraved in brass on the old oak door; it must have been a good building. I rang the doorbell. A woman opened the door. She was very charming. When I mentioned my father's name she began to laugh. 'So you are his son,' she said. 'How cute you look in your long curls.' She was plain-looking but very friendly and warm. She disappeared through a heavy wool curtain and I heard her call my father's name. And then I heard his voice, different, warmer, much warmer than I was used to hearing him, friendlier, more loving. Only years later, of course, did I understand why my mother had sent me; why the endless tensions around the dinner table; why the warmth in my father's voice; who the uncle was and the laughing woman."

So much about Folke made sense to me that night. And when I think of him now, this enormous man in size, in voice, in action, looking for his father in order to bring him back to his mother, I understood that a tiny part of him emotionally never, never had given up, and another part of him never, never dared to believe in love. His last woman, a wonderful person, dark, content, cared for him unselfishly and yet with dignity. The moving part was that she was his brother's widow. She brought him closer to home again.

That night when he told me so much about himself, I went with

127

him into the bedroom. The same blue linen cover with the white crowns that I had bought years ago was thrown over the bed. I folded it carefully before I crawled down between the sheets with him. We held each other. I must have been very vulnerable that night to have once again thought that something could work between us. Was I again looking for security, to be taken care of? Or was it that I so desperately wanted to prove to myself that a relationship could work if *I* tried hard enough? "Why didn't you fight for me? Why did you let me go?" I asked him, tears running down my cheeks. "And why could we not have talked like this then, when we were married?" All those efforts changing men and places suddenly seemed so useless—Don, George, Folke; leaving Sweden, moving from California to New York. I knew the answer was not to be found in us as a couple any longer. I would have to find it in me, as Folke perhaps already had found it in him.

Yet the intimacy of that night was the beginning of a new friendship between us, not the end as it had become twenty-five years ago.

5

It was perhaps bad timing, both for my private life and my work, that Hollywood came through with an offer the following winter.

Kay Brown, the famous agent in New York—she had brought Ingrid Bergman over for David Selznick—had asked for some film clips and a voice-over in English after having seen *Appassionata*. She then approached Paramount and Warner Brothers. The latter came through with an offer. Now followed endless negotiations, telephone calls, telegrams, words, paragraphs, discussions, papers, more papers as well as headlines in the Swedish press about Viveca's "glamorous Hollywood career" to be! It all became real and less glamorous the day I received a cable that I was to leave immediately for Hollywood, U.S.A., to play the lead opposite Gary Cooper in the film *Cloak and Dagger*. For I had begun to realize something about being an actress, as I had about being a mother.

Right after the birth of Lena I had been cast in the part of the bride in *Blood Wedding* by Garcia Lorca at the Royal Dramatic Theatre. It not only became one of the most extraordinary productions to be performed that season, but it also became an important part of my development as an actress.

The set was intensely and painfully beautiful, designed by an extraordinary painter called X. Alf Sjöberg, known mostly in this country for his film *Miss Julie*, directed the play at his passionate best. Opening night became one of the thrills in the Swedish theater. All the passion, all the yearning that the Nordic people feel for the South and its people was touched upon, and the communication between the stage and the house was total. It was a powerful letting-go of emotions on both ends. The reviews were all in agreement. I got much of the praise. But above all, I, for the first time, experienced feelings within me that I had never dreamed of possessing. It was frightening, too, for I did not know how to come back to those heights night after night in the performance. But I knew something had happened to me, for I suddenly felt deadly serious about myself again, about my life, about my work. So much so that I wondered, what else do I need? And what difference does it make where I am as long as I am on the stage?

By the time I got the cable from Hollywood, I was in the middle of playing Olivia in *Twelfth Night*. This time I had gotten lukewarm reviews. It upset me, but it was also a challenge, and with my rushing off to Hollywood how would I ever be able to conquer Olivia, I asked myself.

On the other hand, there was Gary Cooper waiting for me.

Pauline Brunius, the head of the theater, was clear-headed. She looked at me, astounded. "Couldn't Gary Cooper wait until the production is finished?" she asked. She had seen my work and knew what I needed.

I was equally astounded and somewhat annoyed that she didn't get the importance of the fact that I was wanted by Hollywood. It doesn't happen every day. "No," I said, for I wanted to fly with the wind.

"Don't leave for too long," she said, looking at me thoughtfully. "There's always the danger of being replaced."

Oh yes, it scared me, but not enough, for I had other needs, other dreams more real to me, more urgent, too.

It would only be for three months, we all thought. Even so, it would be the longest time I had ever been away from the children and certainly the farthest ever. In those days it took forty-two hours to fly and ten days by boat.

"Mama is going to America. Isn't that wonderful?" the children heard people telling them.

"I will be back," I assured them.

"When?" they asked.

"Three months," I answered. What is three months? A telephone call cost a fortune and a letter took five days. Besides, how do you communicate with children through feelings already five days old?

129

By the time I tried to explain, some awful thing began to turn in my stomach and the only way I could cope was to change the subject. That didn't help the children much, or me.

I don't quite remember why I didn't take them with me. Was it that it seemed too chancy to uproot them? Or was it the image of the sex symbol, the film star, that poked its silly head into the picture, suggesting that I might make out better without them? Or was it that I wanted for a while to be absolutely free?

I was only twenty-four.

The reality of the separation did not really hit me until three days before I was to leave. To my own amazement I cried and cried. I had no idea that I cared that much, that I could feel, that I was that attached to them, to anything or anybody. Who was I, an actress or a mother? Which one should I take seriously? Why either/or? What do I want? What am I looking for, glory or fame? Or what? No answers made any sense!

It even felt good that Folke was coming with me. And Eva Tissell, my secretary-companion, although I would have preferred to have needed no one, to feel strong all by myself. And there is a price for that, too.

"I'm paying a price for it all. I am a gypsy. I am an actress," I mumbled to myself an early morning in April, ready to take off with a plane for the U.S.A., not just the wind. But nothing made any sense. It was like tearing off part of my body, for, had I been a gypsy, the children would have been sleeping in the back of my wagon or helping me drive it! So I wasn't really a gypsy. I was an actress in the twentieth century, and I was paying a price for it, and I controlled the tears only because the flashbulbs were going like mad around me at the airport and all the way out to the plane. They followed me—the photographers, the journalists—for I was the Marilyn Monroe of Sweden. And besides, a soldier's daughter never cries!

Leaving might have been more turbulent than I understood. I still have nightmares about strange new places and people every time I travel. I even lose my dog in my dreams and I am always looking for a lost child. It takes me forever to get organized to go on a trip, even if it is one that I know is going to be exciting. Packing is more complicated than needed. I am often exhausted by the time I hit the plane or the train and easily get sick when I arrive.

Coming home is equally complicated. I am suspicious about

what has changed. I ask myself, is anybody happy that I have returned? Or was it more peaceful without me? It takes me days to settle in and be back. It is perhaps simply the curse of the wandering Jew, of the gypsy, the constant doubt, the questioning around: "Why did I leave the place where I was born?" On the other hand, perhaps the question is as inappropriate as, "Why did I leave the womb?" for the answer is, no doubt, in the doing—often so much more vital than the question. And maybe worth the price.

I have never regretted that I went to America. Not really, only that I felt I had to give up Sweden. In those days it was either/or for me.

V

The City of Angels

"A sex symbol becomes a thing . . .
I just hate to be a thing . . .
I don't want to make money . . .
I just want to be wonderful . . ."
MARILYN MONROE

TURN AROUND, VIVECA! Smile, Viveca! Wave good-bye to Sweden!" I was standing on top of the landing to the SAS plane ready to take off for New York, U.S.A., eventually Los Angeles, California. The other side of the globe! I had been waved goodbye by friends, relatives, press, photographers, cameras, cameramen, news cameramen.

My mother was crying. What did she really feel? Amazement, or even envy for this daughter, the youngest one, on her way to become an international star? Maybe. Worried? Certainly. Anybody going to America either makes it big or is destroyed. Was she tough enough, Viveка? Was I, Viveca?

I was loved by the Swedish people. I could do no wrong. Would I be able to function without their support? I know I had a strong lust for life, and it would take me far if I could hold onto it. At this point in my life I hadn't lost it enough times yet to doubt it. Why the lump in my throat?

My father hugged me. I sensed he wanted to connect with me. I couldn't; I wasn't ready. I was never ready. It was always too late with him.

"Turn around and smile, Viveca. Wave goodbye to Sweden." I did.

"Elsa Viveca Torstendotter Lindfors Rogard . . . Blue eyes . . . Brown hair . . . 5'6" . . . Married . . . Female. . . ." "Stockholm, March 1946"—the last stamp in my Swedish black passport that I still have in the drawer at 95th Street. My next one would be green. I became an American citizen within two years. I emigrated. I became an immigrant. Maybe that's why the lump in my throat.

During the eighteenth century, one third of the population of Sweden immigrated to America. The myths were many and contradictory. It was either finding gold on the streets or disaster in the gutter. For most of the immigrants the myths faded when the reality of life, for better or worse, took over. The struggle was often honorable and invigorating and paid off in more ways than one. For Sweden and the Swedes it was a turbulent experience. The feelings were conflicting: envy of those who dared to take the risk and envy of those who didn't take the risk. Suddenly a choice existed about where to live. It had only applied to gypsies and Jews before. I once asked a Swedish-born artist why he had come to this country. "I inherited my ancestor's dream," he said. "The America fever was in my blood." It was in mine, too.

My father had been to New York once for a few weeks on business. I was eleven, maybe twelve, when he came home filled with enthusiasm for the people "over there." It was the yes-to-life quality that had excited him. He had that, too.

Did my father know of his influence on me? That it was he who had started me reading poetry? That was the beginning! I knew he was proud of me. Would he always be? Even if I failed? And worse, what if I lost my courage? I was his daughter and a Swede, and "No one ever comes back from America" was the myth!

"Turn around and smile, Viveca." But nothing made any sense, and the lump in my throat was still there.

I had said goodbye to the children in the morning, before taking off for the airport. They went to the park to feed the geese and play in the sandbox as usual. By now they were probably back home, looking through the apartment, perhaps, for Mama. But she had flown away with the wind because she was an actress.

The next morning my picture was on the front page of all the papers. I was dressed in a brown, tailor-made suit from one of the best houses in Stockholm. I was thin, almost as thin as Katharine Hepburn! All the baby fat was gone. My hair was thick and reddish-brown, hanging over my shoulders. I looked beautiful and the lump in my throat didn't show.

But when the door to the plane was shut and I sank down in my chair by the window looking out, knowing that nobody could see me anymore. I started to cry again. I, the mother, I, the little girl. But within a few hours, flying over the ocean to a faraway land, the feeling of strength came back to me, and it didn't worry me anymore whether the choice was right or not. I was living my life, feeling it all the way down to the bone. Doing what I wanted for myself and therefore hopefully also for my children. I was a woman.

A woman across the aisle—maybe she saw me crying, she certainly saw me shiver, and it was freezing cold on the plane—offered me her second coat, a Russian sable. We started to talk.

She was a literary agent, sophisticated, gorgeous, without necessarily being beautiful, careless in her elegance, generous and friendly. I had been in love with the image of the American woman for years, as I had seen her on the screen—Irene Dunne, Claudette Colbert, Joan Crawford. And the night I saw Katharine Hepburn in *Morning Glory* I had to walk all the way home across the bridge, overwhelmed by her, by the possibilities she opened up in me. I couldn't stand taking the train. I had to keep on moving, or I would blow up from longing, from happiness, from frustration of not being like her, *now!*

I was filled with her. She, and all of them. They seemed to combine the love of a man with a sense of themselves, a sense of independence; they seemed to be above the sickly suffering of the women around me, women longing for fantasy, for myths! I wanted to be like her! I wanted reality like hers! And here *she* **was,** across the aisle!

The coat was sensational, too, beginning at the top of my head and ending at my feet. I was warm. The only thing that seemed slightly contradictory to me was that *she*, the agent, should own a coat like this and not me, the star. Wait, I mumbled to myself, it won't be long until I have one, too.

I still don't, but it doesn't seem contradictory anymore.

The last I saw of the literary agent was in the customs office, sitting near her jewelry box. She had placed them all—the rubies, the diamonds, the necklaces, the bracelets—on her fur, as in a display window in a jewelry store. She herself was sitting on top of her trunk, smoking a cigarette, her legs crossed, barely looking at her fortune.

Her name was Carol Brandt. It didn't mean much to me then, but it does now. She was quite famous. Still is.

On the other side of the glass wall stood Kay Brown, my American agent, waving at me with red roses in her arms, and Warner Brothers' publicity man was doing his best to get me through customs as fast as possible. We soon stepped into the big black limousine waiting outside the airport at LaGuardia where all planes landed in those days.

We zoomed into New York and the Pierre Hotel, just like in the movies, and as we wandered into the vestibule, I saw *him* standing at the counter—the man I had been in love with at the age of eleven, the man whose pictures had been hanging all over my bedroom, the man I had secretly been making love to without knowing anything about it.

"Meet Charles Boyer," said Kay. "Viveca Lindfors, a young Swedish actress." My face turned red in a flash of a second and I wanted to be pale and gorgeous like Garbo. I put my hand out. "I was in love with you when I was a teenager," I stuttered, as gracefully as stuttering can be.

He was wonderful. He smiled that unbelievable smile of his and looked at me with those gorgeous black eyes that make you feel so much like a woman. He kissed my hand. "*Enchanté*, Madame," he said. Charles Boyer, my idol, my secret lover, an extraordinary actor with exceptional intelligence, grace, and wit, one of the few foreign male stars who made it big in Hollywood, kissed my hand.

Would my dream come true? Would I star, maybe, opposite Charles Boyer?

A glorious beginning to ten glorious days in New York!

Eva and I went to the theater every night, even the first one. Forty-two hours in the air didn't stop us. We saw *Dream Girl* with Betty Field. The production was gorgeous and Betty Field was brilliant. At the time she was married to the author of the play, Elmer Rice. The image was perfect.

Years later I worked with her. She was now divorced. We went on tour together to South America. She was brilliant in a Tennessee Williams play called *Suddenly Last Summer*. But only *some* nights. Others she was too drunk to know what she was doing. I didn't see her again for several years but was struck by the tragedy of her life when I heard that she died of a heart attack on a warm summer day on a beach in Cape Cod. She was only fifty, and she left a record behind her of work that was only a fraction of what it should have been.

She, like me, like so many actors of my generation, was seduced by the film star image, by a period when actors felt provoked to play games for glamor and fame rather than to develop themselves seriously as actors. Since she was a woman, her time was more limited and her chances less. Did she know it? Did she try to adjust? And when she couldn't, did she blame herself? We only know that she died at the age of fifty!

My first night in New York when I saw her, I thought nothing could possibly go wrong for her or for me.

I fell into bed that night, my head filled with images of this new country, this wild city, New York, a new language, and the possibility of a new life. I felt like an actor who suddenly has found the key to her role and was taking off.

Marvelous, terrible, wonderful New York. Time went by like a whirlwind—photographers, interviewers, lunches, dinners, people, theater, films. I was high. My mind was going one hundred miles an hour. The publicity campaign put on by Warner Brothers was something I had never experienced. Meeting the American press astounded me. I was talked to like a thinking person. They didn't treat me as a sex symbol. They weren't interested in with whom I slept. They asked me about my theatrical background, about Sweden, about politics.

Only one question threw me. One newspaperman asked me ironically—and he was the only one—"Why did you leave a country like Sweden where you made such wonderful films? Don't you know about Hollywood films?"

I started to defend myself much too furiously.

The truth was I hadn't really thought about it at all. I had gone with the wind, following the path of others. My myth was far from the reality of what life in the U.S.A. or Hollywood really was. I dreamed about becoming rich and famous and I learned that I don't really care that much for money or fame. I like it but I can live without it. Work is the important thing. I dreamed about finding a man who would make me feel the way I thought those gorgeous American women felt on the screen. But I learned that that feeling has got to be in me. No one can give it to me. I dreamed about fabulous Hollywood directors! Svengalis, releasing some special brilliant quality, the genius in me. I learned that I had to do it on my own. Oh, it helps when "they" allow it, it's glorious when "they" affirm it, but it is in the end up to me.

Thinking about it now, how could I have put it into words? I didn't even understand it myself. It was a feeling, though, a strong feeling of wanting to belong to the world that motivated me, a desire to free myself from old patterns: from Sweden and authority, rules and regulations, even Folke. Not only a feeling, but a want, a need.

Sweden was small, and although we didn't suffer from the war as other countries did, we no doubt suffered from the isolation. We had been totally cut off from the outside world for years. No foreign films, no books, no magazines could make it into the country. Even traveling in Sweden was impossible. Because of the gasoline shortage, the few cars that existed were run on coal. And there were even fewer trains and boats. Never mind traveling abroad. I had been lucky to have been as far as Rome.

V-Day in Stockholm was not as euphoric as in Rome or in Paris, but I remember sitting glued to the radio, listening to the excitement all over the world, longing to be with those people and to share with them that kind of euphoria. I thought of Heinrich and my friends in Berlin and I wanted out! I wanted to be part of the struggle the next time. The pain, too. I knew, perhaps unconsciously, that I had avoided it once and I wanted to make up for it. I wanted to be given a second chance.

A week after V-Day, a group of artists who had contributed their own time to raise money for the refugees were invited to participate in a gala concert in Copenhagen arranged by the King of Denmark. I was one of them. It was the first time since before the war that a plane could take off from Stockholm and land in Copenhagen. It is hardly possible to describe the turbulence of feelings all around me and in me. My appetite was whetted.

The auditorium was huge. I had chosen to read a poem about the King of Denmark. He was an extraordinary man, who, the morning after the invasion by the Nazis, rode through the city on his regular morning ride at dawn. Only this morning, around his arm, over his uniform, he wore a yellow armband with a black star— the same armband that all Jews had been ordered to wear in Denmark by the invaders. A leading poet in Denmark wrote a poem about the ride through the city that particular morning. It was smuggled over to Sweden. I had read it often during the war, and I chose to read it again this evening in Copenhagen. I wasn't aware of the fact that many people in the audience had never heard it before and that it was better known outside of Denmark for obvious reasons than inside Denmark. After I finished, the applause broke out like a thunderstorm. It was an extraordinary feeling. I could feel tears well up in my eyes. I was part of life at its fullest after all. I was part of the struggle of the world, after all. I belonged to the world! I wanted more. Well, I was getting it!

I dreamed of becoming a great film star as well as a great actress in the theater. Today, I am not even sure the combination is possible. Not so far, anyhow, in this country. Film is separated from the theater, not as in Sweden where I can act on the stage at night and be in front of the camera during the day. It took me a long while before I realized that I had to move to New York in order to even come close to understanding what it takes to be the kind of actress I wanted to be. And I know that now. Would I if I had stayed home in Sweden? Who knows? The fact is that I didn't. I only know that it was in New York that I landed thirty years ago, where I became the actress I had in mind to be. It was in New York, with its mess, its poverty, its mediocrity, and its brilliance, even cruelty, demanding the kind of strength from me that I needed to find within myself in order to take myself seriously. The myth came true. I found gold in the streets of New York, gold that didn't look like gold to anyone except for me.

I met the gentleman who asked the question, not too long ago, thirty years later. It was Archer Winston! "Do you remember what you answered me?" he said.

"No," I said.

" 'If you don't like this country, why don't you leave it?' "

I laughed; this time I was wiser. Most of the myths were gone. I understood better why I had left Sweden.

But I was only twenty-five then and hungry for life. Too hungry, maybe, and I didn't know how to admit that or tell Archer that it was my right to find out on my own whom I wanted to be and where and how. That was, no doubt, the source of my fury.

2

One late afternoon Folke, Eva, and I boarded the train at Grand Central Station for Hollywood, California.

Grand Central Station! Gigantic and colorful with its stone floors and endlessly high glass ceilings letting in a soft, strange yellow light, painting everything and everybody with it. Grand Central Station—with its ticket counters and bars and delicatessens and coffee shops, shops of all kinds. There is nothing you can't buy at Grand Central Station weekday or Sunday; so different from Sweden, a quiet country, where everything closes down at 5:00 and it would be a sin to buy or to sell on Sunday. Grand Central Station—with sounds from loudspeakers announcing the trains and the tracks, sounds of people rushing back and forth, sounds of different languages, different accents, people of different places, colors, ages. The future of the world in a nutshell.

Kay Brown waved us goodbye with red roses again. The New York visit had been a success. The newspapers had been filled with photos and articles about the new Swedish film star, comparing me to Garbo and Bergman. As the train huffed and puffed toward the golden West, the reality had been far better than any myth, so far.

I hated the three days on the train. The continuous shaking made me seasick. I slept badly. I was bored. I got constipated. I was gaining weight. I tried to exercise by walking back and forth through the train, getting off at every station for the few minutes it stopped. Breathe some fresh air!

I was worried about my looks. "When I step off the train in Los Angeles I have to be beautiful and gorgeous! Exciting and fabulous! So that they love me and feel they did the right thing in bringing me over all the way from Sweden!" On the second day I looked at my face with horror. I was green and puffy-eyed. "Christ," I asked myself furiously, "who's going to want to put *that* face on the screen?"

Folke was not much help. He read, he slept, he ate, he drank wine, he smoked cigars. He was heavy and didn't care what he looked like. He loved being away from telephones and office problems.

For him it was a holiday. He was to stay with me for a couple of weeks and get me settled. Then he would return and take care of the children. He didn't mind that at all. He wanted to be a father differently from what he had been before. His daughter from his first marriage grew up with the mother. He only saw her on holidays.

I watched him on the train playing chess with himself, envying him for dealing so much better than I with his leisure time. For him, nothing was at stake, I thought. Not even our sex life.

Being together on the train for two days and three nights was too intimate for Viveca with a c. It didn't fit in with the image of a couple the way she had created it—the older manager-lawyer-husband with his young beautiful actress-wife. He, no doubt, more in love with her than she with him. She was rather spoiled and not very nice about it all, for she had in mind to meet the "king" one day and take off.

I'm not sure I was so comfortable with this double game.

What did Folke think about my going to Hollywood? Really? After all, he was the one who had done the contract. The option allowed them to keep me for seven years although it might end up being only three months. But, if so, what was his plan? Move? He was the head of a big law firm! On the other hand, could the marriage survive a separation?

Perhaps Folke sensed my withdrawal—or let's call it ambivalence. And maybe he knew well that I might leave him one of those days, but decided to take the risk, hoping for the best. In many ways, he was a modern man and he had maybe more faith in me

139

than I had in myself. He wanted to help me to become independent in a way that his father never helped his mother. He certainly was aware of the traps that Hollywood might set for a young woman like me, as hungry as he knew I was. For he had been hungry himself. He was a Swede. And as vulnerable as he knew I was, for he, too, was vulnerable. He was a Swede. "Lillian," he used to call me, meaning little girl, and the combination of hunger and vulnerability is a dangerous one, and maybe that is why he insisted on having Eva go along to look after me, protecting his interest as well as mine.

Today Eva and I are the best of friends. But in those days a woman's friendship had no value to me. What could women do except depress me and remind me of my own weakness? It was the men in my life who had been helpful, who had gotten me into a position of power, even giving me feelings of love and worth. Eva's slightly dry manners frightened me. I took it as unfriendliness. Not true, really. Perhaps it was something about her that scared me. Something I wanted for myself and dared not ask for. No doubt her need for independence had always, all through her life, been stronger than her need for the love of a man and whatever that love in those days seemed to demand from her. She saw no way to combine the two. She worked all her life and supported herself at a time when most women looked for a man to support them. Eventually she opened her own play agency in Stockholm, most successfully.

No play takes place without her being involved on some level, if only as a friend to the producer, the actor, or the director. Looking back I can see why she wasn't too enthusiastic about either being my companion or being in Hollywood. We talked about it years later. "No, no, Viveca. It had nothing to do with that. I was going through a different period. I was impossible to live with."

It was the same old story. Eva, like the rest of us, did not want to exclude love from her life. She had married an Austrian Jew, a refugee who sought refuge in Sweden for a while. He couldn't stand the quiet and somewhat controlling security atmosphere and left it and Eva when the war was over. Eva went to look for him one summer, figuring she ought to know whether her "husband" was alive or dead. She found him well and living in Spain with another woman, writing movies.

"Folke knew about all this," Eva said to me. We were sitting in her apartment looking out over the rooftops of Stockholm. "And when he offered to send me to Hollywood with you I was grateful for the opportunity to get away."

"I wish I had known then," I said.

"I'm not sure I could have told you," Eva said.

I laughed. "Like me. I probably wouldn't have been able to listen. It's just as well. Here we are *now*."

Eva does not live alone. She lives with Johan, her adopted son, also an Austrian, who was brought to Sweden to play the part of a dwarf in a stage production. He had simply stopped growing when he was eight years old. When he was fourteen Eva took him under her wings. She found a medical specialist who thought he knew about lack of growth. "My treatment will take four or five years," he said. Johan stayed on with Eva. It has been more than ten years now and he is still with her, although he only grew a few inches. His body is still six years behind his mind.

"So what?" I said to him that day. "You are a super spirit and what does the size of your body matter."

Johan is a Buddhist. Eva's bedroom, that used to be in pale Swedish colors, now has a mattress on the floor, a shrine, a smell of incense, and walls covered with Indian drawings and paintings in exotic dark colors. And Eva's office is her bedroom.

At the time when Eva should have had a child she couldn't or didn't want to or whatever. She was ready when Johan came along. The two of them provide each other with a mother-son experience they both must have needed and wanted. Life pays little attention to rules and regulations when it comes to finding ways to fulfill basic needs, and is even quite divine and fair. It was true about Eva's and my friendship too. It is for real now. She is the first person I call when I step off the plane today, coming home to Stockholm. Eva and Johan. And so it doesn't matter that we missed each other that spring and summer in Hollywood. And looking back I realized now that just the knowledge that she was there with me was valuable. Folke was right. I was too vulnerable to be alone, not like Garbo, and who knows if she really was?

On a foggy day, the train with Folke, Eva, and myself huffed and puffed into the small town station in Pasadena, so different from Grand Central Station with all its excitement.

I had washed my hair in the barber shop in the morning in lukewarm water and didn't eat all day so that I would look pale and gaunt as a film star should. The key was to *look* fragile and interesting, but *be* strong and healthy.

A tiny group of people came toward me. I had had fantasies of men talking loud and tough, smoking big cigars, and gorgeous dames, reporters taking notes, cameras rolling, and lights flashing.

And of course Jack Warner himself, kissing my hand as I stepped off the train. Instead there was a female, unmarried, sad, a distant cousin of his, meeting me, and another one with blond hair and red roses in her arms. I couldn't see who she was for the roses, but I heard her Swedish accent. It was Karin Eklund, an actress-friend of mine, to begin with, a competitor. She had been the number one candidate for the part of the teacher in *If I Married a Minister*, my first big box office film. She was much better known than I was then. It must have been painful for her when I suddenly showed up in the arena and was given the part. What was she doing in Hollywood? "Welcome to L.A., Viveca," she said and handed me the roses. "And meet your agent." Christ! What was she doing here with *my* agent? I didn't want competition from another Swedish actress on my very first day. It was the last thing I wanted, to be met by her.

Nothing seemed right anymore, not even my expensive tailor-made brown suit. It felt all wrong in the balmy, sticky air of the hot afternoon. Silently, I stumbled into the limousine and together we all took off for the Beverly Hills Hotel.

I thought I had left that sullen, stupid girl of my childhood behind me forever in Sweden, and here, seeing Karin with her blond hair like my sister's, I ran right smack into her again. I felt the prison bars, the feelings of competition, of having to fight for my life, closing in on me, strangling me. I wanted to get rid of her forever, that stupid, sullen girl in me. I didn't want her in my life anymore. I wanted something else, something passionate, something wild and strong. Dear God, don't let me lose that feeling, not now! Not now in the U.S.A.! In the City of Angels!

3

The big black Warner Brothers limousine drove through Los Angeles suburbia. There was and is nothing glamorous about Los Angeles suburbia. It's lower middle income homes, ugly, unimaginative, uncreative. Suddenly it switched. We were in Beverly Hills. I had never seen such luxury, one mansion more magnificent than the other, pink ones, yellow ones, white ones, gray ones; mansions made out of brick, out of stucco, out of glass; green lawns, flower bushes, trees, and through an open gate one could even catch a glimpse of swimming pools and Cadillacs parked in front of the garage. Like in the movies.

Everything in Beverly Hills was and is just like in the movies. The Beverly Hills Hotel topped it all. We had our own bungalow with flowers and trees outside and luxurious bathrooms. I couldn't have cared less. Exhausted, I crawled into bed. My first night in Hollywood was very different from the first night in New York. I fell asleep thinking, tomorrow I am going to the studio. Tomorrow I am going to meet Jack Warner. Tomorrow he will kiss my hand and tell me all the marvelous plans he has in mind for me. Tomorrow, tomorrow, tomorrow.

Tomorrow turned into a week. I kept asking the agent, who was better looking than Jimmy Stewart and ought to have been in the movies, "When am I meeting Jack Warner? When am I starting the film?"

"Relax and enjoy yourself," he kept repeating.

It took me a while to catch on to the fact that the part opposite Gary Cooper had gone to Lilli Palmer. "They want to prepare you for something much bigger," was the agent's explanation. "What are you worrying about? Relax."

I hadn't come to Hollywood to relax. I didn't even know what the word meant. I soon learned "relax" means, "Lay off me, baby. I don't know what to do with you and you're getting paid, aren't you?"

Why couldn't I have finished the season at the theater in Stockholm? Moved the kids to the country myself? Done things more smoothly, more responsibly? Instead, I had rushed over to the other end of the world. For what? Questions nobody was interested in answering.

I tried to use the time. Folke went back to Stockholm and the office and the kids. It felt reassuring that they had at least one parent at home.

Eva and I moved to a house south of Hollywood Boulevard. I obviously needed a car and an American driver's license. I had been driving in Sweden for years and thought it would be a matter of formalities to get one. I flunked the test. I cried walking away from the dingy building in Hollywood. It seemed more of a slap in the face than finding out about losing the part in the Cooper film. It's called culture shock.

Finally the day arrived when Mr. Jack Warner was ready to receive me. We met on the lot. He was a small, heavyset man with a kind of restless energy that I have come to get used to in this country. And he didn't kiss my hand and tell me about all the marvelous plans he had in mind for me.

Instead, he kept repeating, "Don't be nervous. Don't be nervous."

I wasn't. I should have been, and I was eventually, but not that day. "I'm not nervous, but my feet hurt," I finally said. We had walked all over the lot. It was a hot day and Warner Brothers is a large, cemented city without trees or flowers or grass. With security guards all over the place, it looked and sounded more to me like a concentration camp or a large factory with the noise of air conditioning and generators booming out from the barracks-like building.

The boss laughed. "My feet hurt, too. I'm a Jew from New York. But I want to introduce you to the stars." He did!

Gary Cooper, tall, lanky, attractive, with the same humorous glint in his eyes and that same quiet intimate way of talking. It seemed unreal for a girl from Lidingo to see him in the flesh. Bette Davis too, brilliant, vital, and intelligent. She came over to me, shook my hand. "Welcome," she said. No competition, only generosity. I stood there watching her work, in awe of her, particularly of the way she talked to her director. There was no little girl and big man game between them. There was only respect and vitality. Bette Davis had survived in a man's kingdom on her own terms in a place where most women forced themselves according to man's wishes. Will I ever know what she knows? I wondered to myself my first day on the Warner Brothers lot.

It was also to the credit of Curt Bernhardt, the director. He had escaped as a German Jew from Germany to England and from there to Hollywood. We became close friends. To begin with, we flirted wildly with each other until I got to know his wife, a beautiful young English woman, a dancer who had given up dancing when she went with him to Hollywood, a superb mother for their two children and a wonderful wife to Curt. It is tragic and impossible to understand or accept that she died within a year.

From Bette Davis' set we wandered over to Joan Crawford's. It was the year, the last, for interesting women on the Warner Brothers lot. Joan Crawford was a far better actress than ever given credit for. She greeted me warmly. "I want to give a party for you," she said after a few moments. A party for me? I was stunned, hoping secretly that she was kidding.

A week later her secretary called and confirmed. "Next Sunday we will pick you up in the limousine at 3:30," she said. Help!

I tried to protest. I had my own car now, a small black Ford. I had finally gotten my driver's license. The studio had connections. A nice man from the Motor Vehicles Department came out and took me gently around the back roads. I loved my independence, coming and going as I wanted to. But my protest was of no use.

144

"You are the guest of honor," the secretary said, and no chances must be taken. She was a good organizer, Joan Crawford. She could easily have been the head of a studio, and a good one.

Eva didn't want to go along. She probably spent the afternoon with Bertolt Brecht! He was living in exile with his wife and children in California, like many refugees from Nazi Germany.

Years later, when I was doing *Brecht on Brecht* in Stockholm, she told me about her Sunday afternoons with him.

"Why didn't you ask me to come along?" I said indignantly.

"You wouldn't have been interested," she answered. "You were too involved in playing the Hollywood game."

Was that really true? Would I have appreciated Brecht's genius? Was I that dumb? Certainly unaware.

I had nothing to wear for the Crawford party. The few Swedish clothes I had brought seemed all wrong for the California climate. In Sweden in those days one owned a dress for a winter, one for the summer, and another one for parties. The same thing went for shoes. Besides, I was used to having my clothes made by a dressmaker and had no idea where to go to buy them here. The female distant cousin of Jack Warner, who had met me at the station, suggested I go to the wardrobe department and borrow an outfit. I had visions of divine clothes from the stars. Wrong. They either hide them, or steal them, or buy them after the film. There was nothing divine available for me to borrow and I ended up with a ghastly purple wool suit. At 3:30 Sunday afternoon, on the dot, a chauffeur-driven limousine pulled up in front of my house.

I stumbled into the black limousine, tense as a stick. I tried to converse with the driver during the ride but he wasn't interested in talking with me. Maybe he smelled my tension!

We finally pulled up in front of Joan Crawford's mansion in Brentwood, a rambling English Tudor house covered with ivy. A maid in black and white opened the door and she seemed disappointed that I didn't have a glorious wrap to give her, and when she showed me to the powder room and I said I didn't need to go she gave up on me. She shrugged her shoulders and showed me down the garden path. Below I saw the pale blue-green pool, and on the opposite side of it an enormous pink tent, raised for the occasion, with individual tables laid all in pink for at least a hundred people. The lawn around was filled with chairs and tables, lights and candles. Waiters were rushing back and forth. I got more and more nervous. How can I live up to all this? Suddenly Joan appeared, coming out of the poolhouse like a goddess, exquisitely beautiful with her white skin and red flaming full hair; dressed in a black delicate chiffon dress and elegant satin shoes. My heart went down into my stomach. My feet got bigger. My borrowed outfit from the wardrobe department felt duller than ever. What am I doing here? I asked myself for the hundredth time, wishing I was home in Stockholm, playing with the children, being taken care of by Folke. I lost all my guts. Why couldn't I have said to her, "You are gorgeous, Joan. I came to this country because of women like you. Here you are for real, beautiful, successful, and competent." Instead, my English became nonexistent. "Gee," is all I managed to say.

"Hundreds of people are coming to see you, to meet you," Joan said. I died another thousand times.

The guests arrived. All the stars that I had ever seen or ever read about were at the party—Spencer Tracy, Katharine Hepburn, Cary Grant, Bob Young, Gary Cooper, Rex Harrison, Lilli Palmer, Jimmy Stewart—you name them, welcoming *me* to Hollywood. American curiosity! American generosity! For a Swede it was hard to live up to. You have to give back, and we are slow people. After about two hours of saying "How do you do?" I couldn't take it any longer. I found Joan. "I want to go home!"

She looked at me with those enormous eyes of hers, bigger than Garbo's. "Impossible!" she said. "We are having supper in the tent in a few moments and you are the guest of honor." I died a few more deaths again, but stayed, although I doubt that anybody would have noticed if I had left. I didn't quite understand the whole situation. Was it just a generous gesture by Joan? Or was it a clever move to give a party for a young Swedish star? Or maybe she was just looking for an excuse to give a party. Everybody was eager to forget the war and bring back the glamor of the past, the Hollywood of the past. Joan's party was one of the first big affairs given after the war was over.

It was hard for everybody to face the fact that things had changed. The men had changed. The women had changed. People's attitudes had changed. It soon became apparent that things were not working the way they had in the good old days, and when TV came panic hit Hollywood. The studios began to close down. People who had been under contract for twenty-five years were fired. Lesser films were being scheduled. Nobody cared about the quality. Many of the European artists, who had lived in California as refugees, decided to return to Europe. McCarthy was around the corner. One began to sense the danger of fascism. Within a year or two, he succeeded in cutting off the balls of the gutsy, radical writers and directors. Then the women's image went down the drain. Gorgeous women, women of intelligence and beauty, integrity and wit, like Joan Crawford, Irene Dunne, Greta Garbo, Claudette Colbert, Katharine Hepburn, were slowly replaced with the girl-next-door or the sexpot image. Only a few of the real actresses survived, mainly those who dared to return to the theater.

Hollywood, more than ever, had become a man's world. Had the American War Hero image gone to its head? The American soldier was loved and adored by women all over the world. We fell in love with him on the screen to begin with, and when we met him in reality we continued to see him through those eyes. We were ready to do anything for him for nothing, or, at the most, a Hershey bar. He was allowed heaven and earth, having romantic, transient affairs without complications or responsibilities, as well as dreaming of and belonging to the girl-next-door. The Hollywood producers were quick to cash in on the romantic image that threw a pink spotlight on the situation, a situation that might have been much more tearing for everybody than was allowed to be seen or felt. When the man returned from war, he did not see, or didn't want to see, that the little girl next door had grown up and become a capable woman running the business while he had been fighting the war. The woman, almost as confused as the man by her newly found freedom and strength, withdrew in bewilderment. She was hungry for love and peace and gave up for the price of what she thought was love.

I met Joan Crawford years after the party she gave me. She had retired by now from films, although she never used that word. The fact is she rarely worked after the age of forty, except for an occasional film, which is not enough for a talent like Crawford's. She was "too old" to be the star and "too big" a star to play smaller parts, according to the Hollywood standards that had also, unfortunately, become hers. When I spoke to her about living in Hollywood versus New York where I had moved partly to escape this deadline standard for an actress today, she said very simply, and without any trace of bitterness, "Hollywood is my home. I have no other place to go." I admired her for her feelings for a place that had rejected her during the best years of her life. I did not admire her lack of insight. Had she understood her potential, she would have found ways of using her talent in different ways from acting in films where her age was in the way.

Film, the wonderful invention of this century, has changed the boundaries of our profession. With the camera having registered our wrinkles in the eyes of the audience, we can no longer play Juliet or Ophelia or Hamlet or Romeo much beyond the age of thirty-five. Much less beyond the age of sixty, as Duse and Bernhardt and Kean could and did. It's slightly more acceptable for the male actor. Burton was in his fifties when he did his Hamlet and nobody questioned it. They would have if Gerry Page or I or even Liz Taylor had played Ophelia.

Actors, however, have to find other outlets for their talents today. In directing or writing or producing. Age makes us deeper, wiser, and more competent. To waste us because of it would be a sin.

There is no doubt in my mind that Joan Crawford or Bette Davis would have made fine directors or producers. But it did not occur to anybody, not even perhaps to them at that time. It might have seemed too threatening for "the feminine mystique" to be in charge. I understand that feeling. And Hollywood in particular is a tough town for a woman to establish herself beyond the sex symbol image. But it is changing even in Hollywood.

It was my good luck that I met a woman like Sophie Rosenstein. She was the head of Talent, in charge of the young players under contract. Warner took me to her office above the make-up department that first day when he walked me around the lot. I didn't see him for months, but he couldn't have left me in better hands. Sophie was an exceptional woman. She worked creatively, lived creatively, loved creatively. She was true to my myth about the American woman. She became my teacher and my first real woman friend.

Sophie greeted me warmly. She was a tiny, delicate woman. Her face was not beautiful, but her smile was such that one never thought about it, one way or the other. I instantly trusted her. She had received her training in Seattle at the university. But with her exceptional curiosity, she sought out everything new and extraordinary in the American theater and passed it on to her students. She had studied with Lee Strasberg. It became my first exposure to The Method.

She had set up a small theater in the back of the lot where she worked with the young players and every third month or so put a show on for the producers and directors to become familiar with the talents on the lot. Above all, it gave the new talents a chance to grow as actors, which is hard in a place like Hollywood where everything is concentrated around becoming a personality and selling oneself in one way or another—a lousy way to spend one's time if one is to become an actress.

Sophie immediately provided me with a schedule, and for the next three months I went to the studio every day for classes. I took dance, speech, and, above all, English.

She suggested I work on a scene and perform it at one of her showings with her students. It was unusual that an actress of my stature would, but I needed it. Besides, Sophie probably suspected the ambivalence of the bosses about what to do with me and knew that it couldn't hurt to have them see me work.

Sophie chose a scene for me from *The Glass Menagerie*, between Laura and the Gentleman Caller. "Laura," I said. "You mean the clubfooted girl who can't catch the Gentleman Caller?"

"Yes," she laughed, and looked at me with her friendly eyes. "It will give you a chance to use your fragilities," she said. In Sweden I was looked upon as healthy and sexy, and I would not be cast in a part with the complexity of Laura. That she believed I could do it moved me.

I was as unaware of my own fragilities as I was of others around me. The young man who played the Gentleman Caller opposite me committed suicide a few months after the performance. I had not sensed it in him at all. And I thought, I never sensed it in my brother, either. It hadn't even occurred to me that anyone would commit suicide. One reads about it in novels, but "it can't happen to me."

Burt was a young actor under contract, and when the studio dropped his option a few months after we performed the scene he gave up. He was found in a small, messy, half-empty, unattractive apartment in Hollywood. He had been dead for several days. No one had noticed. Oh my God! I had paid no attention to him, either, I thought when I heard it. It had been all involved in myself and Laura only. It was my first encounter with the kind of loneliness and despair that is often experienced by young actors coming to Hollywood to seek fame. Yet it was in Hollywood that I, for the first time in my life, was encouraged to deal with unknown areas and fragilities within myself.

After five months in Hollywood, instead of the expected three, it was obvious now that the studio had no plans for me. I was becoming impatient. I had expected Hollywood, Warner Brothers, to know how to build my career better than Lux Film in Sweden. The opposite was true so far. What they paid me in salary with trips and living expenses had seemed like a lot of money at home, but I now realized it was of no consequence to them. I was still a hot property because of all the publicity around me, and had I known how to promote projects for myself, or Eva, my secretary, things might have been different. Certainly the opportunities were there, but only in the last ten years have I known that fifty percent of the initiative must come from the actress. But then, times have changed, too, and I did come from a different cultural background.

Socially I had a marvelous time. I ran around with one of the men from the agency. He was not interested in me sexually so I could flirt with whomever I needed to flirt with. We seemed to make a good working team together, except not much came of it all. After five months, I began to feel enough is enough. I could no longer justify spending my time on taking dance class or learning English or giving an occasional performance on the back lot or having lunch with reporters, telling them about my life, or having drinks with directors hoping they would cast me in their films, or going to the gallery and having my picture taken day in and day out. There must have been thousands of me in various dresses, hairdos, poses: "Wet your lips, Viveca. Look this way or that way, up or down, over your shoulder. Look sexy, Viveca. Wet your lips, Viveca." At the end of the day I went home exhausted. From what? The dilemma of this century's actress. Acting in front of a thing instead of a human being is as exhausting as masturbation. You have to do it all yourself.

What am I? I asked myself. A model? And where were those pictures going to be used? I knew by now that the people in the publicity department were simply busy creating situations for themselves, justifying their salaries, petrified of being laid off. That was true about the photographer and the hairdresser and the make-up man and the dressers and the body make-up man, on and on. At the end of five months I couldn't have cared less. "I will throw up if I get another call to go into the gallery," I thought.

After all, I was twenty-five years old. My career had started with a bang in Sweden and I had not forgotten the white light of creativity I had experienced on stage, that I had a life to lead—in Stockholm too. There wasn't only a theater where the work went on for twelve hours a day resulting in a performance, *and* a film company that was ready to offer me leading parts in three to four films a year. There were, above all, two small children waiting for me. The nightmare was that I began to forget them.

What about Folke? It was more complex, even threatening. He

had been a good father for the children and he was there waiting for me, representing a sense of security that at the time I didn't much like to acknowledge. Nor the responsibility that I might owe him something back. It was mostly the children, I felt, and the fact that I wasn't working, that made me want to leave Hollywood. Made me feel I had to.

I gave Warner Brothers an ultimatum. "I am an actress," I said to my agent. "I am here to work, not to relax. I am going home September first, film or no film." It worked!

"They've got a picture for you, Viveca," my agent called me. "Beginning September 15th. *Night unto Night* co-starring Ronald Reagan."

"Who?"

"Never mind. A young star under contract. Come to the studio tomorrow morning at ten AM and meet the producer and the director."

"Will I be home for Christmas? Can I tell the children I will be home for Christmas?"

"Yes, you will be home for Christmas."

Promises, promises.

4

Night unto Night was not the perfect set-up. The formula was to match a new foreign girl with a big American star. Ronald Reagan was not that. The director was fairly unknown, too. He had made only one film so far. My agent wasn't sure I ought to accept the whole package, but it scared me to go home without having done a film. That might be the end of my Hollywood career. I said yes. I must have wanted it.

"Meet Don Siegel, your director," Sophie said. We met outside her office. He came wandering down the cemented road. He had black curly hair and a smile as if he had a pleasant secret. He was low-keyed and intelligent. He was my age and in the same profession as I. I had not had sex with a man for several months. I was hot and hungry.

We had been shooting for a few weeks when it came to a head. Don took me for lunch in the private dining room on the lot. Only directors and the big shots, plus guests, were allowed. We all sat at a long table. In the middle of the broiled sole, and I don't remember who said it first, "I love you." "I love you."

I was in love again. I hadn't been since Rydeberg.

151

Don had a girlfriend, Kathy, a redhead. I had Folke. They planned to get married. We were married. They had planned to buy a house together. We had a house together and two children. The signal I had gotten was that he was free. The signal that he had gotten was that I was free. When *I* found out and *he* found out, it didn't bother either one of us. We were arrogant. Yes. We were in love, but we didn't *make* love. Not yet.

Folke was coming for a visit within two weeks. Did I want to give our marriage another try? Can one, under those circumstances? I couldn't.

After Folke arrived, I kept inviting Don home to the apartment after work. Eva had returned to Sweden and I had moved to a small apartment all by myself in Beverly Hills. We were together, just the three of us. Don and Folke played chess while I cooked the dinner, my desire for Don increasing. I couldn't wait for Folke to leave. I took him to the plane one late Sunday afternoon, kissed him goodbye at the airport. In love and war everything is allowed! Is it really?

Don was waiting for me in a restaurant not too far from there. We drank champagne, had dinner, and went home. In the middle of the lovemaking the phone rang. It was Folke. Something was wrong with the plane. He was still at the airport, had thought of coming back, taking the next plane in the morning, instead. But when he didn't get an answer in the apartment he decided to stick it out.

I swallowed hard and explained that I had stopped off for a bite to eat with Sophie. I wished him a safe trip. I still wasn't ready to tell him the truth—that I was making love with Don for the very first time; that it was stupendous; that I knew I would never be Folke's wife again. But I had no doubts about what I wanted. Everything was going my way. I was accepted both as an actress and as a woman now in this, my "maybe" new country. I was ready to burn my bridges. It was only a question of how and when.

Sophie was my confidante. She was in love herself with Gig Young, an actor ten years younger than she. Sophie was married to Arthur then. She knew the pleasures of the game. "What do I do about Folke and the children, Sweden or America? What's going to happen?" I asked her.

She laughed and said, "Viveca, this is the best part of the love affair. Enjoy it! Don't worry about the future."

When the love affair with Gig became serious, everyone warned her, "Sophie, ten years from now you will be too old for him and he will leave you. Arthur never will." But Sophie was an ageless creature, a spirit. Ironically it was she who left Gig. She died two years later, but after two years of bliss with him.

Night unto Night was the first major film for Don. His story was a typical American success story. He started at Warner Brothers as a messenger boy. He soon advanced to the editing room and from there into director of special effects. He won an award for his work and was tops in his field. He was then given his first feature-length film, a small mystery with Sidney Greenstreet, *The Verdict*, a year before I met him, and it turned out to be sensational. He was looked upon as the young genius on the lot. As a director he was low-keyed. There was nothing dominating or bossy about him. He was curious about what the actor brought to the part. He had a terrific sense of humor. It was easy to perform under his direction.

Being in love with the director of my first Hollywood film was marvelous! Who would come between him and me? "You are in a special place, baby! And you know it." Was it good for the work? Maybe. It made me less tense, also less *intense*. There was more than that going on. A look at each other in the studio while lining up a shot, Don behind the camera and I in front, and the blood would go wild. Life was a dance between us. We drove off after work in separate cars, bumping each other gently at intersections. Meeting in a bar, having a drink before taking off, and meeting again in bed. Yes, life was a dance!

The production was not without dramas. There was a strike going on, and we had to pass the picket lines every morning to and from the studio. Ronald Reagan was, at the time, the president of the Screen Actors Guild and, although openly on the side of the strikers and the actors union, did not join the strike. He, being in a target position, was not safe. Some violence had occurred, and on the fourth day of shooting I heard one studio patrolman tell another, "Take Reagan home and stay on patrol all night. He is established in the picture now, and we don't want to take any chances." A typical Hollywood story. Today, since he is the President of the United States, his life is in constant danger.

Maybe the strike, with its risks, made him realize where he belonged. Among the Republicans. Watching him on TV years later running for the presidency and being on the opposite side of the fence politically, I thought to myself, in spite of it all he really hasn't changed. He was as bland and smooth and seemingly pleas-

ant as in those days. I don't remember a single conversation with
him of any substance. I do remember some chitchat about sex,
which was up my alley, since I was in love with Don. Ronnie, at
the time, was married to Jane Wyman. "It's best in the afternoon,
after coming out of the shower," he said, and then he laughed
the same, slightly embarrassed laugh that he did on TV the other
day. Nancy was sitting listening to him during the speech. I kept
thinking, "Does he still like it in the afternoon? Does she? I hope
so!"

The creative part of making a film in Hollywood wasn't much
different from making a film in Sweden. Only the physical set-up,
the preparations, were different. Everything was in a separate
building—one for editing, one for wardrobe, one for eating, one
for make-up, even a building for toilets. It was very different from
the studio in Stockholm where everything was in one place and
much more convenient.

I missed my simple dressing room with cotton prints and my
Marianne, my all-in-one helper, bringing me coffee, listening to
what happened in my life and I in hers. It was more human than
all those people around you at the Warner Brothers Studio—all
those experts and specialists, each one exaggerating his own thing,
looking for a piece of hair out of place, or a hem being too short
or too long, instead of being creative about the image of the
character and the actress. By the time she is ready to go in front
of the camera, each one has taken a tiny piece of her unless she
is able to build a wall around herself, one that quickly can be torn
down, for once in front of the camera she will have to be naked.

The biggest shock for me was the falsies. I had never heard
about them. The wardrobe lady took me into the dressing room.
"They want to see you with these on," she said and held two
strange looking rubber cups with nipples on in her hands, shaped
like real breasts. I still didn't get the idea. "You put these inside
the brassiere," she explained, "so that your breasts look bigger."

"I don't want that," I said. "I like them the way they are." I
suddenly realized why everybody had looked at my bosom in a
strange way before. Wasn't it enough that I wore a bra? And a
girdle, and now rubber cups! No, thank you.

"They want to see you in them," she said, quietly and firmly.

Sulking, I put them on. "So what?" I thought. "It isn't a big
enough battle to fight. Save your passions for something better,
Viveca."

I wandered onto the set. The bosses looked at me approvingly this time.

The filming took longer than planned, and around Thanksgiving I began to realize that I would not be home for Christmas. I got upset, much more than I had expected, furious, too. I went up to the executive offices and saw Jack Warner's righthand man, Mr. Trilling. Equally short. Equally stocky. Equally bald. He didn't smoke a cigar or kiss my hand, either. It was a large office. All executive offices in Hollywood are long and empty and large, the desk in one end, the door in the other so that "he," the big man behind the desk, can watch me, judge me, inspect me as I walk over on my high-heeled sexy shoes. Maybe even embarrass me or put me off guard.

Not this time. I was more furious than I knew. I found myself slamming my fist on the table and screaming, "You told me I would be home for Christmas. The children are waiting for me. If I am not coming I must tell them, and *when* I will."

It worked. He gave me a definite date. Two days after Christmas Eve I could leave.

Christmas Eve was gray, heavy, humid. We worked in the morning. Eggnog was served all over the place. Christmas Eve in Sweden is beautiful and spirited. I missed it all and the children. Not even loving Don seemed to help today. By two o'clock in the afternoon, everybody was drunk in the studio and happy, except for me. It was ridiculous to try to accomplish anything. I felt the pressure. "How will I get out of here in three days?"

We were invited to the Bernhardts' on Christmas for dinner. As I drove along Sunset Boulevard from Beverly Hills to their house, it started to rain. It poured down in buckets. I slowed down. I crept with my lights on. I was swept by waves of homesickness, a strange sense of loss. "What am I doing here so far away from my children, from my country, from my home?" Don seemed more and more like a stranger. He was, of course. I had, after all, only known him for three months, but I was not kind to myself in those days. And to doubt was a sin.

Some of the feelings disappeared during the evening in the warmth of the Bernhardt family. And at night, my body against Don's, his penis inside of me, life seemed real again. "Nothing is lost, but it changes," says Anais Nin. Oh yes!

Three days later the film was finished and Don put me on the plane. It was a brilliant sunny California day. I couldn't wait to come back.

I stopped overnight in New York.

I had supper with the Bernhardts at the Gotham Hotel. They were on a holiday, just the two of them. They were warm toward me. They knew my trip to Sweden would be not only pleasure but that I was facing the breakup with Folke. But we all felt strong and good about the future and our friendship. We kissed each other good night. It was the last time I saw Pearl.

When I arrived the following morning in Stockholm, Folke was waiting for me at the airport with a cable from Curtis. Pearl had died that same afternoon. No, not she! Why? How?

They were getting dressed to go out for dinner. She was standing by the bed in her slip, laughing. "My head," she said suddenly. She moved her hand up to her neck and fell on the bed. That was it. Her life was over. A tiny vein in the back of her head had broken. It could have happened any time before, now, later, the doctor said. It happened now. Never mind why. I couldn't grasp it. How could Curt? They had been married for twelve years.

I couldn't grasp twenty years later that George was gone. He didn't die: he just left. It's all the same. The tie between two people who are physically and intimately involved with each other, although you can't touch or see it, is filled with a substance of such strength that, when cut off, suddenly, it dangles there, in shock, bleeding, lost, unable to grasp what's happening, unable to heal, until fumblingly, out of survival instinct, it begins to seek another tie, somebody else's blood and feelings—and only that strange mixture of substance makes for the healing, the soothing, for the restoring, for survival, and, finally, for life. Happy is she or he who understands the mystical strength of the tie.

It was heavenly beautiful when Folke and I drove through the woods to Backa by the sea. The snow was coming down in big flakes. The silence of nature was all around us. Our own silences were in between us.

The children occupied my thoughts. Nine months! Would they remember me? John was three going on four, Lena only two. "Mommy is coming home," they must have been told. "Mommy who?" A boogie-woman on the front page of the newspaper. I was a grownup and in spite of their pictures hanging all over my bedroom they had begun to be unreal to me.

I can't stand the fact that I remember nothing from the moment when I saw the children for the first time after nine months! Was it guilt, or that I was too preoccupied with finding words to tell Folke about the end of us? Conflict makes for more conflicts. Distracting from the basic quality of life. Weakening antibodies.

Did I understand that they had perhaps forgotten me—Lena more so than John? He knew me longer and therefore better. Was I patient about that? To Lena I must have been an image only, a word. Did I spend enough time with them, real time within the next couple of weeks making up for lost time? Or was I too busy being a film star? The photographers were all over the place. Did the children sense that when we sledded down the hill or built a snowman that it was partly for the cameras, for the press? Within a few years they both refused to be photographed. Feelings were too valuable to them to be played around with. My God, so much of my life has been playing with feelings, posing with feelings, photographing feelings.

And Nana. How did she feel about my being back? I was the real mother. Had she, while I was gone, given into feelings, quite justified, as I had with Henry, my stepson? "This is my child. I don't want to give it up. It is mine now." Why not? Nana had been there, not I.

Whether I liked it or not—and I did not always like it—I was totally dependent on Nana. I became even more so later in the U.S.A. To be a working star with children wasn't part of the picture in Hollywood 1947. It has changed some. On the Altman set of A Wedding the only rule was no pets. Otherwise everybody was allowed. Girlfriends, boyfriends, wives, husbands, grandfathers, grandmothers, and children. Mia Farrow and Geraldine Chaplin brought theirs all the time. Altman's own children were working in various capacities. They were part of the grownups' world. What a preparation for the world.

When I worked in the studio in 1947, I left the house at six in the morning and didn't come home until seven at night, including Saturdays. I often had to leave for location on short notice and be gone for days. I had to have a loyal and reliable person for the children. Nana was that.

When she was fourteen years old she lost her own mother. She was the oldest of ten. She had already been her mother's helper for years, ever since she was old enough. When the mother died, she became the one and only to take care of them. From then on she never saw herself in any other capacity except as mother to someone else's child—a "nana." It became her way of life, her commitment.

157

She stayed with us through stormy years and various marriages. She now lives with Lena taking care of *her* children. Love for the children has kept Nana and me together. The price and the reward of an actress, 1950. The price and the reward of a Nana, 1950.

I had only six weeks to accomplish the move: Stockholm to California; six weeks to straighten things out with Folke, to pack up the furniture, to organize the children's departure as well as my own. The pressure of time, the need for efficiency was helpful in one sense. It did not allow doubts or regrets or useless confrontations. On the other hand, it made it too easy to avoid useful ones —dealing with the continuity of the relationship between Folke and the children. We did not know how to work that one out. And John and Lena did lose their father. In those days it was most unusual that the man would get the children. I, the mother, did. I was, on every level, in a stronger position. I was the one who wanted out of the marriage. I had a lover, a life waiting for me. I was twenty-five. Folke was fifty at the time. I was quite insensitive to his pain, but I got it back. It was Folke's fourth marriage, as it was mine when G.T. left! Everything one does to others . . .

Folke did not want a divorce. He was hoping that this was a passing phase and that I would change my mind. He insisted on a two-year separation. I gave it to him. I didn't really care, but he must have panicked when he saw the furniture go and then soon me, and then, last but not least, the children. I sensed it all, the rage, the hurt pride, the fear. And also the recognition of himself. Folke had moved with ice cold swiftness from one marriage into another. There had been little compassion in him for his wives when he left them. There was little compassion in me for Folke. I told myself, "He should not have married a young girl like me. He must have known what would happen." Besides, I'd been told he had a woman during the summer while I was gone, before I had Don, and in front of the children, in front of the maids. "I don't have to feel sorry for him."

Excuses, excuses, excuses. I knew perfectly well that he had no intention of breaking up our marriage. It was a fling only or a way to keep the ego intact. It was the only way he knew how. I did the same years later while married to G.T. But I needed to catalogue Folke's crimes in order to justify my choice to leave him.

It was like an efficient nightmare those two months—packing, buying, arranging, moving to a new life far away. There were too many questions never asked: Aren't you jumping the gun too fast?

Do you really like it over there? Is Don the right man? Will he like the children? Will the children like him? Why do you burn your bridges? What about the actress? Your chances at home were far better in films, and there is no theater in Hollywood. Can you overcome the hardship of an accent? Have you forgotten about the quiet water and the stepmother violets? Should you turn your back on a place that has given you so much love? Think, Viveca. Think.

I couldn't. I didn't want to. "Look back and you turn to stone," the Bible said. I chose to believe that.

There was a reward waiting. Love. Pure love, total love. I had found him, I thought—my brother, my father, my friend, my comrade, my lover—all of them in one man. Life was going to be beautiful. It was worth giving up security, roots. Yes?

As I got off the plane in New York and heard Don's voice on the other end of the line, I knew it was all worth it! Love surged through my blood. I felt safe again. Yes—love coming from a man made me free.

Don met me at the airport in Los Angeles. We drove over the hills into the valley. He had the top down on his car. It was a warm day, a clear day, the air filled with brilliant smells of desert nature. We stopped on top of the mountain overlooking the valley. I hugged him. "I love you. I am so happy to be back," I mumbled, my fingers stroking his skull, feeling his black curly coarse hair. I stood up in the seat. I stretched my arms toward the sun, feeling its heat on my face and embracing the whole world. I felt free. So, so free.

The children followed a few weeks later, accompanied by Nana, of course, and Edith, her younger sister, red-haired and terrifically bright.

I had worried about the children and felt anxious as I stood at the train station in Pasadena, waiting for their arrival.

Ten days by rough sea. John had had an ear infection and all of them had been seasick. Folke had driven them to Gothenberg, the sea town where the ships leave for the U.S.A. and other faraway lands, where Henry had left for America several years earlier. Folke took them to a photographer to have a last picture taken with them. They looked serious and beautiful in their gray flannel traveling outfits. "How wonderful! You're going to America," people must have said to them this time.

"Wonderful?" they might have wondered! "Why? And

America? What is that?" They knew their apartment in the city and the park and their friends and they knew the grass and the trees and the sea and the strawberry plants in the country. In the evening Folke had kissed them goodbye on the ship, the same ship where Harry had kissed Henry goodbye. It had been a gray and rainy day.

"I was very angry," John told me years later. As angry as a four-year-old can be without getting into too much trouble.

I saw them step down from the car. Lena discovered me first and ran toward me. "Mama, mama, mama," she called out and jumped into my arms. A second later, John was there too. They love me! They know me! Children are beautifully generous and pure. All my worries were gone.

We piled into the new station wagon. The small black Ford had been fine for a free, independent actress with no responsibility, but I had a family now. Don was the driver and I sat in front with John on my lap. He looked thin and pale from the trip. Lena sat in Nana's lap behind me. She had dealt better with the trip than John. She was two years younger and she had Nana, who loved her as if she were her own child.

It was late in the afternoon when we drove up the driveway, around the wisteria tree gently shading the low, rambling California ranch in Tarzana where John and Lena had come to share my life in the U.S.A., now also theirs. We slept quietly that night, under one roof.

I had to leave them again within the next three weeks. The film, *To the Victor*, was to be shot in Paris. It was typical of the studio to have mentioned it quite casually one day. I couldn't stand telling the children right away. It seemed so much harder than leaving them in Sweden at Backa with Folke. I waited for days, which wasn't helpful at all, either for them or for me. There was no time to ask questions or to express feelings.

"Do you have to go?" John finally asked at the airport as I was ready to take off and was kissing him goodbye. He didn't say "Please don't leave. Please."

His eyes were big and black, and when I answered "Yes, I have to," he accepted it.

Astounded, I realized that I was wanted, needed, and loved. I stumbled onto the plane, promising myself no more trips without them. I finally recognized a feeling that had been growing within me for some time. A desire to be a mother, a real one, not a ghost-mother, not a photograph or a word, but a mother, ready to share a life with my children. Finally, ready to share all the ecstasies and agonies that go along with being one.

5

Paris 1948, right after the war. The limousine took us through the streets. There was singing and dancing.

"Why?" I asked the chauffeur.

"Bastille Day," he answered. It was the fourteenth of July. How could I have forgotten?

I had a flat on top of the Georges Cinq Hotel, with a terrace overlooking the rooftops of the most beautiful city in the world. I was the star of a major Hollywood film, *To the Victor*, produced by wonder-tycoon Jerry Wald, written by Richard Brooks, directed by old-time director, Delmar Daves. Warner Brothers had scrimped on nothing. The studio was behind it, this time, and me, one hundred percent. It was the picture that was going to make me a Hollywood star.

The four weeks of shooting locations in Paris were glorious and seductive. Dennis Morgan, my co-star, might not have been the greatest actor, but was a divine friend. He had a glorious voice and was a happy man! We ate, we drank, we danced. We lived it up in Paris and Dennis signed all the checks! Warner Brothers paid! Those were the happy days of expense accounts. Delmar Daves and his wife Mary Lou were full of love and enthusiasm.

Thirty years later they came to see my *Woman* show in San Diego. At supper afterwards Delmar toasted me. "I knew when we were working in Paris that you were many women in one. I loved you for it then and I love you for it now," he said. His hair had turned white. That was the only change. He died a year later, a happy man.

Coming back from Paris, Don and the children met me at the airport in Los Angeles. They seemed in good shape and the children had learned some English. And Don had learned about the children.

Living on a farm had its glories. By now we had three dogs, several cats, and chickens galore. The box that had arrived with the furniture from Sweden became a superb, red-painted playhouse, and Edith had learned how to drive, speak English, and had a boyfriend. Life was lived.

It was Sophie who introduced me to the American theater. It became a habit of ours to go to New York together every fall during the next six years. "Come with me to New York, Viveca. I am going for ten days to see theater," she would tell me.

And I always said, "Why not? I am an actress. I need to see the theater."

In ten days we managed to see fifteen productions. We had a glorious time! We were drunk from the city, the theater, the people we met.

It was during our first visit that Sophie introduced me to Lee Strasberg. I didn't know then that he was a brilliant teacher. I met him as a director. The play was *The Big Knife* by Clifford Odets. Lee asked me to audition for the part of the wife opposite John Garfield.

I was unfamiliar with the system of auditioning. "Should I?" I asked Sophie.

"Of course," she said. "If you get the part and you like John better than Errol," she laughed—I was going into a film with Flynn called *Don Juan*—"you can try and get out of your film commitment and if it doesn't work, you have met some great people and they have learned about you."

"Learned about me?" No doubt I was spoiled by my early and fast success at home, and, like many other European artists, embedded in a false security.

But Sophie, in her warm way, made me understand that life for an actress in America was much tougher than in Sweden. Also more invigorating. "That is what you wanted. Isn't it, Viveca?" she would point out.

Auditions are part of the American actor's existence. It can be challenging, but the system is also abusive. Actors sometimes audition seven or eight times for a part. They give their time and their talent and are often the only ones not on salary. The producer has, by this time, raised money and is on salary included in the pre-production expenses, as are the director and the stage manager. The writer's play has already been optioned. For the actor, the risk is one hundred percent.

"The only way to look upon it," I say to my students, "is to use it as an exercise. At least you are acting, and in front of an audience, however special and small. That alone justifies your efforts working as waitresses at night." Most of them work late shift hours so that they can be available during the day for calls and auditions. It's a brave life with no security as to where it might lead. But the opportunity to suddenly get a lead in a play is also there, and through auditions.

The audition for *The Big Knife* took place in Lee Strasberg's office. I was not able to function as intensely as I could have. John Garfield was standing behind me, massaging my neck as my husband in the play, while I was reading the dialogue. I was unused to this kind of quick intimacy. I didn't get the part. "Because of my accent," I was told.

I wasn't ready.

"An actress must always be ready," Sophie used to say to me. "You never know what is around the corner. In a competitive place like America there is no room for carelessness." At the time I was convinced that I would lose my accent completely.

It didn't even occur to me for a moment that I, maybe, would have problems being a foreigner. All the attributes that the word "woman" is loaded with in man's dreams were given the European woman. We were goddesses, ever-forgiving, passionate, and generous. To begin with I benefited from it. It carried me on a wave. It was my luck that the American male thought that I was better in bed than his American girlfriend or wife. I was used, perhaps, to make her jealous, to teach her to be more "foreign," meaning feminine, more submissive. I was unaware of it. I believed in my role and played the game to the hilt.

The wind didn't always blow in my favor.

Years later, I was past thirty-five and things were rougher. Besides, I was almost an American woman now, not a European goddess anymore on a pedestal at a safe distance.

I remember asking the producer of *Who's Afraid of Virginia Woolf*, "Please, please let me play her." It was way after the opening and they were looking for replacements and casting for the road company.

He laughed at me and said, very warmly, "You are a lovely actress, Viveca. But the character is a neurotic American woman. A European woman would never behave as she does."

I couldn't make him see that I, as a Swedish woman, knew every breath, identified with every second that the woman in *Who's Afraid of Virginia Woolf* experiences. The fact that I was well-kept and still beautiful, that I had not let my conflicts defeat me physically, was also against me. A woman in pain would have to be ugly.

Elizabeth Taylor broke the myth in the film. She was sensational in the part, in spite of her looks. Money talks. No doubt she was cast because of her box office appeal. This time it turned out to an advantage.

I began to understand that being an actress both on film and on the stage in America is different and more difficult than in Sweden.

I don't know if I could have faced moving the children to New York if I had gotten the part, although, artistically, I obviously would have preferred playing opposite Garfield in a play rather than opposite Flynn in a film. The Spanish Queen in love with Errol Flynn, one of the six female stars around him, was definitely less attractive. I was never very good about standing in line. Still, I was relieved that I wasn't confronted with the choice.

It was an experience to work with Errol Flynn, in spite of the fact that he was drinking heavily. After 3:00 PM he was out, and all close-ups of the rest of us, the other actors, had to be saved until then. (His way of rebelling against the system, staying in charge.) Saturdays were a total loss. He would be there next to the camera, incoherent but charming always.

While endlessly waiting between takes, he used to lecture me on drinking. "I have one book at home," he said, "in one room. It tells me why I should drink. So, I take a drink. Then I go to the other room and there I have a book telling me why I should *not* drink. I immediately stop! Until I go into the *other* room and read why I *should* drink, and then I take a drink again!" He looked at me with his famous smile. "Won't you have one with me, Viveca? One is so much nicer when one drinks," he said. "All the pettiness just goes out the window, all the nonsense."

We all go our own crooked ways to stay sane!

Flynn was a sex symbol as much as Marilyn Monroe; taken advantage of by the studio for his charm, his sex appeal, his body, as much as she was; and he was as vulnerable as she and knew as little as she about how to defend himself against the system. He ended up in his own little beauty-box prison, just as she did. And he drank himself to death to get out of there. He was a brilliant actor. A genius. And didn't know it. He went fishing, and fucking, and paid no attention to his talent. It was only in one of his last films, the Hemingway picture, that he lived up to his own genius. By that time he had lost all the trash around him. He was ugly and fat and puffy, but brilliant. Couldn't he have gotten to it sooner? Did he have to destroy himself first? Yes. What he had to do he did. There was nobody there to help him or point the way for him. Jack Warner didn't. He was in his own fog.

Errol Flynn had enough power through his beauty and his sex appeal. To give him credit also for his brain would have been far too dangerous. It's ironic that Errol's father was a British academic professor. Why did he not help his son? Did Errol not help his? Sean Flynn, to begin with, followed in his father's footsteps, but changed the course of his life and became a photographer. He went into the combat zone. He tragically died while photographing reality instead of fantasy.

By the end of the film I was frustrated, fat, bored, and ready to embrace the Flynn philosophy. I had sat around for six months. During that time I worked perhaps a week altogether. I was dressed in uncomfortable dresses, laced so tight I couldn't sit down; with hairdos so complicated I couldn't lie down. Besides, I was twenty-seven and didn't want to either sit or lie. I wanted to act, to feel, to be. It seemed I spent more time fitting dresses, changing hairdos, waiting for the stagehands to polish the enormously large, black, shiny floor in the throne room where I had to reside as the Spanish queen in love with Don Juan, than I acted.

On top of it all, *To the Victor* opened and was a flop, in spite of all the money spent and all the fuss made. It was worthless that I was good in it, that my reviews were brilliant. It was still a flop. I went to an afternoon performance on Hollywood Boulevard. I sat among the audience in the balcony. I didn't understand the film. I hadn't understood it when I read the manuscript, either. At that time I figured that "they" knew better than I. Now I knew that "they" did *not*.

What was I doing in Hollywood? I felt even more humiliated when they threw me into a fourth picture, a mystery story, a B-class thriller, *Backfire*. I was to play the sexy and pathetic girlfriend to Dane Clark. I hated the script. I hate mysteries. I hate violence, on the screen and in my life. I really didn't want to be part of it.

I went to see the producer. "Why are you doing a film like this?" I asked him senselessly. "I won't want my children to see it. Do you want yours?"

"No," he said honestly.

"So why do you do it?" I said, putting him on the spot.

"Because Warner wants it done and I am a producer, hired to do it." He was very blunt.

That made me even more furious. I called my agent. "I won't do it," I said. "It's an immoral picture. I've done three pictures in a row for the studio. I have fulfilled my obligations. I am turning this one down."

He called me back within a few hours. "You are on suspension," he informed me. I was stunned. How dare they treat me like this? How dare they not give a damn about what I think, what I want, who I am?

They dare, was the answer.

Suspension means no pay! I looked at my weekly household bills, the private school bills, the payment on the car. I couldn't fire Nana and Edith. I couldn't pack up and go back to Sweden for a million reasons, one being a sense of defeat. Sweden doesn't always look kindly at its returning sons and daughters. I had left with such fanfare! I was never going to return! And then there was the fantasy about the sinful sister returning, begging the good one for shelter. I couldn't face all that. Another reason was that I didn't have enough money to get us all back home, and there was no Folke around now anymore to solve my problems, to take care of me and the kids, for Don was no Folke, especially now that he was fired from Warner Brothers—not just on suspension, but fired. They didn't pick up his option. Where were all those promises from the time we first met—the young genius director on the lot and the foreign girl star? A magic combination! *Night unto Night* had been put on the shelf for the release of *To the Victor*, which was a flop. Had we brought each other bad luck? I hated myself for those thoughts. But I had them. I felt trapped and I was trapped because of that.

I picked up the phone. "I'll do the film," I told my agent. Like the producer, like a lot of people, I copped out. My guts ended up in the trash can in Warner Brothers' lot. It lay there like a poisoned cockroach, waiting to crawl out. I loathed every minute of the shooting, and that was not necessary. Whom did I want to punish? I didn't know yet that one could create magic, no matter, like stepmother violets.

"What happened to Viveca?" was the question a *Life* magazine reporter threw at me two months later. I answered him in words and in images. I danced my Hollywood story on the lawn in front of the low, rambling ranch house in Tarzana. I danced it all—my hopes, my dreams, the myths and what happened to them. I danced all my characters one after another—the widow in love with Ronald Reagan; the French whore in love with Dennis Morgan, the American soldier; the Spanish queen in love with Errol Flynn; and last, the pathetic sexy girlfriend stuck with Dane Clark. Suffering ladies of the media! I danced them all!

It turned out to be a terrific layout. The reporter picked up all my comments, my ironies, my bitterness, my anger. I don't know if he picked up my fears, my defenses. That shows up more in the photograph on the cover. My face is naked; no Hollywood glamor. It's a Hausman photograph.

A month later it stared at me, lying in stacks outside of drug stores and newspaper stands. "You don't bite the hand that feeds you." A week later Warner Brothers dropped my option and I was on my own. Both Don and I were out of work, fired. I was not so cocky anymore.

We were not the only ones. Whole departments in studios closed down. Everybody was in a panic. Even Jack Warner was nervous. Instead of making three million, Warner Brothers, that year, made only two!

The moment of heat over my Hollywood career passed. My work as an actress had been insignificant, and the result had in no way lived up to the anticipation. The reason I had come to the U.S.A. was to become a bigger star than I was in Sweden. It had not happened, nor had I grown as an actress, and Don, my comrade in trouble, began to seem like a drawback. Oh! The mirror image!

I began to fantasize I might be better off free—free to look around for another man who could help me in my career, free to use my sexuality. It had worked when I was thirteen, when I was sixteen, when I was twenty.

It could still work! I didn't know yet that it wasn't a man I needed. It was me. I was still playing the game "I need Daddy" or "blame is the game."

For a while, Don and I decided not to see each other, at least not go steady. I soon learned, from experience, as always, that I was not tough enough for the Hollywood game, or rather that I didn't want to play that kind of game, and that was good. Even better if I had understood it—all the way down to the bone.

It was David Selznick's wife, the famous actress, Jennifer Jones, who called me. I had met them at a party a few days before. "Would you like to be the hostess at a dinner party here at the house?" she said. "I am going away myself." It sounded like a perfect idea. David Selznick had been fabulous for Ingrid Bergman and many other female actresses. A big black limousine picked me up.

At the dinner table I sat next to Selznick. It wasn't a particularly stimulating dinner conversation. When I went home Selznick insisted on coming with me. The battle began the moment we hit the highway, and it was a long ride. I lived in Tarzana. An hour

seemed like forever. It was ridiculous and pathetic. The chauffeur
never turned around. The window between us pulled up, of course,
and he must have witnessed hundreds of soundless scenes like this
before, in the mirror, and I understood why the windows were
black and nobody could look in, only out. I don't know if Jennifer
knew what it was all about when she asked me to be the hostess at
the table. Maybe she did. Maybe she didn't. I certainly suspected
nothing like this. I never heard from David Selznick again.

It was a lonely and frightening time. The children were my
only solace. The children and nature. We would go for long walks
in the hills. My body moving, feeling the air against my face, their
hands in mine, their bodies against mine, brought me back myself.
I could breathe.

I began to see Don again. I had learned something about needs.
Maybe my brother's tragic fate had scared me, even taught me
something.

I had received a letter about him. "Bjarne is going to America.
Please help him in whatever way you can," my mother wrote.
Bjarne had made the decision to get away from Sweden, from
everything that had dragged him down—a broken marriage, his
father, his mother, silly contests of one kind or another. My mother's anxiety came through the lines of the thin blue airmail letter,
touching my own anxiety off like a flame. Help him? He was always reaching for the moon and the moon was always too far
away. I didn't want to be reminded of that! Besides, how could I
help him? I could hardly help myself and those who depended on
me.

I needn't have worried.

The ship caught fire in the middle of the dark and endless ocean,
so much larger than the swimming pool. This time he made the
final lap, in larger terms, on his terms. If only he could have believed it!

Bjarne was in a lifeboat for ten days. Ten days of no contact
with the outside world! Ten days of not knowing whether anybody would find him and his comrades in despair! Ten days of
heaven and hell. A man died in Bjarne's arms! I was told, not by
him but by the dead man's daughter. She had been told about it by
other survivors and also that my brother had been the spiritual
leader! Without him they all might have drowned, or gone mad,
or given up, they had said. My brother was the poet, the creative
spirit, the hero during those ten days in the middle of the dark and

endless and unknown ocean. Did he not believe it himself? When he was brought back home, to mommy and daddy, to so-called safety, security, to the suffocation and the prison of his childhood, the past with its pattern of defeat took over for my brother, and this time for good.

It ought to have mattered no longer about coming in a pool-length after everybody else in a silly swimming contest. It ought to have mattered no longer that he didn't make it as an officer or a publisher in my father's office or that his marriage had broken up. None of that ought to have mattered any longer, for he had tasted his own standards. He had tasted the real essence of life, and once you have there is no return. He didn't have the strength or he never recognized the glory in his effort, the fight, the struggle to find his own rhythm, his own place in life. He never even saw it. Christ, how much did he have to prove to himself? How much did I?

I saw Bjarne a few months later. I went home to Sweden to do a film, *Singoalla*. Between press conefrences and fittings I managed to visit him in the hospital.

He sat in front of me in his bathrobe, his eyes bloodshot, telling me of new horrors, the shock treatments. As he told me he must have hoped that I could help him out of his hell. Instead, my fear of not providing him with the answer put me into a state of panic. Instead of taking him in my arms, like a sister, loving him, holding him, kissing him, rocking him, I cut the cord between us. I tried to change the subject. I talked about my career, blind to the fact that it made his pain worse.

He punished me. "You will never be a great actress," he said. "You are too shallow."

The words stuck with me. The hurt erased any sense of perspective. Why be serious, like him, and end up in a straitjacket? Besides, how could I tell him about my agonies? They seemed insignificant next to his. In my efforts to defend myself, I couldn't share his pain. It was my last chance with him. It was the last time I saw him.

Twenty-five years later, I was walking along the quay with his son, Anders, who looks so much like him and acts like him, too, and became a doctor as he always wanted to.

The lights from the street and the houses and the boats were glimmering on the surface of the water. We were talking about love. "The moment I commit myself to a person, I feel as if I am suffocating," he said.

"I know what you mean," I answered. "But it is only old, bottled-up fears, old bottled-up angers that pop up and want to destroy what you love the most. But it has nothing to do with your life today. Nothing."

The other day I received in the mail a wedding invitation. Anders is getting married. I wish I could be there. I can't. I am working. I sent him a cable from us all: "We'll send you love from the other side of the ocean. We'll send you love, Anders," and I signed it "Viveca, John, Lena, and Kristoffer."

Work, always work. I wish now that it had been compassion that took me home that time to see Bjarne after the shipwreck, but I wasn't ready and it was far safer to commit to work.

I had been offered the film *Singoalla*, an old, medieval, mystic Nordic tragic love story between a gypsy woman and a Nordic Prince, a story loved by the Swedish people and loved by me. Folke negotiated the deal. He was still my manager. Still, legally, my husband, although we were separated. Financially, it was a splendid deal. They would pay for mine and the children's trip. We could all go back to Sweden. For good, if we wanted to. No doubt, that is what Folke hoped for. I was sure I didn't hope for the same, for I was planning to marry Don in Paris after the film was finished.

I can't help thinking that my decision had something to do with my brother's journey. Perhaps it affirmed in me that life has to be lived positively and lovingly. The rituals surrounding the death of Don's father at that same time reminded me of the same spirit. The funeral turned out to be a deeply moving experience. I had never realized that Don was part of a large family. They all gathered around Ann, Don's mother, and Don. The feeling was warm, spirited, and joyful. I cried. I wanted to be part of that feeling. I wanted to belong. I wanted to be part of a family, too.

Suddenly life seemed more real, more intimate. Decisions about living in Hollywood or Sweden, film parts or no film parts, *Life* magazine, making it big or not, seemed unimportant.

A surge of love for Don came over me. "Let's get married! I love you, I love you, I love you."

Don was with me! Generously! "Yes, let's get married. In Paris!"

I wasn't alone anymore. Alone without a man. There were to be no changes. I was living up to my decisions. There was money and work. I was in heaven. It was easy to leave now. To go back to Sweden—now when I didn't have to stay!

Don put me and the children and Nana on the plane. "See you in Paris!"

Folke and the producer, one of his best friends, were waiting for us at the airport. Folke had brilliantly managed to put together the production. *Singoalla* was a big deal for Swedish production, a film in three languages, directed by a French director—a film for the world market. Yes, Folke and I were a team again. He accompanied me to all the press parties and "getting together" was in the air. Certainly from Folke's side.

The work was long and intense. I did my part in French, English, and Swedish. I had two different leading men. No doubt, Michel Auclair, my French lover, was more brilliant, intense, and romantic, bringing a dimension to the part different from that of the Swedish actor. My performance benefited. The rushes were brilliantly beautiful, and not just because of me. The cameraman, a Frenchman, a genius at his craft, had captured the Nordic mystic landscape in late-winter–early-spring as no one ever had.

During the filming we stayed, the children and I, in our old apartment, now only Folke's. And although I slept in the study, I was treading a thin line, trying to keep the relationship on a friendly basis mostly because of the children. I nursed the daughter-daddy love relationship. That had always worked between us. I was cuddly and sweet until I saw flashes of danger, "desire" in Folke's eyes. He was still in love with me, although he still kept the other woman, just in case.

I played my own games. I had run into Danny Kaye in Central Park en route to Stockholm. We had had a five-minute conversation where sparks were flying. He was unbelievably attractive. In addition to being a genius. Danny kept calling me from all over the world. The phone would ring in the middle of the night in the study. And I shouldn't have encouraged it. It was slightly indulgent on my part, especially since I was going to marry Don, and it obviously added to the tension between Folke and me.

However, when the film was finished, it was clear, even to Folke, that things were over between the two of us. One late afternoon in June I signed the final divorce papers. My name was back to Lindfors.

For a couple of weeks!

6

Don and Viv married at the American Embassy in Paris. Don always called me Viv. The witnesses were the head of the Warner

Brothers studio in Paris and his wife. They had become my friends while I was doing *To the Victor*. My hair was cut short by Alexandre and was still black from *Singoalla*. I was no doubt beautiful. I wore a pink dress with white pearls.

I was marrying an American. My name became Siegel, and outside the high French windows the chestnut trees were in bloom.

After the ceremony, Don and I took off for St. Tropez to swim in the clear blue Mediterranean water.

The children were with Folke at Backa by the sea.

That's when Folke cut me off from all communications with the children. I wasn't allowed to talk to them over the phone or write. When John heard about the marriage over the radio, he called my mother and asked if it was true. "Yes," she answered. She called me in St. Tropez, very upset. "Should I have told him? Was that the right thing to do?"

"Of course you should have told him," I said, cursing myself for not having done it before I left, cursing Folke. Why couldn't he have told John openly, without drama? Whom did he punish? Me? Yes! Himself? Yes! But, above all, the children. I was in a panic, petrified that he would keep them forever. I felt that Folke, being a lawyer, had all the power in his hands and could twist anything the way he wanted to.

My own negligence was that I paid little attention to how much they had loved Folke. Perhaps he paid little attention to it, too. I became painfully aware of it once we had moved to California.

From that moment on Folke ignored the children as though they were hot potatoes. He didn't write, he didn't call, he didn't send them presents, not for birthdays, not for Christmas. Lena was only two and a half, and her adjustment seemed to come more easily. I became aware of her love for Folke thirty years later when I watched her deal with some ugly, unjust details that took place around the closing of Folke's estate. Her loyalty toward his memory was total. John was four and a half at the time of the move to the U.S.A. and had formed a real relationship with Folke. The separation was deeply painful for him. Every morning he would go down to the mailbox in Tarzana, only to return slowly, white in the face, his eyes bigger and blacker than ever. There was no mail from Folke. It was devastating for him, for how could I explain to him, a five-year-old, that Folke was angry with me, not him?

But it was only a beginning.

However, I was wrong worrying about Folke keeping them forever. To bring up children is different from having them visit. We

had no trouble picking them up in Stockholm on our way to the
U.S.A.

It was a clear autumn evening when we drove up the path to
the ranch in Tarzana with the dogs and the cats greeting us, and
the ripening peaches on the trees waiting to be picked.

I had hardly unpacked my bags, gotten the kids into school,
eaten some of the peaches, when I got an offer to go back to
Europe, this time Switzerland, for a film called *Four Men in a Jeep*
—Leopold Lindberg directing, a brilliant script, a valuable film, a
superb part, and the money good. I accepted.

My leaving was easier on the children this time. They felt more
at home. English was almost their language and Don almost their
father now. The dilemma was mine. The twentieth century actress'
dilemma.

The Golden Coach actors traveled and lived like gypsies, always
together. Birds, when they fly south, leave in groups. No one is on
his own. I went alone to Vienna. The first night in the hotel in
Graz, I cried myself to sleep, longing for my family, feeling split,
conflicted, like an abandoned child, although I was the one who
had left.

The next day I went to work. In the evening, Leopold Lindberg,
the director, took me to a wine festival celebrating the new wine.
I drank. I laughed. I danced on the tables. I sang. I was happy. I,
the actress, was happy. I, the mother, the woman, had cried herself
to sleep the night before. Not much had changed, but instinctively
I began to sense I could no longer afford those wasted emotions. I
needed my energy for better things. I had begun to realize that I
must promote myself as an actress. Work would not be handed to
me on a platter, as it had been when I began my career in Sweden
and I didn't have to lift a finger, or even smile. And work was
essential; work was happiness!

My agent had given me an outline written by a Hungarian
writer, a story of a Russian woman falling in love with an American. It took place in London. It was romantic, political, tough, and
superbly written. A meeting was arranged between me and the
writer at the airport in London where I had to change planes on
my way to Zurich.

He was thin, tall, and elegant and picked me up in his chauffeur-
driven Bentley and transported me and the luggage from one airport to another. We had a drink in the bar. To discuss the deal
seemed suddenly unimportant. I got on the plane in a pink cloud.

He was George Tabori.

We laughed about it afterwards. He was broke and tried to impress me; I was the great international star who could make his projects a reality. She, on the other hand, with her usual fantasy about the power of men, thought that he was the one to make it all possible. We were both right. Together we *could* have made it. We got sidetracked by romance! We didn't know how to combine sensuality and business, not then or later. Can any relationship last if you can't separate love from arrangements? Whether it comes to figuring out who is to take out the garbage or make a deal about a film? Ours didn't.

G.T. said that time over a drink at the London airport that he would come to Zurich to discuss the project further, but he never did. Probably didn't have the money. He had spent it on the Bentley and the chauffeur. And I never dared to pursue the project either, scared that I couldn't handle the attraction. I was right about that. What a shame! Don would have been a wonderful director for the project. We could have made a wonderful film together, all three of us!

It would be another two years until I met G.T. again, and another fifteen until I pursued my own projects, and apart from my love life. But it was delicious to be on a pink cloud, on my way to Zurich. I'll never regret that, only that we thought they had to be pink all the time. Pink perfection or black despair. Too bad! Pink plus black equals gray, and it is a beautiful color.

Four Men in a Jeep turned out to be one of the best films I'd ever done. Lindberg, the director, was a brilliant and creative man, an Austrian Jew who fled to Zurich during Hitler's regime and married a Swiss woman, and within a short time became one of the leading directors at the Stadts Teater in Zurich. His production of *Mother Courage*, by Brecht, was one of the first. Theo Otto did the set, *the Mother Courage* set that became identified with the play all over the world.

I loved working for Lindberg. He was demanding but intensely passionate and so I never minded. He had a clear point of view and knew what he wanted, without taking away from the actress' inventiveness. And an extremely attractive man. We flirted marvelously and safely, for he had a wife and I had a husband! The European way! A nonconsequential stimulation, making life more enjoyable. Why not? If you can handle it.

The story took place in Vienna, right after the war, when the four armed forces, Russia, America, France, and England, still had occupation of the city. The four men in the jeep were officers each representing his own section.

We shot some locations in Vienna but it was too dangerous to enter the Russian zone and we did those in a small town called Graz, of similar structure as Vienna and safely located in the American zone in the northern part of Austria. The interiors were shot in Zurich. It was a tough film of international concern.

The Swiss producer didn't understand the value of the film and sold it to television. It received brilliant reviews, but it was too late then to get it the theatrical release it deserved.

It was Christmas time when we finished shooting in Zurich.

I decided to drive to Salzburg and from there take the plane to Vienna. I never forgot the drive over the mountains. It was a crystal-clear, cold winter day. As I came over the mountains, I could see Salzburg lying like a shining jewel down in the valley. We drove into the city late in the afternoon. The old-fashioned street lights shimmered in the snow; the young people were coming out of the universities, wandering across the bridges, singing, talking about music. It reminded me of Uppsala, the university town where I was born. I wanted to stay.

Don and the children met me at the airport in Los Angeles, all happy to see me, telling me about school, about the cats and dogs, and friends. I felt awful, isolated, driving over the mountains. It had been a dry month and the hills were brown and barren, the grass dry. The ugliness of the small towns in the valley toward Tarzana with artificial Christmas trees overwhelmed me. It all seemed so poor in comparison to the deep green and white mountains in Switzerland and the old charm of Salzburg.

It confused me, this feeling, and I could barely hear the children, for I was on a romantic street in an old town, with a lover like Lindberg or maybe Tabori. And although there was no physical distance between me and my family anymore, I felt further and further away from them.

I found myself idiotically intense about Swedish traditions and rituals for Christmas.

On Christmas Eve, Bill Klauson, our Swedish carpenter's son, was Santa Claus. He came late in the afternoon over the hills, dressed in a red Santa Claus costume that I had rented from the studio. He sang Swedish Christmas songs and carried a large sack with packages from Sweden. John and Lena and their friends waited for him. They all still believed in Santa Claus, but their American friends had never seen one, except in the stores. Santa

175

Claus sat down and passed around the packages from Sweden—
except those that came from Folke that I had bought. I couldn't
face explaining to the kids that he had "forgotten" to send them
packages for Christmas.

It was easier for me, the mother, to get close to the children. It
was more difficult for me, the woman, with Don, my man. He, no
doubt, sensed it. He was very quiet. It was his way. He was out of
work, too, so it was rough, for I was the breadwinner, the star in
the family.

The day after Christmas we had a few friends in for dinner. It
was late and everybody was leaving. We had a slight disagreement
about some nothing thing—if there is such a thing. I said, "charmingly," "If you dare do that I won't sleep with you ever again." It
was a silly thing to say, and I didn't think I meant it, but we
hadn't really made love to each other yet, or I hadn't, anyhow. It
was more an act of duty on my part, or an unsuccessful effort to
get close. We both knew that so it was a loaded sentence.

Don reacted as if I had hit him with a sledgehammer. "I won't
have it, baby. Not for much longer," I felt he might say any second. It was the first time I was ever aware of my own terror of
being abandoned, dismissed. It made the tension even more unbearable, for I was also aware that I didn't want to love out of fear,
like my mother. Now I was trapped, trapped, trapped.

I got very ill the next day. I threw up for hours. I threw up my
fears, my resentments, too, of wanting to try to belong to two
countries, two men. I had no way of dealing with it except to get
ill. I threw it all up, the resentment, the ambivalence, the wall between us. I got down to the bare bones in me. "I love you, I love
you. I want you." I came home. We made up that night.

Oh, it's partly the actress in me, wanting to melt into new sur-
roundings with new people, quickly and emotionally, in order to
be part of the action, as with a role, a play. How else can I? It's
the dilemma, too, of the traveler of this century. It's too easy to
change one place for another! Too fast!

Today I know more about coming home and the difficulties; I
know better how to patiently cross the threshold of time and space.

What also scared me, no doubt, that winter in Hollywood, was
that the quality of work offered to me in Europe appealed to me
so much more than what was offered to me in America.

A few days later we went to see a film made by a young, unknown Swedish director called Ingmar Bergman. After the lights

came up, in the shabby art house in downtown Hollywood, I couldn't move. I was overwhelmed by the beauty of the film, the depth of the film, and by my own pain for not being part of it. My God, I had left Sweden in search of this kind of work. To get away from silly, flip, corny films about girls in trouble, and now they are making glorious films over there, and I am here where they make silly, flip, corny films! I was in agony.

I started to write letters to Bergman. "I am overwhelmed by your film. Please do not hesitate to contact me if you need me. Don't consider it a disadvantage that I live in Hollywood. I can come home in no time. I want to work with you."

I never got an answer. I would write a letter like it after each film I saw, each film having moved me more than the last. I never got an answer.

Ten years later, when I was doing *Brecht on Brecht* in Stockholm, I tried to get an appointment with him. Finally, after three weeks, I got one at eight o'clock in the morning. I was appearing at night in a show and didn't get to bed until midnight. However, if he can show up, I thought, I can, too. He was there ahead of me. In spite of the early hour, I had made myself up to the hilt. I looked gorgeous, glamorous, and beautiful. "It's a mistake" flashed through my mind. He prefers naked faces, plain faces, like Liv Ullmann's face, and Bibi Andersson's. But then, I had always wanted to combine being glamorous with being deep, like the American woman on the plane, like Garbo, like Claudette Colbert. I thought Bergman would understand me on every possible level. I had this "Svengali/Daddy" fantasy about him, like most actresses and actors, and he does seem to understand women, especially when they are in pain, as we have been a lot. And it was moving to be taken seriously on that level.

He brings out the deepest in his actors and that is what we want. Now I wish he would go one step further and allow us the strength, too. I missed it furiously in the concert pianist that Bergman portrayed in *Autumn Sonata*. Why didn't he just once let her say with passion, "I am an artist; when I play Beethoven's *Appassionata* I am as big as he was. I need to exercise that quality in me. That is me, too, and you, my daughter, should listen and not press me with your guilt." But, even so, he is a great artist and has the right to express his own needs, his own weaknesses, and he does, brilliantly. I knew it then. I know it now.

We spent an hour together. I left exhausted, as if I had spent an hour with the enemy, a smiling enemy who talked about the soul every five minutes as if I did not have one. And there wasn't one word about my work, or working for him.

"He doesn't like me," I said to myself, going down in the elevator in the Royal Dramatic Theatre where I used to run down the steps as a seventeen-year-old actress. "He just doesn't like me." I wandered out onto the street, the same street where I had run with joy after being accepted in the theater school. Today I was rejected. Why? I am a better actress today! I walked home to the apartment that I had at the time. I took all my clothes off, washed my face, crawled into the bathtub, and screamed, just as Bergman would to Sweden ten years later: "Fuck you. Fuck you. Fuck you all." I was cured. "Just because I love his work doesn't mean he has to love mine," I said to myself. I have never contacted him since.

A few weeks after we saw that first Bergman film, Don was finally considered for a job with Hal Wallis. "Come along tomorrow night," he said to me. "I am going to watch a film with an actress who is going to be my next star—that is, if I get the job."

The star was Lizabeth Scott, Hal Wallis' girlfriend, an actress of questionable talent. If Don happened to say the right thing to her, he might get the job.

"Okay," I said.

"Only you must promise me one thing," he continued. "If you don't like it, Viv—and I don't think you will, because it's not your cup of tea—don't say it too loud."

"I promise," I said, wondering to myself, what is my cup of tea? Where do I belong?

The film we saw was a typically Hollywood B-picture film, tasteless and violent, with one body after another falling down steps, or into rivers, or hit by cars. Finally, when the number ten body fell from the top floor of a building and you could hear the thud of the poor, human fake body hitting the cement, I had had it. "I am leaving," I said, as quietly as I could manage, knowing that his job was at stake.

"I'll walk you to the door," he whispered back, not trusting my behavior. He knew I was allergic to senseless violence.

God! All Don's films are about violence! I didn't know it then. I thought of him in such different terms, such totally different terms.

I grabbed the doorknob in the back of the theater. "Shit, it's closed," I whispered. I began to shake it, pull it, push it, getting more and more panicky, feeling trapped. God, and I did feel trapped. "I've got to get out of here," I whispered in a loud, theatrical whisper. Bang! The door opened. Wrong door. It was a closet. Out again.

Don was already at the next door. Thank God, it opened! I was out! I wasn't trapped—at least not for the time being—at least not that evening. God, why do I feel so trapped!

Don was far too understanding. He had every right in the world to be angry with me. "I know, I know," he said. "It's not your cup of tea. It isn't mine, either. What do you want me to do? I've got to get a job." He was trapped, too. We were all trapped.

"I don't want you to make films like this. I don't want to make films like this, myself." (And I didn't see that it doesn't have to be connected.) "I want to make films like Bergman's, like Lindberg's, maybe like Tabori's, and I want you to be like that," I wanted to tell him, which was unfair, for "to each his own."

Don got the job. He made the film. Now I was the one who was out of work. I hated that. Now he was the one who brought in the check every week. I was dependent on him.

I hated that, too, and soon myself, of course, and with it the courage of conviction began to fade.

It was a creepy time all around in Hollywood. McCarthy was every place. He had crept into the souls, the bodies, the minds. To begin with, it had been romantic and exciting to be part of the movement against him. He was so clearly destructive. I hadn't been in the City of Angels for very long when I went to a party one night and was asked to sign my name to a petition, the Stockholm peace appeal; I didn't hesitate. I soon understood the danger.

John Garfield and his family became friends of ours in Hollywood. He and his wife lived next to us with their two children during the summer. Julie and David played with Lena and John. Later in the fall, John would stop by for dinner on his visits to New York where they lived in the winter. He would tell us with a smile, "I didn't get the job. The agent told me I was too old, or too short, or not popular enough." An actor's ego is fragile. If we are turned down, not liked, not accepted, it's impossible not to take it personally, even if, like John, we know it had to do with the blacklisting, although nobody said openly, "You are blacklisted."

When I heard over the radio, driving home from the studio one late afternoon, that he had died of a heart attack, I started to cry furiously. "Those bastards, those bastards," I mumbled. "They killed him." Years later, I spoke to Robin, his wife. "Why didn't he tell me the truth?" I asked her. "Why didn't he take me into his confidence?"

I was stunned by her answer. "He didn't want to put you in jeopardy."

"You mean by just telling me I would have been in danger?"

"Of course," she answered.

I was luckier than John, those days in Hollywood. My signature went by unnoticed. I was never blacklisted like John. What scared me the most was not the possibility of being called to Washington to testify, but that I might not have the conviction needed to take a stand under the pressure. I still had a long way to go.

I started to go to a religious group that spring in Hollywood. They talked to me about God. I envy them the common cause, the mutual belief, the togetherness in spirit. I longed for it myself. Like coming home. To myself? Or Sweden? Or God? But I had never been religious.

"What's the matter with me" I said to myself. "I have a nice husband who is making money. I have a house, two healthy, wonderful children. Two cars. What am I complaining about?" I still had to learn that lesson—that I could go after what I wanted without giving anything up, without blaming my man if he didn't help me. I wasn't ready to take the risk yet. Not yet. Risks were dangerous.

One late afternoon, I walked into the house and there was that yellow envelope from Western Union, affirming the tragedies of life, the dangers of risks taken too late. "Bjarne's body was found in the water." It was signed by my mother. He had jumped into the icy, cold, black water. It was spring in California, sunny, warm, and beautiful. I stood there with the yellow sheet in my hand, feeling nothing us usual, like the time I visited him in the hospital and he looked at me with his bloodshot eyes, like the time I received that blue, thin airmail envelope telling me that his ship had burned on the ocean and he was in danger for ten days and had held a dying man in his arms. I felt nothing then. I felt nothing now. I made no effort to go home to the funeral and be by my mother's and father's side. I left it all up to my sister.

Why? Defeat had hit too close to home for Viveca.

Don must have wondered about my lack of feelings, although he said nothing, asked nothing. It was his way. It was, no doubt, mine, too. And the silences grew between us. But it wasn't too late. Not yet. Not at all.

A few weeks later Don and I received an offer to do a film together in Vienna, Austria—Europe. *No Time for Flowers* with an

American producer. The script wasn't great, but we were going to work together! Be a team! Life was filled with new energies again.

We put the house in Tarzana on the market, the furniture in storage. We took the kids out of school ahead of time, like gypsies, like the Golden Coach actors. Life is a better school, I finally thought to myself. I am not going to leave them behind, alone, this time. We flew to New York and boarded the Queen Elizabeth. We seriously thought of never coming back.

The trip was heavenly; eight days on the sea, restful and luxurious. We ate. We slept. We swam in the pool. We made love. We thought of nothing special. We spent time with the children. I was wife/mother/actress. It was perfect.

Lena, four going on five, was pretty, very pretty, and bright. She started to disappear from our table in the dining room to sit with a young man, very attractive looking in a New England way. Eventually she began to take her meals with him. In the beginning, I was amused. But when she began to visit him in his cabin, I got scared and decided to interfere.

"I would like you to introduce us to your friend," I said to her. She wasn't too happy about it, but she did. We took a walk on the deck together. He told me that he was crazy about Lena, that she was quite exquisite and extraordinary. I agreed. Then he told me that he was a writer who wrote about little girls and little boys. I was relieved. Lena was playing around us, hiding behind chairs to get our attention. It was quite obvious that she felt he was hers, that she wasn't willing to share him with me. It was my role to flirt with good-looking men. It was the first time I had a sense of rivalry between the two of us, two females—one five, one thirty-five. I was slightly amused. He gave me his card and talked about getting in touch later in America. We never heard from him, and I lost the card.

About a year later, I was reading *Catcher in the Rye.* As I looked at the picture of the author on the back, I realized who it was that had been so crazy about Lena—J.D. Salinger!

Two years later there was another book out, *Nine Stories,* in the book stores. One of the stories was about a little girl on a ship who wanted to kill her brother! She, too, was very pretty.

Once we arrived in London, Don went ahead to Vienna to prepare for the film. I and the children and Nana went to Stockholm. The children were to spend six weeks with Folke out at Backa. I knew the conditions—no telephone communication. I didn't fight it. I should have. I didn't want to make it harder on the children, I thought. And Nana promised to go around the corner and call me once a week. I spent a few days with the children in the country. I kissed them goodbye and told them I would write to them every day. Then I took off for Vienna, work, and Don.

We had a small apartment, a dark, old-fashioned, cozy Vienna apartment, with a maid who loved to take care of us. Vienna was gorgeous, friendly, and pleasant. We were going to make a picture together. We were comrades. We were lovers. All the things that I wanted! We went out the first night to celebrate. We sat in the garden-restaurant drinking wine, singing songs like everybody else, getting gorgeously drunk. We zig-zagged home through the streets and made love as we hadn't for a long time. It was wild. It was super.

A few days later, the news arrived from Sweden. Nana called. Folke had fired her. I should have known. "She had lived with another man of mine, like Klara."

It was a dirty trick then, and it was a dirty trick now. Again, he had thought less of the children than himself. It was a tough summer on them anyway, being transplanted from one country to another, one language to another again. They had not seen Folke for a year.

He even forbade Nana to come to the house to see them or talk to them over the phone. He hired a new, horrid nurse. The children loathed her. Nana had been my one link of continuity with the children at this point. Now I had no way of contacting them. I was petrified as I had been the last summer, afraid that he would keep them forever.

I drew my first calm breath six weeks later when they arrived at the airport in Vienna. The airport was located in the Russian zone and was heavily guarded by the Russians. When I saw the children step off the plane I ran through the guards. Nobody could have stopped me until I had them both in my arms. Nobody did. Guards are human, too. They, too, had been children. They, too, perhaps were parents.

"Never, never will I send them to Folke again. Never, never, until they are old enough to defend themselves," I promised myself.

Our war was in the open now.

I had no idea it would go as far as it went, but pain weakens our antibodies.

It eventually had to do with money. It always does!

I had full custody of the children. I had bought them, I used to say laughingly. I gave up property settlements, and the child support was the lowest the law would possibly allow.

When I got back to California after that summer in Vienna, I went to talk to a lawyer. He affirmed my conviction of not sending them over. If Folke wanted to come and visit them in America, fine. I was open to that. But he wasn't interested. When the children were approximately eleven and thirteen, they decided on their own to visit him. They did. It turned out well. The mistake I made was not having insisted on receiving child support steadily, no matter. It was my participation in the game, hoping that as long as I didn't, he wouldn't insist on his visiting rights. It never works out, those games. Eventually I needed money for their college education. That's when I approached him about it.

I was in Sweden doing *Brecht on Brecht*. To begin with, Folke didn't take me seriously. He tried to charm me, bought me dinner and wine. I finally went to a lawyer, Grufberg. Together we went to Folke's office. The same office where we had gotten married. We sat on the same sofa where I had signed my contract to Hollywood. Folke was pacing the floor. Like a great actor, he was using his emotions to achieve the ends. Whether he was in the right or not seemed irrelevant. I understood why he was so feared in court trials. I had to keep repeating to myself, "Viveca, he owes you child support. He agreed to it in court. He hasn't paid it. Any man has to pay it. Why not he? It's better for him that he accepts the responsibility. It's better for the child. Besides, it's not for me. It's for their education, which he should help pay for anyhow!"

Still, if it hadn't been for Grufberg I might have been affected. "You owe this woman money for child support," he stated, untouched. "You, being a lawyer, know it as well as I."

A few days later Folke asked me if I would mind signing a paper stating that the money could be called "student support" and be paid out to the children directly. It would save him money in taxes and since it made no difference to me I was delighted to do so.

A few weeks later he added two clauses to his will: (1) that the "student support" was an advance to be deducted from their inheritance at his death; (2) that fifty percent of his assets should go to Monica's, his daughter's, children.

It's tragic, too, because I have no doubt that by the time of his death, years later, he had wanted to change the will, written in anger and revenge. By now the relationship between him and the children—no longer children—was deeper and a reality. He had two new grandchildren by Lena and he and I had become friends again. It began that night in the kitchen after having seen *Appassionata*, and I am glad I knew nothing about the will. It would have stood in the way.

"I am settling with my past," he said to me sometime later, when I was in Stockholm on a visit again. It was the last time I saw him. He was past seventy, and I was struck by the ash-gray color in his face.

I went with him to the doctor for his appointment that afternoon. I sat in the waiting room during his examination and discussed his condition afterwards with the doctor, like a mother or wife, or both. Why not? The line is thin. Two months later I was notified that Folke was struck by a massive heart attack, unable to move, to speak, barely able to see.

Lena borrowed some money and was on a plane to Stockholm with her newborn baby girl in her arms within a few hours. She knew that Folke loved her and she could accept his love in spite of the past.

When I asked her, "Why all this effort, Lena?" she simply answered, "He's my father." Again, I had been unaware. As unaware as I had been about myself being a daughter to a father in a faraway land. I didn't get on a plane when he was ailing. I missed out seeing my father before he died; Lena didn't hers, in spite of the hurt Folke inflicted on her.

Her generosity put me to shame but also enlightened me.

That was true about John also, who was in Sweden that spring partly to do research for his dissertation but perhaps more so in an effort to find his way back to Folke once again. He knew now for sure that Folke had been and was his one and only father, and they had begun to spend time with each other. It seemed as if slowly all relationships were beginning to fall into place.

When Lena walked into the hospital room there was a sudden flicker of light in Folke's eyes and a faint sign of an effort to smile.

He died three weeks later. And the will, written in anger, was never corrected. But both I and the children knew that he had meant to, and so, in the long run, it didn't matter. For when he died, he was my friend, and Lena and John knew that he wanted to be a father for them, as he had been a father for them when they were little, that spring I went to America, and he took care of them for nine months, and they knew him better than me.

But that summer in Vienna, with the children safely back with me, life seemed good again and I had little awareness of how to avoid wars.

The film wasn't finished, and we rented a gorgeous old house and a swimming pool for the rest of the time.

THE CITY OF ANGELS

The work had been marvelous. Don was intelligent, clear, and compassionate as a director. He knew every part of the business. It showed that he had started through the back door. The film, too, was funny, warm, and human. It's only strange that I can't remember it ever getting a release, not even what happened to it. In those days, neither Don nor I knew how to protect our properties, our work. Today Don is part producer of all his films.

We seriously thought of staying in Europe. It was obvious that the European film industry was becoming as important, certainly as productive, as the American. But when I received an offer to play opposite Margaret Sullavan in *No Sad Songs for Me*, we took off for Hollywood once more. We rented a house in the Malibu colony, right on the beach. The kids went to school up in the hills. Through the fall and winter that year we went to sleep at night hearing the waves, smelling the salt of the sea.

No Sad Songs for Me, with Margaret Sullavan and Wendell Corey, and Rudy Maté directing—a wonderful script and a good part for me. I played a young engineer in love with Corey, Margaret's husband. She was dying of cancer. It was a sentimental movie, but done with taste. It was Rudy Maté's first film as a director. He was a loving man with superb eyes, having been a top-rate cameraman. Natalie Wood played the child who was to become my stepdaughter. She was intensely talented and professional already at the age of eleven.

Although I had no idea about women's liberation, my role in the film was a truly liberated one, an engineer. The engineer gets the man in the end of the film, and there is no mention of her giving up the job or apologizing for it. Yes, I did like the part.

It was one of the first low-budget, independent movies that tried for quality. The effort was a healthy one. I was used to conditions like this in Sweden. For Margaret Sullavan it might have felt like a step down to participate in this kind of a venture. She was trapped by the star image, with the chauffeur and the limousine and the personal maid cooking lunch for her in her dressing room—even if she had to pay for it herself. It separated her from the rest of the company.

Did she feel that adjusting to new ways affirmed that she was old, no longer in demand, no longer a star? I didn't see the courage and the pride, nor the bravura that Brooke Hayward, her daughter, writes about brilliantly in the book about her mother. I saw more the defense and withdrawal of a not-so-friendly and tired woman.

And yet she had going for her what Joan Crawford didn't—a position in the theater and a talent that had been better nursed than Crawford's.

In the story of the film she portrayed a dying woman who turned over her position to a younger woman. It was meant to be a gallant gesture. It didn't come across that way, quite, for, although her work was immensely talented, she leaned toward choices of the "tragic woman," the "victim." Perhaps it was all too close to home. At the time her marriage had broken up and her husband, Leland Hayward, had married a younger woman who devoted all her time to being his wife.

Margaret Sullavan behaved gallantly about the breakup, according to the book. How "gallant" you can be is the question. Perhaps using her pain in the film became her release.

Of course, I only met the *actress*, not the mother, the wife, and I saw her only through the eyes of a younger actress. I was only thirty-four then, but when I was the same age she had been when we were doing *No Sad Songs for Me* and I read in *The New York Times* about her suicide in the Taft Hotel in New Haven where she was staying for the pre-New York opening of a play, I was swept by waves of pain for her, for I understood her better.

7

It was at the end of the film *No Sad Songs for Me* that I began to feel nauseated in the morning and always exhausted. I took long walks on the beach, thinking it would pass, or that it had something to do with the fact that the film was finished, and that Don was working and I wasn't, and that there were all those gorgeous girls around him at the studio, and I did know all about seducing my director. "Oh, fuck it all, Viveca," I would say to myself after a period of self-torture. I would run on the beach and the blood would circulate and I would feel better again for a few hours, but no more.

It didn't even occur to me that I might be pregnant!

I finally went to the doctor. "I think I will do a test on you," he said and handed me a little glass bottle.

I laughed. "Why should I be pregnant now!"

"I don't know," he said and laughed too!

Sitting in the sterile bathroom at the doctor's, delivering what would tell me whether my body was fertile-producing or not, infuriated that I was not the first to know, conflicting thoughts

flashed through my mind, like. "Oh, how nice. I can give up struggling for a career, take a break, I need it, I am exhausted from trying to make it!—No, no, no! You know better! At this point in
your life you don't want to be stuck with baby bottles and diapers
and worries about another soul. At this point in your life you
want to pursue your craft. You are past thirty-five, time is passing!
—Oh, come on, Viveca! You can do both, just don't get involved
in unnecessary trifles like decorating nurseries or love affairs!
(With a Hungarian writer, for instance.) Use your energies creatively. Read, write, take classes. And wouldn't it be divine to give
Don a child of his own. It would bring you closer!—Help! What is
this need for closeness all the time? Do you have to have a child in
order to be close to a man? You have played that scene before. Did
you learn nothing?"

There is a knock on the door. "Mrs. Siegel, are you all right?"

"Oh yes, Nurse. Sorry, I'm just talking to myself."

"Dear bottle! Please don't be pregnant," I am thinking as I hand
it back to the nurse.

"The doctor will call you Wednesday, Mrs. Siegel."

Sometimes I wonder if I lost my womb years later, when I was
married to G.T., the Hungarian, so as not to be put into the same
dilemma once more, knowing I wouldn't have the strength to say
to him, "I can't cope with one more child *and* be an actress *and*
your woman."

When I came home, there was a phone call from Kay Brown, my
agent in New York. "Viveca, I've got the play for you. This is it.
It's written by your admirer, George Tabori." My heart took a delicious leap. I had not forgotten our last year's ride in a chauffeur-
driven Bentley!

George's play arrived a few hours later. I lay on the bed in the
upstairs bedroom, hearing the waves beat against the sand as I
read it. I cried! My part was fabulous. The name of the play was
Flight into Egypt.

I called back. "I love it, I love it, I love it!"

"Good, Viveca. Elia Kazan wants to meet you on Wednesday in
L.A." Wednesday! The doctor will call you on Wednesday, the
nurse had said! Never mind. To be pregnant is out of the question!
In any event!

Kazan! New York! The theater! Maybe a love affair with a Hungarian writer, tall and elegant, with or without a chauffeur-driven
Bentley! I felt terrific!

Wednesday morning, I was all dressed up to go and meet Kazan when the doctor called. "Congratulations, Viveca. You're pregnant." I hung up the phone. Help!

We met in a dark, seductive bar in Beverly Hills. Kazan was unbelievably attractive. The meeting was definitely positive. I began to feel guilty about taking up his time. After all, I hadn't decided completely what to do about the pregnancy. Or had I? On the other hand, I certainly didn't have to tell Kazan, a stranger, not until he offered me the part. Not even then. It was none of his business. It was mine and Don's.

That much clarity was too much for a Swedish girl who had changed the spelling of her name from Viveka to Viveca. "I think maybe I am pregnant," I stuttered as charmingly as stuttering can be, adding a little white lie to keep the door open. "I will know in a day or so." Naturally I hoped Kazan would help me out by telling me how fabulous I would be in the part, that he couldn't do the play without me, and I wouldn't have to make the decision. It would be made by him!

But Kazan smiled his warm, famous smile. "Congratulations! A child is more important than a play. Let me know." The man had spoken. God, help, help, help! But God was a man, too.

I ran to Sophie. She had my interests at heart! My career!

"This is your chance, Viveca; don't fool around. You can have a child some other time. Don't let *anything* stand in your way."

"She is right. I mustn't. I mustn't. I am an actress, I am an actress," ran through my head as I drove along the ocean to our Malibu house. Sophie had no children herself. She meant well. She was my friend.

But when Don and I walked on the beach that night, with John and Lena running around us, laughing and playing, and I asked the father of my unborn child, "What do you think?" and Don said, "You must do whatever you have to do. I will understand it either way"—he was quite marvelous about it, leaving it up to me —I wasn't so sure anymore! I hadn't been able to have an abortion when I was pregnant with Lena and I was still the same person! The peasant woman in me emerged again, that night, walking on the beach. She who wanted to challenge life on all levels, wanted to say yes to nature and nature's way, felt she could hang on to joy, no matter what, knew how to wait, to live and let live. She who believed a hundred percent the more she said yes to life the more there would be of life.

I turned down *Flight into Egypt*, Broadway, New York, and the possible love affair. Kristoffer's fate was affirmed.

Our Christmas card was a photograph of John and Lena on the

beach, tenderly printing in the sand: "Merry Christmas from Viveca, Don, John, Lena, and It!"

John and Lena had been magic in their wonder about having a new brother or sister. I had told them one day when we were driving down the Pacific Coast Highway, the sea on one side, hills on the other. Their eyes suddenly got large and quiet. There was much love inside that green, old Ford station wagon.

While I was still pregnant with It, Sophie and I took off for one of our yearly theater trips to New York and caught a preview of *Flight into Egypt.*

Just as we were leaving the hotel, a special delivery letter arrived from It. I read it in the theater before the curtain. It told me how much It appreciated being born, that It understood the difficulties in the choice that I had made, that It would write a play for me one day that would make up for it all. I laughed and cried and loved Don, myself, the unborn child, and the world.

The performance was disappointing and lacking in point of view. It had been given the Broadway treatment and drowned in the process. Nothing was spared: Elia "Gadge" Kazan directing it, Irene Selznick producing it, Boris Aronson designing the set. Yet the excitement I had felt reading the play was gone. There were a few brilliant performances by Zero Mostel and Paul Mann, but it didn't save the evening. The audience around me was as alienated as I was, and so were the critics when it opened two weeks later.

I didn't see George at the theater. Perhaps he sensed the failure written on the wall as well as the friendship with Kazan coming to an end. Circumstances in the play, from another time not too long ago, another place not too far away—so similar to those now in the U.S.A., had undermined the production and its radical point of view.

It was a vicious time. McCarthy's witch hunt was at its peak. Everybody involved in the production was radical, left-wing minded, including, to begin with, Kazan. Perhaps working on the play he was hoping for an answer. Did the fact that it failed influence him in his decision to become a cooperative witness in Washington in front of the Un-American Committee? He had just finished the movie *On the Waterfront* and was under pressure. It was either give up his career as a film director or name names. He made his choice. He went to Washington three days after the unsuccessful opening. He gave names of close friends, some of them actors in the cast. It was an unexpected and a stunning shock for everybody.

189

"I was sitting in the theater with Gadge a day after the opening night performance," Irene Selznick, the producer, told me. "I sat behind him. He was sitting in the row in front of me. He turned to me. 'Do you love me?' he asked me. I put my arms around him, thinking he was upset about the fate of the play, blaming himself. 'I always will. You know that,' I answered. I was very close to him. I thought I knew every thought, every feeling he had. I was wrong! The next night, in the evening paper, I read about his testimony. It was like being hit by lightning. The conviction among us, already weakened by the reviews, was shattered now. The captain had left the ship. The rats were taking over. We closed two weeks later."

"A child is more than a play," Kazan had said. Kristoffer is twenty-six years old today and together on the stage we are acting *My Mother . . . My Son.* I had made the right choice.

The other day, thirty years later, I heard Kazan speak about Harold Clurman, who had just died. "I went to see him a few days before and found him deeply involved in a discussion with his wife about compassion and justice. It was very moving."

It was moving, too, to hear Kazan say it. He never became the Hollywood director one thought he had set out to become at the time of the testimony. In fact, he stopped directing altogether and started to write. Journeys, journeys.

I learned about all this months later from G.T. himself. I had run into him at the Farmers Market in Brentwood, a few days before Kris was born. When I spotted him I tried to hide. It wasn't easy. He caught me and we spent ten sparkling minutes between us, my stomach like a football keeping us at a safe distance. We decided to get together for dinner with the wife and the husband at our house.

The dinner was sensational. G.T. told us about the production of *Flight,* about Kazan, about theater in New York, about Brecht, about the theater. I sensed that evening in Brentwood what I learned later to be true—that G.T. was brilliant as well as committed to the arts. I sensed that evening that he could help me become a more aware person, a more aware actress. It was through his knowledge that I began to build, politically as well as artistically, a courage of conviction. Without it supporting me, I might never have been able to overcome my fears of taking a stand. For that I am forever grateful.

Yes, that evening in Brentwood I sensed a promise in G.T. to help me become the person I had always wanted to become. The sensuality between us became less important now that something more real had been added to our fantasy relationship.

We stayed up, all four of us, until the wee hours of the night, talking and eating watermelon. Their car got stuck in the driveway; we all pushed it. "It's perfect exercise for me," I said. Kristoffer must have agreed. A few hours later he gave me the sign. At first I thought "it" was the watermelon. "It" was a boy!

Don took me to the hospital. I didn't like to say goodbye to him. But in those days fathers were not allowed to be present. The experience became mine and my baby's only. Once more.

Kristoffer, my third child, my last child, was born August 4. My first childbirth without fear!

Each time the doctor came in and put his hand on my stomach, the work stopped. "Leave me alone, doctor," I said. "Let me do the work alone, me and my baby." I was laughing as I said it, and he didn't mind.

"Does it hurt?" he asked. "Do you want a shot?"

"No! No! No! We are doing fine."

The final moments were purely sensual. It was large and slippery, this thing coming out of me, like one enormous orgasm. "A boy," a voice came from someplace. "A big boy." They held him up over my stomach, the navel string still uncut. My head rolled from one side over to the other to take in this whole body of my son. He seemed enormous. I heard him cry. They had cut the string. They took him away, washed him off, and dressed him in swaddling clothes. He was on his own.

Oh, I wanted to feel that body wet and bloody against mine, against my tired, powerful body. I wanted to lie there with him, my child, still part of my flesh and my blood. I wanted to lie there with him and wait until I was ready to bite off the string myself and he might then cry, or scream, or breathe air instead of breathing me, breathing through me. I would have licked him clean with my tongue, even if it made me vomit, my own smell, my own blood. I wanted to gorge myself on him, my own child, my baby, my own flesh and blood.

Oh yes, I had made the right choice!

A few days later, in the middle of the night, while I was feeding Kristoffer for the first time, I received a cable from G.T. It was beautifully quiet around us. The nurse had tried to teach him how to take my breast. He screamed. "Leave us alone," I said laughingly. "We know how." She did, and while nourishing my child I read the cable. "Writing play for you and son. George Tabori."

A week later I was offered the lead in a play by John Van Druten called *I've Got Sixpence*.

Three months later, I left for New York—it was October now—to begin rehearsals. Although still nursing Kris, I left him behind to go all by myself. Now, thirty years later, I get furious with myself. I had left babies behind me before. Had I learned nothing?

Oh yes, New York is a tough place, and all efforts must go into conquering this new field! And I had paid my dues as a woman! Oh yes! I felt all that, and I was justified in thinking that I couldn't cope with living in hotel rooms with diapers hanging in the bathroom, trying to learn my lines and live up to the image of being a new exciting star on Broadway. Oh yes, and it is tough, almost impossible.

But above all, it was true that I was excruciatingly hungry, after five slumbering years in Hollywood—I hadn't even understood how slumbering those years had been, how much I had wanted to be on the stage again. Oh yes! It was like a bomb exploding when I hit New York. I was back in a city again! Back in the theater!

I loved rehearsals. My energy was endless. It was all possible again. Oh yes, I was hot and vibrant, beautiful and sensual, as if childbirth had cleansed my body, when I ran into my Hungarian writer, George Tabori, at the election party for Adlai Stevenson against Eisenhower at Kay Brown's. The evening was a disaster politically, but it didn't matter. I had not forgotten G.T., nor he me. He made no secret of his passions. Our love affair was unavoidable. He was elegant and softspoken, European and brilliant. He was a writer and in the theater. He lived up to every fantasy of a man I had ever had. The picture was completed. Oh yes!

We went to hear Edith Piaf sing, and when we danced and I felt his body against mine, I knew I had one foot in heaven and the other in hell . . . Oh yes . . .

8

Did you have to die now, Sophie . . . when I need you so much . . . when everything finally is the way we dreamed it could be . . . I mumbled to myself through tears as the train was rushing toward Boston.

We were on our way to open the out-of-town tryouts of *I've Got Sixpence*. Van Druten had asked me to come to his compartment. Why? Was something wrong with the performance? I sat down. His friend and producer, Walter Starke, was with him. They were lovers. Starke was younger than Van Druten, who was in his early sixties. John was an impeccable gentleman in every respect, from his gray flannel suit and elegant silk tie to his superb way of speaking. He loved words. He studied them: where they had come from; how they had changed; and why. He made a chart a page long on my name. It came from the Latin and was connected to the word "life."

"Don called this morning," he said. "He wanted us to tell you in person, rather than for you to hear it over the phone." I stiffened. Tell me what? Had he heard about G.T. and me? But the world did not only concern itself with me and my lovers.

"Sophie died last night in her sleep," John continued. Sophie died? Oh, my God. No!

Train rolling on. Telephone poles passing by. Life goes on. Proved by us three alive in the compartment. Sophie is dead! No emotions, yet. They must have wondered about that. I wandered back to my compartment. I started to cry. That's when I saw her way up in the lefthand corner of the moving, shaking train compartment. She held her hand up, her fist gently clenched. She was smiling. She seemed to be saying, as she always did, "I am here, Viveca. Carry on. Life is terrific."

She had had a hysterectomy ten years earlier. Did they not cut the whole beast out? What started him roaring again? Was she filled with fear about not being able to love a younger man? Did she feel the loss of her womb more so, now? Was the conflict of love and work too much for her as for me? I never saw her angry. I never heard her blame. She was a superb human being. Why did she die ahead of her time? What did she want that she didn't get?

I miss her still! I miss her!

The first time I realized she wasn't quite well was the day after one of the performances on the back lot. We were having lunch together. I was telling her about one of the unknown stars in the show, a terrific looking young man. " 'You are going to be as big a star as Gregory Peck,' I told him, I think. His name is Rock Hudson. But I'm not sure he believed me," I said to Sophie, while looking over the menu.

"I think he knows," she said. She didn't order much food. "I can't eat too much," she said. "It makes me nauseated. At least I am losing weight."

I looked at my pregnant tummy. "I can't say the same," I said. We were both laughing.

It was at Kris's christening party right before I went into rehearsal in New York that I began to worry. She looked pale and much too thin. There was no way one could joke about it anymore. Still, it didn't occur to me at the time that it might be cancer. Today one suspects it at the slightest provocation. The fame of the beast has spread its sick sperm since then.

Gig knew all the time that it was hopeless. He kept it a secret from us all in order to keep it a secret from her. "She never knew," he told me after her death. We had gone to visit her grave. "She never knew," he repeated. "It would have killed her spirit." He grew taller with the human challenge. The last couple of weeks he sat by her bedside, reading aloud to her, which she loved. She died in her sleep, free of pain, her hand in his.

Not too long ago, years later, I read in the papers of his suicide. He took the girl he was married to with him. He knew what it was to be left alone. I identified. My own fear of death is mainly that no one will be there to hold my hand.

G.T. was waiting for me outside the stage entrance after the opening in Boston. He had flown in from California. "If we let our moment of love pass we might lose it," he said. He dropped out of the film he was working on. He didn't want to continue, or couldn't. G.T. was always afraid of losing his talent as a writer by working on material that wasn't creative for him. He simply packed his bags and left. I was impressed and moved by his gesture. Scared, too.

The performance had gone well, at least for me. I loved my part and had little awareness of whether the play worked or not. When we entered the restaurant across the street, the people applauded me.

Later G.T. and I went dancing in a funny little restaurant around the corner from the hotel. We hadn't slept with each other yet. We both knew this was the night. I went with him to his room at the hotel to drop off his bags, and never left. It was wild. Too wild, perhaps, for when I woke up, and I must have gone back to my room, my whole right side was paralyzed. "I am dying," I said to myself, as if a tiny part were still alive inside my body. "This is the feeling of death. I am dying."

Oh yes! One part of me was afraid, but another was very much alive.

The love affair between the actress and the writer, the Hungarian and the Swede, the gypsy Jew and the Nordic beauty with her three children, had begun.

The production went from Boston to New York. It was apparent now that the show had problems. It was a tender love story with radically political undertones. Eddie O'Brien's character was the one that carried most of those ideas. Although McCarthy was not yet in power, it was in the air. Eddie and the producers became scared and insisted on changes to soften the political statements and to bring the second act up to the fluffy level of the first. But the excitement that had made Van Druten's plays successful in the early days did not come easily for him anymore. He had wanted to try to write a deeper, more serious, tougher play. Under the pressure he became unsure. The play never quite made it. It's sad, for it was his last play. He died a year later.

This was my first experience with the Broadway theater—with tryouts and rewrites and constant changes. None of that happened in the Swedish theater. It was all new to me and it didn't occur to me that I could make any suggestions as far as the script was concerned. It was far from my conception of being an actress. I was also unaware of the life and death struggle that goes only with all Broadway productions.

The pressures caught up with me in New York. I felt ill. There was nothing wrong with me. "Relax, Viveca," the doctor said. "Get some rest." How?

No wonder I was exhausted and tense. Don had joined me in New York for the opening, and in order to carry on the love affair with G.T., I would get up sometimes at six in the morning to see him (and not just to see him!) in his hotel. Then I got back to Don in our hotel and gave some excuse about wanting to walk and think. Of course I was exhausted and tense! "Christ, Viveca. Tell them both to leave you alone until the opening," I mumbled to myself. But then the other me was saying, "Come on. You love it. Actresses lead flamboyant and turbulent lives. It's part of their repertoire."

I don't know if Don suspected anything. I think he trusted me completely. We all spent time together, like friends; as Don and I had done with Folke—and we never knew if Folke suspected anything either. Circles! Circles! It got easier when G.T.'s wife arrived. On opening night, all three were out front. I stood in the wings. "I will be punished," I thought. I was scared. I made a pact

195

with myself. "I'll give up G.T. and our love if I can be brilliant tonight," as if paying a price were the answer. I had a long way to go about my craft.

My crazy love life didn't seem to have hurt my performance. The reviews were all in praise of me but not the play. I was lucky! I quickly gave up the pact!

We went to Sardi's afterwards—me and Don, G.T. and the wife! Around twelve o'clock *The New York Times* was brought in and Brooks Atkinson's review was read aloud. "It won't work," I heard the PR man mumble. One man's opinion—and months, years of work was down the drain. I experienced it for the first time, but nothing quite penetrated. Being in love cast a pink shimmer over the grayest truth.

Don went back to California after the opening. I was to follow when the fate of the play was certain. The producers tried to keep it alive, but by the third week the notice was up on the board. It finally began to hit me. How could I live without New York, without the theater! They were in my blood now, and so was G.T.

We lived it up those three uncertain weeks. We dined, we danced, we made love. G.T. talked about writing plays for me to star in. The image of the theatrical couple was all within reach. He was tender, too, and sensitive, interested in my soul. I was even convinced that he was the father for my children. He seemed never to disapprove. I pushed Don out of my head. I dared not think of him.

The last performance of *I've Got Sixpence* was a few days before Christmas. The next day I was to leave for California. There was no reason for me to stay any longer. I had to get home for Christmas!

It was late Saturday afternoon when G.T. picked me up at the stage door after the matinee to have dinner with me at Sardi's. We walked through Shubert Alley. New York was magic, filled with Christmas spirit, lights, and sounds. The snow was coming down heavily and heavenly. G.T. stopped halfway. He put his hand into the large pocket of his yellow duffel coat where I would put my hand, for years to come, when it was cold. He took out a tiny Tiffany box. Inside was a sliver of a platinum ring. He slid it gently on my finger. It fit perfectly.

That I already had a wedding ring flashed through my mind. I wasn't wearing it, hadn't been for the last couple of weeks. I was afraid of losing it. (Having to take it off every evening in my dressing room was my excuse.) The girl I was portraying in the play was not married. And so I left it in the hotel room.

I ought to have said to George, "I am not free. I am already married to somebody else. I love you—I think—but I have a family. I need time. I don't know what it all means." I couldn't. I didn't want to put the pin in the balloon. The pink cloud seemed so much more real in that moment. I wanted him sexually all the time. I trusted that feeling more than anything in the world, always had —more than speaking up, more than facing trouble. I trusted it as much as pain. That was real, too. One or the other. And pain was around the corner. But not that night, or the next, or the next. Maybe for the first time, I acknowledged that it would be more than just my pain. But not that night. That night, everything was wonderful.

"Will you marry me?" G.T. said. The snow was still coming down heavily and heavenly. I could feel the snowflakes on my eyelashes. I must have answered yes.

The next day, on my way to California, half of me with G.T. in New York, the other half on my way to Don and the children, it began to hit me. I felt weak. "I hate to live this way," I mumbled to myself. "It seems I have felt this way before. Damn it!"

Don and the children met me at the airport, as always. My state of mind interfered with the quality of the time just as it had years before in Sweden when I had been away for nine months in the U.S.A. and came back in love with Don. Had I learned nothing?

Kris had changed. I barely recognized him. Had he forgotten me? What was it like for him that I had disappeared so suddenly, and, with me, the flow of milk? He seemed to know Don much better than me now. They had seen each other every day for the last two months. Oh God, how can I rob a man, once more, of his child? And myself of a father for him? For the first time in my life I began to feel it wasn't only my child. It took me days to confront Don. The feelings that had seemed so clear in New York were all muddled now when the reality of my past life confronted me with open arms, with so much love, and then it was Christmas! The house was beautiful! The children had bought the Christmas tree and dressed it beautifully. How can I tell them now? I must wait until after Christmas. Thank God for Christmas!

"Don't you love me anymore?" G.T. asked me over the phone from New York when I explained to him I hadn't been able to tell Don yet. I was standing in a phone booth on the San Vincente Boulevard. John and Lena were playing outside. Did they sense anything? They had courageously taken to the new house and the new school—their fourth. My God, how can I uproot them once again?

"Viveca, don't *doubt!*" In the long run they will benefit from New York.

Then there was that other voice: Why not wait and make sure? How do you know G.T. will be a good father, a good husband?

I didn't know.

We had been to the library, the children and I, that afternoon. I wanted to find a book by G.T. I wanted to read his writing. Unconsciously, I knew I needed to know him better in order to trust him with myself and with the children.

They only had one book in the library in Brentwood—*Beneath the Stone the Scorpion.* I read quickly two chapters, then switched to the last, turning colder and colder. The man in the book was poisoning his wife because he couldn't bring himself to tell her "I don't love you anymore." The whole book was about that. "That was during a bad period in my marriage," he explained long distance. "I wish you hadn't read that one, not now. Don't you love me?" he repeated.

G.T. had a wife, yes. He had given me the impression that she barely counted and that the marriage had been over with long ago, that it was just a question of signing papers. Wasn't it true? Did he say that to Uschi, too, about us?

When he went into rehearsal with his next play, *The Emperor's Clothes*, there was a wonderful part for me in it. When *Sixpence* closed, however, I was not offered it. It would complicate things more than necessary with the wife, he explained to me.

I didn't like the fact that I had to give up a part to protect his wife, but I put it under the heading of humanity and decided to think positively and not wonder why he hadn't said it to begin with. Or if he lied about this, would he lie about other things, too? But I didn't want to think that way, certainly not now when I was about to take such a risk and cause so many people pain.

"The children," I said. "I'm worried about the children. It's another upheaval for them." At least I did say that.

"Don't worry. Don't you think I will make a good father? I will. I love them already."

What is love? What is being a father? How did he know that he could be a good father? I had heard others say the same.

"I have found a house on 71st Street. It's perfect for us all. And some friends of mine are talking to the Dalton School about getting the children accepted there."

198

Why did I doubt him? Go with love, Viveca! Go with the yes feeling in life! You're strong enough.

Am I?

"Don't you love me?" He repeated it twice. Finally, slowly, I answered yes. But I wasn't quite sure that I loved him enough to make such an enormous decision. The reward seemed so far away in the distance, beyond my reach, at that moment. "It will be better once I tell Don the truth," I thought.

"I have begun to tell my wife," G.T. said. "Don't you love me anymore?"

I told Don that same night. We drove home after a dinner party. I have totally blocked out where we were, with whom we had dinner. I only remember the drive back, the rain coming down in buckets—like that first Christmas in California. Does it always rain on Christmas in California? It's supposed to snow on Christmas. The earth is supposed to be white and pure. But the asphalt was black and shiny and wet that night. I was staring straight ahead. The windshield wipers kept going, zoom, zoom, zoom, desperately trying to keep the windows clear. I hoped we would crash, swirl, have an accident—anything—so that I wouldn't have to say what I had decided to say.

Nothing happened. Finally, words came out of me, as if someone else had said them, from far away. "I am in love with George Tabori."

Silence, except for the sound of the windshield wipers and the rain and the other cars passing by us, with passengers quite content and happy with life, not like us. Don still didn't say a word, just drove on faster and faster. "This is when the accident will happen and what a relief it will be," I said to myself.

But nothing happened! He didn't even yell at me, "I am going to kill you, you bitch!" He just continued speeding.

He didn't fight for me. Don, who fights studio heads, editors, stars, everybody—whose films are filled with violence—didn't fight for me, for himself, for us. He just drove on, faster and faster. Not even the rain stopped. The windshield wipers kept going, zoom, zoom, zoom. We didn't have an accident.

Nothing happened, except that the marriage was over with.

It wasn't as easy as leaving Folke. "Come and sleep with me, Don. Please, let's hold each other. I want you. Please." Some nights seemed unbearable. But Don steered clear of me. He was in pain. He couldn't afford to accept me now that I had told him I was in love with another man. Besides, he was still out of work and

broke. He knew I was sick and tired of worrying about five cents
here and five cents there. So was he. Neither one of us knew that
success was around the corner for him. *Invasion of the Body
Snatchers* was one. He became a big name director, even a cult
director.

"I'll never let you do the dishes," G.T. used to say to me, those
romantic weeks in New York. What a fantasy that was! We never
had any money. To raise three children in New York takes a
fortune. I did the dishes a lot. G.T. was always broke. It was Don
who became the millionaire.

Four weeks of insane efficiency followed, of moving, of packing, of arranging, of planning. Four weeks of denying the past, of
avoiding confrontations, good ones as well as bad ones. Four weeks
so desperately similar to those five years before, when I had left
Sweden and Folke, in love with Don. Only the nightmare seemed
more real this time.

Such a waste of time! You could put on a play with that kind of
time, or write a book. Breaking up a marriage is expensive in more
ways than one.

"We are moving to New York," I told the children. "A large
city. It will be wonderful, fantastic. I will take you to the theater,
to museums. You will meet exciting people." And I answered their
questions. "Yes, you will go to new schools. Yes, you will get new
friends. Yes, you can take the dogs with you, even the hamsters.
Don't worry; yes, we will find a house." By God, the house in
Brentwood—I loved it. I had spent so much time making it beautiful and perfect. Efforts wasted again.

Come on, Viveca. What is a house? Furniture? When magic is
waiting for you? Life as you dreamed it could be!

"Is Don coming, too?" the children asked. I was back in reality
in no time.

"No, not now. Maybe later he will visit us and you will see him.
Yes, yes, you will!" "It is my last move, my last man," I said to
myself. It was my last move, but not my last man.

It was Don who broke the news to them. I sat in the house,
waiting anxiously, wondering how they would take it. Was the
word "divorce" mentioned? Did they understand what that means?
I heard the ball go thumpety-thump against the pavement outside
the garage. "Get involved in a physical activity," the psychiatrist
advised us.

We were clever enough to have sought advice about telling the children. Why we didn't about us is beyond me, for we needed help. I was spaced out. Don't remember the place, only that it was a man. "Let Don tell them," he suggested. "If Don tells them, they will know that he is not angry with them, that it is not his decision, but that they are moving because of your work, Viveca. Most children easily take on a guilt feeling of breaking up a marriage," he said. "It's better to try and avoid that. Time and distance will help!"

I sat in our bedroom. It was late in the afternoon, a glorious time of day in California in December, cool and crisp. There were dark, long shadows from the trees, old trees around the house, barely moving outside the window. I heard no screams of delight when the ball hit the basket hanging on the garage door. It seemed much too quiet. How will they adjust to the streets in New York, so different from our backyard in Brentwood? Oh, but that's not all that life is about, Viveca. There is music and painting and books and art and spirit and there is G.T.! But would he play ball with them like Don? Or take them fishing like Don? Or buy them a dog? Or water the lemon trees with them, like Don? Would he?

"Be sure to make them understand that you are not disappearing," the shrink had said to Don. Don did disappear, totally, out of the lives of John and Lena. Like Folke. He dropped them. Almost his own son, too, for a while. And I didn't insist for I still knew nothing about faces disappearing and ghost-fathers turning into boogie-men.

The New Year had begun when we boarded the plane for the East. I and the children, and Nana, of course, and Berit, her niece, who had taken the place of Edith, who had married her Irishman, and Lady, the most extraordinary dog, and Bosse, the poodle, probably even some birds and maybe some hamsters. Kristoffer was lying in the basket next to me on the seat. John and Lena were waving goodbye to Don, standing at the airport. And in spite of some sadness, a certain excitement took over as the plane lifted. We were off again, and this time together, for a new place, a new man, a new father, a new horizon. Doubts began to fade. Magic time was coming up! Magic was G.T.! Magic was New York! We were ready to reach for the moon!

VI

New York

> "Such a wonderful lot of
> terrible things did happen.
> And now it's you, who can tell
> me, 'Sorry, baby. Sorry.' "
>
> BERTOLT BRECHT
> Polly in Threepenny Opera

T HE MAN I LOVE is coming to visit us," I told the kids.
We had been in New York for ten days, half settled in a
funny, old, dark, through endless rentals neglected brownstone house on 71st Street. G.T.'s play *The Emperor's Clothes* was
back from the tryout tour and was previewing on Broadway. He
was still living in a hotel with the wife. It didn't occur to me to
ask or even to worry about what was going on between them. I
implicitly trusted him to love me forever, as I did twenty years
later. I was either too romantic, or had a very large ego, or both.

I was fixing tea in the kitchen when I heard the doorbell ring.
As I opened the door for my elegant looking Hungarian lover, I
saw Lena coming down the stairs. She looked angelic and exquisite,
all dressed up in a gray velvet dress, her blond hair loosely and
frizzily hanging over her shoulders. She had braided it in the morning and it framed her delicate face like a shining moon. She was
eight now, going on nine, soon a woman.

Behind her came John. He was dressed in cowboy clothes, boots
and hat and a gun in his holster. He was ten, going on eleven,
soon a man.

Lena put out her hand. G.T. kissed it and handed her a gift.
John put out his gun. G.T. didn't take it, but handed him a gift,
too--English lavender soap. They were more astounded than disappointed. It was obvious that they were in for a whole new experience. The same was true for G.T.

It was clear that this time they were out to get a father for themselves and one that would not drop them the moment their mother
left him. Or vice versa.

Lena didn't have to worry about G.T. From that moment on
they were close. And still are.

John and G.T. were never as close. Maybe being the same sex stood in the way. Father-son competition? No doubt, John, rightly so, was suspicious of any man falling in love with his mother and making him change his life once more. But he was open to love, and when, a year later, the CIA came to investigate G.T., John took all books in reference to G.T.'s left-wing politics out of the library and hid them in his own room on the top floor. John was only ten at the time.

The Emperor's Clothes opened a week or so after we had moved to New York. The opening night party was at the house. Everybody involved in the production was there—the two stars, Lee J. Cobb and Maureen Stapleton, producer Robert Whitehead, director Harold Clurman, and others. Clurman kept asking Lena for a kiss. "If you give me a dollar," she said. He did, and kissed her.

I wore a pink chiffon dress. "He who has you cannot fail," Clurman quoted one of the lines from G.T.'s play, looking at me.

Spirits were high until the PR man got the telephone call and Brooks Atkinson's review was read over the phone. It quickly got very quiet around him. He got even quieter. It was clearly thumbs down. The play would not run. Months, years of work was down the drain.

People started to leave. "Goodbye, Viveca. Good to see you." "Goodbye, George. See you tomorrow. Let's see what the other papers are saying. Let's get some sleep." Exhaustion set in, finally. The efforts of the last couple of weeks, the strain of opening night took its toll now, when the payoff was gone.

Soon only G.T. and I were left. We stood by the mantelplace in the disarranged living room, holding each other for a long while. In the short time that we had known each other, we had experienced three flops. We didn't know then that the ratio on Broadway is one hit to ten flops. We might have another seven to go.

No play, no pay. Necessity has no laws. Georgie moved in with us on 71st Street, whether we were ready for it or not. We started the Tabori family.

The wife, whom I hadn't seen since that time in Brentwood, must have faced it all and gone back to England. I hadn't given her much thought and thank God she didn't insist on confronting me.

I paid little attention to her, whether she was in pain or not, whether she was hoping that he would change his mind and come back to her or not, but then I hadn't been abandoned yet, except by Rydeberg, way back in my youth, and I had decided it was never, never, never going to happen again. Obviously G.T.'s wife wasn't glamorous enough, or maybe loving enough, or maybe even

fabulous enough for him, as I was. It wasn't a question of age anymore—I was getting close to thirty-five myself! And I didn't feel
like an old hag at all! It didn't seem to hurt my career, either.

New York was an exciting place for actors in the beginning of
the fifties. TV had just begun to become an important medium. All
the good TV shows were made here, live. First-rate stories done by
first-rate talented people who hadn't yet made it in the movies,
either because of youth or by choice. I did one show after another.
I worked with top directors like Bob Mulligan, John Franken-
heimer, and Sidney Lumet. They, too, did one shown on top of another, acquiring an experience that Hollywood would never have
given them. My favorite show was *The Bridge of San Luis Rey*,
on "Playhouse 90," based on a novel by Thornton Wilder, produced by David Susskind, and directed by Mulligan. I played a
famous Peruvian actress whose face is destroyed by smallpox. The
cast was sensational—Hume Cronyn, Judith Anderson, just to
mention a couple. The sets were creative and elaborate. We rehearsed for three weeks, then spent two days in the studio on
technical rehearsals, and last, a full day on camera before the final
performance in the evening—live—watched by thousands of
Americans. It was like an opening night in the theater.

Good actors were required for live TV, actors used to rehearsal,
trained for the theater. New York was becoming like London,
where actors could participate in more than one medium at a time.

It's a pity it had to end. Seven years later, the television industry went out West and live television went out the window.
With it went seventy-five percent of the quality, certainly as far as
drama is concerned.

An hour of filmed TV on the screen takes one week to shoot—
no rehearsals, no time to prepare. The result has to be different.
But the studios are occupied in the City of Angels and everybody
is working. TV saved Hollywood. New York had to go on living
without it, as it had before. And it has.

Most important for me as an actress that spring in New York
was that I discovered the Actor's Studio.

It was by pure accident that I got involved. Mickey Knox, a
friend of G.T.'s, needed a partner. "Would you assist me?" he
asked. I remembered Sophie talking about Lee Strasberg and the
Studio and, not knowing enough about it to be scared or nervous,
I said, "Why not?" I must have been good, for afterwards Lee

spent a great deal of time talking about my work although I was not a member and Mickey was. No one had ever talked to me like that. There was no sexual interest. There was no bargaining.

He took me seriously, and when he said, "There is much more in you to be used than Hollywood was ever aware of," I felt like heaven was opening up. I decided immediately, "This place is for me!"

It made it hard to leave New York and accept an offer to go to London. J.B. Priestly had seen me in *Sixpence* and offered me his latest play. It was also difficult to leave because of the children. But I felt I had finally gotten back to the stage and I couldn't afford to pass up the opportunity. I accepted.

George took it for granted that he should come along with me. After all, London used to be his home. Besides, his mother, a Hungarian woman who miraculously had escaped her husband's destiny, lived there.

"Yes, of course you should come along." I had other wishes, not expressed: "What about the children? Shouldn't you stay, take care of them, get to know them, become their father . . . ?" At that point my conviction came to a halt. "Like Don? Like Folke?"

Maybe he's right. We should be together. Isn't that what I wanted, too? I had left out that part with the other men in my life. "Yes! Do come!"

Next question. Who should pay for the ticket to London? Not Priestly. He paid for mine only. "We can sell the station wagon. We don't really need it in New York." It was my suggestion!

Anything to keep the romance going. Maybe I really believed that you have to pay a price for love.

We took off for London, leaving the children again with Nana. Don was in California and, like Folke, had withdrawn, wasn't able to pay attention to the children anymore. Couldn't. Then there was the distance and that was real, as with Folke. And so the children were alone this time, without both parents.

London was bitter and cold and no place to be unless you could afford to stay at Claridges. G.T. and I rented two rooms from a neurotic lady on Eton Square, and I was only warm in the bathtub, which wasn't often since hot water was a rarity. My teeth were chattering most of the time. Also on the stage. English theaters are drafty! I was dressed in bare gowns and there was no chauffeur-driven heated Bentley waiting for me at the stage door.

The play was a love story. Priestly, now in his later years, had remarried a younger woman and was full of romance. Everybody was in love. The producer, too, and with a real "Lady" lady. He was shot by her real "Lord" husband, in the hotel room. He caught them rehearsing one of the seduction scenes from the play, over a bottle of champagne.

They had admitted to G.T. and me that it was their favorite pastime before they would throw themselves passionately on the bed. It all ended with a gunshot. It hit him, not her, of course— not too seriously, but enough to put a stop to the romance.

The play was as ridiculous as the events around it. Dreadfully directed, too, by a British, mediocre comedy director. It was obvious already in Dublin, where we opened, that we were a flop. But the pistol-wounded producer insisted on continuing to the West End in London. We almost got booed. That was my one and only theatrical experience in London so far.

In the meantime, cables were coming from New York, asking me to take over for Deborah Kerr in *Tea and Sympathy*, with Kazan directing. How perfect! I can go on the stage every night! I will be home with the kids, I can go to the Actor's Studio! And we will eat! Fabulous! But there was a 'but': Kazan's testimony in Washington and my lover's experience with him. My own newly found social conscience was put to the task. I turned it down. It wasn't easy, but, on the other hand, my lover was writing a new play for me. Dreams were coming through! Me and my man working together!

G.T. had begun writing *The Jealousy Play* when Mickey and I were rehearsing the scene for the Actor's Studio in our bedroom. I had no idea about G.T.'s feelings until I read the first act, in London, several months later.

"Were you really jealous, or just dramatizing?" I asked him. It was painful for him to admit, but he did. "How weird," I thought, "I am in love with him. It hasn't even occurred to me to flirt with Mickey, or anybody else. Yet he is jealous." If he didn't trust me now, how could he ever?

The woman in G.T.'s play reacted the same way. When the husband has wired their bedroom in order to catch her in the possible act with another man, she screams at him in fury, "You have no right to check on me. My body is mine. It belongs to me. I do with it whatever I want." I never said it like the woman in the play, for the insecurities, whatever they were, his or mine, were solved through physical intimacy.

Since the play wasn't ready for production yet, I agreed to a summer stock tour of *Bell, Book and Candle.* G.T. seemed depressed. Had he hoped that we would stay in London? "I have no choice," I said to him. "I've got to get home to the kids. I've got to pay the bills." I really didn't want to stay in London. I had just moved us all to New York! Besides, I was dying to settle in, root myself, go back to work with Lee Strasberg, be a mother, actress, wife!

"Come on, Tabori. It's all waiting for us over there," I said. "And the children need us, Georgie!" G.T. still seemed depressed. He said he was worried that he would be refused a visa to return to the U.S.A. It wasn't inconceivable. He was a British subject and a radical, left-wing writer, although never a member of the Communist Party.

He finally agreed to apply. We spent a tearful day of goodbyes, planning on how we would meet, someplace, somewhere in the future. It all added passion to our love affair. We went to the tearoom at the Ritz Hotel, across the street from the American Embassy. I kissed him goodbye, went to the ladies room to wipe my tears and powder my nose. As I got back and opened the newspaper, G.T. reappeared. He pulled out his British passport. "I got it, just like that," he said. "I can't believe it."

"Believe it, darling," I said. We started to laugh.

I hadn't completely understood his anxieties. I was a Swede and he was a Jew. G.T. rarely talked about his story of horror or the death of his father, nor did I talk about my father's death. Perhaps G.T. felt he had no right to the mourning, as I didn't to mine. Perhaps I wasn't able to listen to G.T. as I hadn't to Raoul Wallenberg. Although both G.T. and I were uprooted and had something in common there, his was much more turbulent than mine. He fled his country whereas I left mine of free will, or so it seemed.

Still, at that time in London, there was something courageous about our efforts to want to adjust to a new life together, a loving life. It was only more complex than we understood.

I went home ahead of G.T. The children seemed to have adjusted. They were amazingly independent. Lena was only eight and John soon ten. They took the bus to school by themselves. Both of them talked very little about the experience of a new town, a new school, new friends. Lena spent a great deal of time in a pet shop around the corner. They must have wondered what happened to Don and who was this new man in their mother's life. Kris was perhaps too small to understand. Yet the children were amazing in their love toward me.

One night I found myself crying. John must have woken up. He came into my room. "You're crying, Mommy."

"Yes."

"Why?"

Yes, why? What were the silent conversations with self in the middle of the night with the sounds of New York outside the window, hearing only the frightening ones—the sirens, the police cars, the fire engines. So different from California nights, with cricket sounds and long shadows on green lawns, friends living around the corner, Don next to me. No! No! No! No!

One no is enough!

Hurting Don still haunted me, as did exposing the children to a new life, a new father! I was not able to communicate with G.T. about it. After all, he had never been a father. Besides, they were not his children. But he wanted them; he said so.

Another flop in London. Flying back alone to New York, not yet to a home. We must get settled. I am a peasant Swede! I need roots. And then the bills. And nothing to pay them with. Had never been completely broke in my whole life, not like this. Trips, moves from West Coast to East Coast, are insanely expensive. Was it really necessary? Yes! Yes! Yes! Yes!

One yes is enough!

G.T. wasn't rich. I knew it now. A playwright is as rich as his last play runs. And it hadn't. Nor the one before. Nor the next one. The one he is writing for me. Yes. Why can't I stop crying? What's the matter with me? I have everything I asked for and I got it. G.T. seemed unperturbed by it all. He was the gypsy. "Our love will overcome it," he says. I am envious. I want to be as free as he.

"Mommy, you are crying." John is crawling down next to me. And suddenly Lena is on the other side. They don't say, "Don't cry, Mommy." They know better. We go to sleep, the three of us, holding each other. The next day is easier to get through. I am not alone. Once again, I experience their love. Loyal and beyond doubts.

G.T. came back from London. Things didn't change much, except for a few sublime moments of extraordinary connection between two lovers.

No doubt the move, the adjustment, was tough on G.T., too. He was more rooted in London than I had ever been in L.A.—even I understood that now. This time he returned to New York with no play of his waiting to go into rehearsal, no possibility of a hit, success, money, fame, but, rather, three children waiting to be fathered and a woman waiting to be husbanded, more than just courted. A breadwinner, too, at least half of one. New, too, for G.T., to have a woman with a career, needs of her own to be considered equally with his. The wife in London had no other needs but to fulfill his.

If he had any doubts, he never told me. I never asked him.

Just thinking about it—my doubts or his—scared me, and then the next thought was, of course, "I must get close to him again."

Efforts, efforts. To be the loving woman. Was it the same for G.T.? Efforts, efforts, to be the loving man, not knowing, either one of us, that magic must be found in daily life and has nothing to do with place or time.

We decided to send the children to camp so we could spend the summer alone with each other.

In spite of the children begging me, John particularly, "I don't want to, I don't want to go to camp, I want to be with you and George," my mind was made up. I was unbending. Trunks were packed, tears were wiped. Off they went to camp. And Kristoffer went to California. To see Don for the last time for years to come. Nana went along, of course, to pack up the house.

How insane, this need for exclusivity, when I needed the opposite, as did the children. As did G.T., perhaps, too.

The best decision I made that spring was selling the house in Brentwood and buying one in New York.

We drove up 95th Street—the Hellgate block, as it was named way back in time when there was nothing but hills, woods, and the stones that the city is resting on. It was spring and the vines had just broken out and all the brownstone houses were covered in soft, green-colored leaves. We went in and looked at ours, gave them a offer, and the next week the deal was made. We never saw another house.

It didn't help at all that G.T. and I were alone, just the two of us, touring the countryside in order to find love "on the middle-ground." It made it worse. I had no excuse now for not being a loving woman. I broke out in a sweat before I went onstage every night, petrified I would forget my lines. For the first time in my life, I experienced anxiety. It crept over me like cockroaches.

I felt no right to my pain. I didn't understand why, when I had everything I had asked for and gotten. And I told G.T. nothing.

We had more in common than we knew. Oh, the mirror image!

Finally, one summer night on the beach along the southern coast of Virginia, it became unbearable and I dared, for the first time in my life, to share anxieties about love with my man. It was a revelation. G.T. was wonderful, understanding and tender. "It's been too hard on you. Perhaps you should talk to a shrink," he said. "A friend of mine goes to a good one."

We became instantly closer. Oh God, how fast feelings move within us, from black to white, from shade into sunshine. I felt sure he was my man again.

The following week I made an appointment for me. The moment I walked into the doctor's office, I began to cry. By the end of the hour, he told me, "You have broken up three marriages! It is essential that you understand why or the fourth one will go to pieces too."

I felt an enormous sense of relief. Never in my whole life had I been confronted with the fact that it was unnatural to keep moving from one man to another. I was only aware that a wall was creeping up, at times, between me and the man I loved, or between me and life: a glass wall where I could see her on the other side—the happy woman—but not touch her.

I had no idea that the glass could be broken, without cutting myself bloody, through a conscious effort on my part with the help of someone who knew *how*. My brother hadn't known. He had only known straitjackets. Still, it took me more years and more doubts before I went into analysis. Like so many people, I thought it was a sign of weakness to go for help. The opposite is true. It is a sign of strength to admit you need help. It is even harder for a man. It didn't even occur to G.T., nor to me, that he might need help, too.

The family got together in August. We rented a cottage in Connecticut. Nature, no work, taking long walks in the woods, alone or together, swimming, eating, sleeping, sunning, accepting each other, settling in with each other, watching Kris take his first steps, doing nothing, became the temporary answer. By Labor Day we were ready to move into the house on 95th Street and to root ourselves.

The day the furniture arrived from California, we made love on my bed. It became ours now. That same early evening, we walked up the street together. I felt his body close to mine. "I have your penis inside of me. I will feel it in me always. I love you," I mumbled to him. He pressed me against him. We were happy. We were in love. We were one. Who needed a shrink anymore?

"We will build a fire around our love," G.T. said. Yes. Our love would solve everything. Love and work. Yes! Work!

2

I went into rehearsal in the middle of September in *Anastasia*, a play about the youngest daughter of Czar Nicholas of Russia and his wife Alexandra. Anastasia was the only surviving member of the Czar's family during the revolution. Maybe!

It is still an unsolved mystery whether she did or did not survive the massacre at Ekaterinburg, the palace where the family spent their summers. The rumors about her continue.

Someone insisted that they had seen that her body was missing from the heap of dead. Someone had seen her crawl away. Someone had seen her in the woods. Someone had seen her, there.

The story came alive again when an unknown woman was found in the canal in Berlin, half-dead, years later. In her unconscious state she kept insisting that she was the Princess Anastasia. Her broken face, her destroyed body, her desperate eyes seemed to have nothing in common with the young, beautiful Anastasia of the past. The only close human being still alive to recognize her, to affirm who she was, was her grandmother, the Dowager Empress, still living in Denmark. She refused the unknown woman admission. Why? Bitterness, perhaps, or vulnerability, or fear? Let the dead be dead. Anastasia withdrew, one more, into the Black Woods and obscurity, stamped as the impostor, left only with herself to tell the truth.

Today she lives in Virginia, U.S.A., married to an Englishman. When a TV interviewer caught her, not too long ago, in her obscurity and asked her who she really was, she furiously spat right into the camera. It was her answer to an insensitive world.

The story, whether she is or isn't, is heartbreaking. Marcel Maurette, a French author, turned it into a play, which Guy Bolton in turn adapted for the English-speaking stage. But unlike the unknown woman in life, Anastasia in the play is recognized by her grandmother. It was tried out in London unsuccessfully, but became a success in New York at the Lyceum Theatre, with me playing Anastasia and Eugenie Leontovich the grandmother.

The recognition scene in the second act between the two of us was emotional—big, and marvelous—filled with the intense insistence on love, of the life force that uniquely exists in all families and has to be affirmed in order to re-create love again.

As the curtain comes down, Anastasia alone on the stage, in a feverish faint, calls out the names of her dead sisters and brother, calls out for her mother and father, in Russian. There is no doubt any longer who she is. She can love them again, and therefore herself. There was rarely a dry eye in the audience. The applause came, as if on cue, every night. The recognition scene made the play into the theatrical event it became.

Eugenie Leontovich, born Russian herself, and having escaped the revolution, was an endless source of background information. "They were taught that death was around the corner, always," she told me. "They were taught to behave with grace and nobility in the face of death." Leontovich behaved much like it herself.

She was not only a superb actress, but a superb human being. Slowly a relationship developed between the two of us, two different actresses, two different-generation women. She would bring me some old remedy to treat my throat if it was sore, or some Russian delicacy to nourish me, or Russian fairy tales for my children that they came to love. She never stayed to chitchat or gossip. She knew about the need for space, for bareness. We came to love each other.

Opening night was a triumph. G.T., John, and Lena were waiting for me in the dressing room. The press photographer took a picture of us all, surrounded by flowers.

There was no opening night party this time. Instead, we all went home and sat in the kitchen with a large bottle of champagne and a large cheesecake with thirty-three candles. It was my birthday. Around one in the morning, the phone rang. Brooks Atkinson's review was a winner. Thumbs up this time! Hooray! I can go to the theater every night and still live at home in my own house. I can help the children with homework. I can go to the Studio and we are eating tomorrow! What a way to begin the New Year! I was a hit on Broadway. My one and only, for years to come. Thank God I didn't know it then!

Lena was nine by now, and John eleven. For the first time, they experienced in reality "my mother, the actress." And I experienced sharing my work with them. In Hollywood it was never particularly desirable to have children running around the studio. The theater is a friendlier place. There is less money and therefore more human cooperation, like in large families. It's healthier to include and make children part of our society, our lives, and it's only in (the latter part of) this century that we don't. In the old days, the child was around the mother when she was milking the cow, or the father when plowing the fields.

Both Lena and John loved coming to my dressing room on

matinee days. They did their homework while I was on stage. We had dinner together and then went home after the show together. They knew where I was and what I was doing. Kris was too little, but he made up for it soon.

My small but cozy dressing room in the beautiful old Lyceum Theatre provided me also with a room of my own. I came to love the quietness of it, the privacy of it before the performance. I hadn't even known how much I had needed it.

I would get there early. The subway ride from 95th Street to 47th and Broadway gave me the distance from life and daily trifles to the journey and life of Anastasia—my own, too. I would lie down for half an hour to rest, to get in touch with myself and the play. The room was filled with pictures of Anastasia as a child, as a young girl, with her parents, her sisters and brother, or alone. I had pictures of the impostor, too—the unknown woman with the broken face and the desperate eyes who lived alone in the Black Woods, alone, unwanted, pushed out, denied.

"All that research is good, Viveca," Lee Strasberg said to me one day. "But most of it is only useful if you add to it the research about yourself. It is your own life experience that will give Anastasia reality." I put up pictures of myself as a child, of my father, my mother, my brother, and my sister, too. Above all I began to get in touch with a feverish desire within myself—like Anastasia—to be recognized for better or for worse. For myself! Even loved, like Anastasia. Through the work at the Studio, through the work on the part, I began to see how I could use my past, however painful.

"Emotional memories are an actor's gold mine," Lee told me.

Paula, his wife, said, "An actor must have an emotional card file. Every time I go by a bakery store I start to cry. The smell from the freshly baked bread reminds me of my mother. I know it now and I can use it in my work."

My card file is my mother's thinning black hair, my mother's bluish, swollen hands, swollen from frostbites as a child; my brother's black, sometimes bloodshot eyes; my father's hands. My card file is stepmother violets and green moss and the smell of the woods in my childhood country, and nightmares about a little girl not daring to be herself.

I was thirty-four years old. I finally took my work seriously.

Louella, my dresser, a wonderful Black woman, brought me coffee on my half-hour. She was a marvelous listener and never judged, and when I complained about George, she never took it seriously. "Christ, Louella," I would say. "Do you think he would get up on Sunday morning (Nana's day off) and take Krissie to the park? No! I'm the one who has to do it, while he is snoring in bed or reading the Sunday papers!" She would just laugh and say something about her own man or men in general, identifying with me. And, like me, not see that a change was possible.

G.T. was writing. By spring he had completed *The Jealousy Play*. Producer Saint Subber loved it and took an option on it. He planned to open it in the fall with me as the woman. Everything was going our way!

When the producers of *Anastasia* asked me to take the national tour, I said no.

My agent called me, astounded. "Viveca, you're turning down $35,000. Can you afford it? You don't have a contract for *The Jealousy Play* yet."

"I am sorry," I said. "I can't go on the road. I am doing George's play." A few months later, the roof fell in.

G.T. had met Sidney Poitier and decided to rewrite the part of the young lover for him. Sidney was, at the time, unknown. He ran a hamburger stand up in Harlem for a living. But he was beautiful and brilliant, and G.T. used his background, his language, his life story to its fullest in the play.

Saint read the rewrites and didn't like them. He called G.T. over to his apartment. A few hours later, G.T. came home devastated. Saint suddenly had turned unimaginative and prejudiced: "Don't you dare tell us Americans what's wrong with this country," was his attitude. (It was even more ridiculous since one of Saint's lovers was a Black.) The play was canceled.

It wasn't easy for G.T. to be turned down by Saint. He had two flops behind him on Broadway now. It wasn't so easy to raise money for a Tabori play any longer, and *The Jealousy Play* was never produced.

In those days I had no way of understanding how to help, to take it to another producer, or a regional theater, or to put it into workshop production. They were less available then, but they did exist.

I did take it to Tad Danielewski, a young Polish director, and we did a few scenes from it at the Studio.

In the session afterwards, Eli Wallach and Mike Gatsell both pointed out that the scene was unclear. When asked what they meant by "unclear," they could not answer. Was there a feeling of embarrassment among the men in the Studio about a Black being in a white woman's bedroom? It was 1954. It is hard to believe today.

Marilyn Monroe was in the audience. She stuck her hand up in her own hesitating way—as if she had to test the air to be sure she wouldn't be hurt by something or somebody.

"Yes, Marilyn." Lee had spotted her, of course. He adored her and her talent.

Barely audible came in a whisper from Marilyn, "They say that it wasn't very clear. But life often isn't very clear."

Marilyn had an extraordinary perception. She was one of Lee's pet pupils and almost on her way to tearing down the images of the sex symbol. Had she only had the courage to stick through this vulnerable period of adjustment, letting down her defenses, unavoidable when you open yourself up to the kind of work Lee and the Method demanded, she would have become a great actress. I understood, for eventually I had to go for help myself. Marilyn did, too. But the analysis wasn't enough for her. The screams within her were too filled with pain, or fury, or both. She gave up. A tragedy for us all.

The night her death was announced and headlines splashed all over the front pages, I was performing *Brecht on Brecht* at the Theatre De Lys. Sitting on my stool with Brecht's oversize face behind me, I was filled with Marilyn. She was in me and around me and I wanted to share it with the audience. "In memory of Marilyn Monroe," I announced before the section "Hollywood Elegies," Brecht's brilliant poems: "I fled from the tigers. I fed the fleas. What got me at last, mediocrities." It was deadly quiet in the house. Truth happened that instant.

It was too late for me to get the *Anastasia* tour. I was unemployed and soon broke again. That's how fast the cookie crumbles.

In the meantime the film opened with Ingrid Bergman in "my" part. At the time they were casting, I didn't think I cared—I was on the stage every night. I finally realized the loss when Alan Schneider, who directed the play, and I went to see the film one late afternoon around the corner from the Lyceum Theatre. Alan was out of work at the time, too. We were holding hands. One moment I was furious for being dismissed, another delighted when they failed, the next frustrated that eight months of work could have been used and wasn't.

I was either shortsighted or afraid to fight. Probably both. True, there was a great deal of commotion around Ingrid Bergman at the time, and *Anastasia* was to be her return to the U.S.A. after having been penalized by Hollywood for the love affair with Rosselini. True, the investment was heavy, both emotionally and financially, on everybody's part. And true, it surely didn't help that we had the same agent. On the other hand, I could have found a new one, an agent that was for me only, and no doubt I would have felt better if I had fought for what was mine, even if the chances were small. I didn't even insist on being auditioned for the film, or meeting Anatole Litvak, the director.

Years later, Anatole and I became good friends. "Why didn't you come to see me in the play?" I asked him.

"I didn't want to be influenced in my approach," was his astonishing, but to him justified, answer. The Hollywood system is as blind as a woman in love! It had taken us weeks to find that impalpable nerve, that need for recognition of self that pulsated all through our production and brought it beyond the level of mediocre melodrama. Anatole would have benefited from seeing it; even the famous recognition scene between Anastasia and the Empress was dull in the film in comparison to ours on the stage.

In my workshops today, I urge young people, "Take your career in your own hands! Fight for what is yours! Fight the system! Change it!" At that time, twenty-two years ago, I felt completely out of control of my destiny as an actress.

It was partly my security-fed upbringing. In Sweden you are not even allowed to be fired. Once employed, always employed. A trap of its own. Making money can be a healthy driving force. Besides, I am happiest when I work. I have learned all that here in the U.S.A., and I might never have gotten *I Am a Woman* together if I had not been forced to find my own initiative. But I didn't know that then, and it was hell the first couple of years after *Anastasia,* opening *The New York Times* every Sunday morning and not finding my name in the Broadway section. I had been a hit. People had come to see me. Where was my name now? If someone had told me that I would not be in another Broadway play for years, I would have laughed. I didn't always, but it has been twenty-five years now.

I did learn that I can do without it. I would rather *not!*

The Actor's Studio became my haven. It provided me not only with a place to grow as an actress, but also a place where I could function, to be part of the theater.

You can spend whole days there, preparing and rehearsing scenes, even complete projects. "Use the place for what you need it for and it will serve you." Lee is adamant about the actor taking the initiative. I did. Within a year I was a member, and for the next four years I "lived" there.

Words like Lee Strasberg, the Method, the Actor's Studio are inseparable. It's impossible to mention one without the other. It is extraordinary how this tiny man, the son of two Russian immigrants, who came to this country as a small child, has created a kingdom of his own, yet one so much a part of the American theater, therefore American life, therefore the world. The Method, Lee Strasberg, the Actor's Studio, and the group theater represent a new kind of acting, a new kind of theater, identifiable not only with this country but also with this century.

The Actor's Studio is located in an old church on 44th Street, a building donated to Lee. There is nothing special about the small, not terribly well-kept place. There is never enough money to fix or paint anything. There is a small library with a few books, a rehearsal room. The performance space is adequate, a few lights hanging from the ceiling. There are bleachers climbing up on the three sides. The Studio can in no way measure up technically to the hundreds of university theaters with their perfectly equipped stages all over the country. And although it is ludicrous that an internationally famous place like the Actor's Studio cannot find funding from the government, it proves that technical equipment is the least important thing for creating theater. "Three boards and a passion" is all that is needed, Alexandre Dumas pointed out years ago. And nothing has changed in that respect. It's the people and what happens between them that matters. And magic goes on at the Actor's Studio every day.

Only members are allowed and a few observers, after careful checking—actors from other countries or other towns, or an occasional journalist writing about the Studio. The list of members is impressive: Marlon Brando, Jane Fonda, Eli Wallach, Anne Jackson, Ellen Burstyn, Marilyn Monroe, Paul Newman, Geraldine Page, Rip Torn, Al Pacino. It goes on and on. There is barely an important actor in this country who is not on the list. You apply for auditions in the spring or in the fall. The jury is made up of older members, and, for the final audition, Lee himself.

The acting sessions meet Tuesdays and Fridays. The directing and writing sessions meet other days. The doors open at 10:00 in the morning. Actors well known and not so well known stumble in. Directors and playwrights, too. There is coffee in the backroom, and talk, and a kind of friendliness that comes from knowing that we are all after the same thing.

At 11:00 everyone is seated in the theater for the first part of the session. Once the scene is being performed, nobody is allowed in. Lee sits in the first row, in the middle, with a card containing the name of the scene and the actors performing in it. There are notes on the back from earlier work that the actors have appeared in. Lee guides you carefully through the rehabilitation process, the retraining of your tools; even the very young ones seem to have to go through a similar process.

The more you give, the more Lee gives you back in return. Everybody in that room is hungry for affirmation, for centering of self, and, in turn, making the awareness into a useful tool as a performer. Eli Wallach always does a scene before going into rehearsal for a new production, "to warm up," he says. Jane Fonda worked regularly the years I was there. After one of the scenes she explained, "I have difficulty being bitchy in life. I figured I have to exercise that muscle."

I saw Gerri Page do a scene from *The Good Woman of Szechuan*, about teaching her unborn child how to live. Gerri was quite pregnant at the time, her belly round, and she used it to the fullest, making us part of the experience with her. Gerri Page is one of the great actresses of this century. In my view she can rarely do anything wrong. Had she lived in the nineteenth century she would have been acknowledged like Sarah Bernhardt or Eleanora Duse. Not to say she is not recognized by the American people or the world, but times have changed, and attitudes about actresses of her stature with them. The superstar image has muddled it.

After the performance, the actor speaks about his work. Lee is insistent about making *you* your own best judge. Then the group speaks up; if destructive, Lee interferes. Otherwise, he waits. When he speaks he is always revealing, always constructive. Demanding, too, in the sense that he wants the utmost from you. He encourages you to stretch yourself. Helps you find hidden, dark corners of your soul. Helps you accept that there is nothing you have not experienced at one point in your life, even murder, if only in your head. Or, if in life, through the killing of a fly. The fury is the same. He makes you realize that you have millions of colors within yourself, millions of tones, millions of feelings, and that it is your responsibility to make them available for the profession, to share them, good, bad, or indifferent. No secrets. Lee makes you aware of all that, never once forgetting the logic, the choices, making you into an "actor of the Age of Science," as Brecht says. To put the two elements together—the brain and the emotion—is the task, the lifelong task of the actor, of us all, maybe.

Lee affirms in you that nothing is impossible. We are ageless and endless. We can reach for the stars and touch them. And it's up to us.

By the end of the year, I was filled with a sense of curiosity about myself and my work when the producers of *Anastasia* came back to me and asked me to take over the West Coast tour in the spring. I immediately said yes.

We opened in St. Louis and ended up in Los Angeles. I knew Eugenie Leontovich had been angry with me for not having gone on the road with her in the fall. She was right. My consciousness as G.T.'s woman had won out over my consciousness as an actress. Leontovich's dedication to the play and the theater was far deeper and more socialistic than mine in spite of her being a "White Russian" both in life and in the play and my being the socialist, and our relationship was never quite the same after.

However, nothing seemed to interfere with the work between us. The tour was a triumph.

The last performance of *Anastasia* at the Huntington Hartford Theatre on Hollywood Boulevard, where we played for three months, was unforgettable for me. At the moment when the Dowager Empress finally accepts Anastasia as her grandchild, I felt utterly naked on the stage. It was just she and I, two naked souls on the stage. Nothing else. As we walked off, with the applause thundering behind us, I turned toward her, wanting to share the experience with her. With a gesture identical to that of the Grand Duchess, yet so much her own, she seemed to say, "Viveca, please, we are simply two actresses working!" saying perhaps, too, "It contains everything, Viveca; it is the infinite magic of our work. It is all that matters."

3

Anastasia ran for eight weeks in the City of Angels. It was summer again. We rented a house on the beach. The beach always made me happy. Always! Long walks, alone or together, G.T. and I, the children running around us.

We decided to get married on a Sunday morning.

We asked the judge to come to the house. The ceremony took place on the porch at ten in the morning. The children were there,

too, this time, except John. He was in camp. He tells me that I
didn't inform him, as I hadn't when I got married to Don.

I always felt I was looking for a father for John, one that my
father had not been for my brother. Did I think he would not ap-
prove of my choices? Had I let him inherit my brother's eyes,
looking at me, judging me? Otherwise it is hard to understand that
I was so insensitive. Or even careless.

But Kristoffer was there, chubby and curly blond, in Nana's
arms, and Lena, all excited. She was ten going on eleven, becoming a woman, in love with George, like me!

When I was her age, my father discovered my sensuality. It put
me into the sunshine, out of the shade. I knew for sure then I was
his favorite.

Why wasn't he here today? It's been so long since I saw him. It
was my fourth marriage. Would he not have approved? But I always felt he understood and accepted everything I did. Was California too far away? Was it too costly to travel?

My mother wasn't there, either. If I missed her I wasn't aware
of it. I knew I missed Sophie, but her best friend was there instead of her and I wore a gray bare sundress. I could feel the sand
from my morning walk on my bare feet. The sun was trying to
break through the mist but never quite made it. But then I like
gray, misty days on the beach. The sound of the waves was our
wedding march. G.T. and I looked at each other all through the
ceremony. Only I couldn't stop crying. I really didn't want to.
I wanted to be joyful with my man. And a soldier's daughter never
cries!

Maybe it was just that women cry easily, especially at weddings.
My mother always did.

G.T.'s mother wasn't here, either. We were on our own.

After the ceremony, more friends stopped by. We all had lunch
together. In the middle of the broiled fish and champagne, Lena
made her entrance with a dead snake in her hand. I screamed.
Lena was ecstatic, but G.T. took me in his arms and fed me champagne. We laughed, and in the afternoon we made love while Lena
and Kris were playing on the beach, and it didn't matter that the
sun never broke through the mist.

It is the only wedding of mine that I remember clearly, the only
wedding where both the woman and the actress were present.

Ten years later, Lena married in the house on 95th Street on the
last day of the old year.

"I want anemones all over the house," she said. We picked

them up, she and I, at six in the morning on 9th Street. Through the lush colors of the flowers, the candles were flickering in the cold winter night. The snow lay like an enormous wedding cake on the round garden table, outside the window of the dining room, where the ceremony took place.

I had just turned forty-five myself.

"Happiest of all is that her gentle spirit commits itself to yours, as to her lord, her governor, her king."

She was getting married to Marty, a director. They had fallen in love the summer before up in the Berkshires where G.T. and I were running a theater festival. We are a growing theatrical family, the way I always wanted. Kris is an actor. John is here this time, too. We are all together, the whole Tabori family. John and Kris are reading a poem together, and I am doing Portia's love speech to Bassanio from *The Merchant of Venice.* "Myself and what is mine to you and yours is now converted. I give them thee with this ring."

I had done the play during the summer in the Berkshires the year before in a production directed by G.T. I used to think of him and our wedding on the beach. On the stage I am always total and giving. It is not true, always, in life. But I want to change the pattern.

Lena never took her eyes off Marty during the entire ceremony. Not once. I loved it. Yes. Only why doesn't G.T. look at me tonight? He looks at Lena only.

"I'm in love with Lena," G.T. used to say when she was becoming a woman, when she was twelve, going on thirteen. I couldn't blame him. I had seen her taking a bath one day and saw her breasts. They had suddenly become like hills and valleys. She was beautiful. *Lolita* was popular, and G.T. was a writer with a rich fantasy life.

G.T. had staged the entire ceremony. She had asked him to. I felt left out. Of what? The trust between them? But I always wanted that for the two of them, the way I'd had it with my father. Was that true? Yes! But up to a point only.

When I was twelve, going on thirteen, when we moved to Lidingo, when I was becoming a woman, I started to avoid my father. What happened?

I used to sneak up the kitchen stairs so as not to have to say good night, not to have to feel his lips against my chin. "Viveca," he would call out. I was caught. I had to go into his bedroom and answer sullenly his questions, receiving unwillingly his kiss on my cheek. No doubt, he loved me. No doubt, I loved him. What was I so afraid of? He always accepted everything I did. He was the first, almost the only man who has done that. It was he who taught me to affirm the vitality of life, and, without his image of joy and strength, I might have drowned like my brother, or become a cripple like my mother. What was I so afraid of? That he would treat me like my mother or that he would find out that I was like her after all?

I used to hear my mother cry at night. My father had mistresses now. I took his side. I didn't want to identify with her, the victim. I would rather be the mistress.

I had just met my first boyfriend. "You have stars in your eyes," he said. It was a snowy night on top of a hill.

"You don't have to leave your father in order to have a lover," someone said. But for me it was always either/or. It got all screwed up. Damn it. I wish I could have moved on gently.

G.T. and Lena are still very close.

Am I jealous of my daughter? She looks exquisite tonight, dressed in black and white cotton and a red veil over her shiny, long, straight hair, colors of purity and sin and passion. I was dressed in gray again, this time glittering gray, my hair short and curly and Clairol-formula brown with a dash of ginger hiding the gray. Maybe the dye went into my bloodstream; I felt poisoned. Lena's hair was pure chestnut brown like her father's. To be jealous of my daughter? I knew by now it wasn't too corny to be true.

I had coped badly when I discovered that men were finding Lena as attractive as me, or even more so. Yulin was a brilliant and although not so young, yet younger than me, actor. We had a marvelous time working with each other, and he turned me on sexually. It soon became clear that he preferred Lena as a woman. They fell in love. One night, I don't remember what she said, only that I felt she was showing off about him. She was on her way to see him. I hit her in fury. Did she not know that I had liked him, too? Probably not. It was probably far from her imagination. She probably just wanted to share her joy of love with me, her mother. I was stunned by my own fury, by my own behavior—as stunned as she was. In self-defense she laughed. She is proud, my daughter, like me. I ought to have taken her in my arms, kissed her, and asked her forgiveness.

Was I jealous of her youth? Am I still? No, no, no, not her youth, but the hope she feels. That's what I am jealous of. And the way she looks at Marty. The way Marty looks at her. The way G.T. and I used to look at each other. Something has changed.

There were all those young girls around him that summer in Stockbridge. One of them, a redhead, too much in need of a father, the age of Lena, was around G.T. a lot, assisting him, doing research for him. I can't blame him for maybe having a fling with her, I thought to myself, not for a moment allowing myself to feel threatened by the competition. "I am too wrapped up in my work to bother about it!" I thought to myself. I wasn't even jealous when I found the slip from a motel in the Berkshires. There was only one reason why G.T. would go to a motel in the Berkshires.

I paid little attention. I too had had love affairs and it hadn't interfered with the marriage. Not really. I didn't for a moment believe it would for G.T. either. Was that true? Or did I take it out on Lena instead of confronting him about our darkness? That was unfair. It was simple, safer with my daughter. She would never leave me; did I think he would?

My father never left my mother. Only death did do them apart. In spite of the mistresses.

One of them was my age when I went to the Royal Dramatic Theater School, same age as Lena now. She mentioned his name over and over again and looked at me in a peculiar way. I hated it; I hated her. I wanted to tell her, "He's mine. Lay off him."

My what? My father or my husband? Confusion! Damn it. It got all screwed up.

I said nothing to her or to my father or my mother. I avoided it all. The fear of being replaced, the fear of feeling I have no rights. I avoided them, too. Thank God I found my way back to my mother before it was too late. But not to my father. I avoided him forever. Even in the moment of his death.

I realized the loss for the first time that day in Stockholm when I took the trip into my past . . . when I walked into the building where I had lived as a child. When I got to the top floor and I saw the door to the attic. I remembered I used to go there with my father. He would open it with a big key. Then we would wander up the old, cold stone steps. It was scary. There were the strange smells from air not let out for months, air from summer, air from winter, air from fall, air from spring, and thin streams of light coming through in a few places. It was scary, but not when I put my hand in his. In the winter we looked for the sled; in the summer, for the bicycle.

I never talked to G.T. about my father. G.T. never talked to me about his, either, or about his need for revenge, the fury, the anxiety, that must have choked him about the killers, the Nazis. He finally dealt with it; he wrote *Cannibals,* the first play where there was no part for me, no parts for women, only for men and about violence and a dark, winding road in search of hope, in search of a father, in search of dignity and hope in the face of ugliness and death.

He never knew the details of his father's death. He could only fantasize. Now Berlin wanted the play. It seemed too far-fetched to believe. G.T. never wanted to put his foot in Germany.

"Will you go?"

"Yes."

The road back to those we love is long and winding. No one can live with hate or fear. We had more in common than we knew . . . wanted to know . . .

Lena was planning to go to the opening, to be with Marty. He had directed the play in New York and was doing it in Berlin also.

Would *I* go?

If there is time, if I can, because of my work.

If I can find it in myself, don't know if I can share his dark, winding road, don't know if my road goes hand in hand with his.

I am feeling G.T.'s right arm crossing my left. I am holding Lena's right shoulder with my left hand and Marty's with my right. G.T. is holding Marty's shoulder with his right hand and Lena's with his left.

As part of the ceremony, we, their friends and family, lifted them, rocked them, lifted them again, way up high so that they could touch the stars. I want everything gray behind me. I want to use my experiences only in order to be stronger, better, wiser. A woman—a total woman.

I see Kristoffer, blond and serious. I see John, too. My father used to talk about family ties. I understood him now . . .

George is standing next to me . . . we need to be rocked, too . . . lifted and rocked . . . I don't want to be sophisticated any longer, Georgie . . . So we have been married for more than fifteen years . . . So we have been angry with each other . . . So we have had lovers . . . but I don't want to be sophisticated, Georgie . . . I don't want to . . . I just don't know any other way to deal with it sometimes, but I don't like it . . . I am hungry for you, for us . . . I want to love you in a new way . . . Just exist with you, live and let live . . . Joyfully . . . Do you? Silent conversations, words never spoken, questions never asked, answers never receievd . . . not yet . . .

Gently, gently, G.T. and I, side by side, ever so gently lowered them down to the ground. There was only a thin, cork floor between them and the ground in the garden room, between us and the ground, between the stars and the earth, with the snow outside, and the candles flickering in spite of the cold, the wind, the snow. Only why don't we look at each other tonight the way we did once? Something has changed. Something is in the way. Anger? Whose? Mine or his?

4

It still haunts me that I had been so careless or unaware of my father's death. He loved me, I loved him!

I was his favorite, yet I avoided him even in the last moments of his life as if I didn't want to grasp that he might die and I would have to face him as his daughter, simply as his daughter, with the love and the hate and the fears and the joys that involves.

My father died a few years after my brother. He drowned in his own saliva. The medical term is emphysema. He had waited for me; I knew it. I had said I would come that weekend, on my way to Madrid where I was to make a film, but I got delayed, and death has no patience with film stars with their changing schedules or daughters who are unaware of their love for their fathers. I arrived in Stockholm a day too late.

I was wild that spring. I didn't even "hear" that my father was ill. I had lost my womb in January. I had caught a glimpse of my own death and couldn't cope with anybody else's. My best friend Sophie had died of cancer.

I only wanted to know about life. Once I regained my strength after the operation I threw myself into rehearsal, wanting to live more than ever, as a woman, above all as an actress.

The play was *Brouhaha*. G.T. had done it in London with Peter Sellers the summer before. He rewrote the part for a woman, for me. And although I kept receiving letters from home: "Father is ill. Try and come," I ignored them. How could I leave now? And what if we were a hit?

We were not. The reviews were awful. We opened and closed in a week. The public relations man, as usual, had them read over the phone, this time in our dining room on the first floor. His face made it clear: thumbs down.

By now, everybody in the cast had gone home. There were empty wine bottles and glasses all over the place. There were just a few of us left. The director's wife started to cry. It was obvious

225

we were closing that following weekend. For G.T. it meant, once more, years of work down the drain. For me, the actress, it meant not to be allowed to function on the stage.

The scene had repeated itself. "How many times?" I asked myself. G.T. must have asked himself the same, but we didn't hold each other that night the way we had on his first opening night, in front of the mantelpiece in the dining room on 71st Street . . . years ago . . . nor did I get on the plane to Stockholm the day after closing night, a week later, to hold my father's hand. I was too exhausted, too devastated. Failure meant weakness, like illness.

I hadn't told my father about my hysterectomy. My mother had lost her womb when she gave birth to the baby boy, her fourth child, that could have been my partner. Did she lose her sensuality too? Would I? Is that why my father took mistresses? I could hear her cry at night. I never asked him; he never told me.

Besides, there were other questions at the time, seemingly more real, like: How de we eat tomorrow?

Miraculously, my agent called me two days after the opening later and offered me a part in the film *Jesus Christ*, to be made in Madrid.

I cabled home that I would stop in Stockholm on my way over, but I caught a cold and went straight to Madrid, planning to see my father the following weekend instead.

My first evening in Madrid was marvelous. In no time I reverted to the life of a film star with limousines and luxurious suites at the Hilton Hotel. In no time I washed off all sense of failure, worries, dirty dishes, homework, cleaning up after dogs and cats, and struggles and useless efforts and bad reviews, operations, and fears. But death had its own schedule. In the early morning, as I happily wandered into my room, I found a yellow cable from Western Union. "Father is dying. Come home."

My sister met me at the airport in Stockholm. She rushed toward me, white in the face. "Poor Viveca; it's too late." She was crying. I felt a sting of resentment. I was the one who missed out seeing him. I was the one who wanted to cry.

"He called me that same afternoon that you were supposed to arrive from New York. 'Come over,' he said. 'I need you,' " my sister Marga was telling me, years later. She had been there.

"He wanted to take a ride around the city. He loved Stockholm, as you know. In the early evening he went to bed. I thought he had fallen asleep. I sat in the living room. When I suddenly heard the bed squeal something terrible, I went in as quietly as I could. I saw him sit up in the bed, holding onto the sides of it, struggling to breathe. I sat myself down on a small chair by the doorway, very quietly, for I knew he wanted to die alone. He had told me that many times. But I was also afraid to leave him. When I shifted my leg and the chair squeaked, he discovered me. He couldn't speak. With enormous intensity and dignity, like a king, he pointed to the door, indicating that I must leave. I did. I sat in the living room. After a few hours it suddenly became very quiet. I went to tell mother. She was deaf, as you know. I had to yell in her ear, 'Father has died. Father is dead.' "

As I listened to my sister, even now I dared not even ask her if he had inquired about me, for I should have been at his side and my mother's, too. I knew it now, when it was too late. It wasn't that I had been replaced. I had chosen not to be there. I was in Madrid, drinking champagne, listening to the gypsies sing.

"Why do I cry so much?" I asked my analyst years later. Yes, I was finally in analysis. "Tears withheld are like old wine in bottles. If not aired they explode." "What about words, feelings, thought?" "Yes, it's the same. It's all the same." "Yes, yes, yes."

But I couldn't cry. Not then. Not that day.

We were at the cemetery in Stockholm at the family grave, where my brother was buried inside the deathhouse.

"Viveca, go see him alone," my mother said to me. She was dressed in black and heavily veiled. "You haven't seen him yet," she said. There was no disapproval in my mother's voice, only sadness.

My mother was alone now. It didn't seem to matter. Nor that my father had not asked her to share his last moments with him. It was obvious that she had accepted and understood that he wanted to die as he had wanted to live—his own way. That she was his woman, and, like Strindberg's Alice, she knew she must have loved that man.

And I?

I stood in front of my father's body. I was cold, shivering. I stood there for half an hour and yet I wasn't there at all, only my body. I felt nothing. I couldn't cry! I hated myself for pretending I wanted to. How insane. There was no one there to watch me. I was free to feel anything: joy, pain, love, hate—but I felt as if I were in a prison, stifled, turned off, as if I had to live up to a role. Which one?

"What they call depression today, we thought of as lack of courage in my time," my father wrote in the introduction to a book of his poems. He was a man of a certain generation, and he might not have understood then why I went into analysis, but had I been able to explain to him that it was in order to give up all masks, all myths, even to find my love for him again, he might have grasped it, for he was a man who wanted to say yes to life.

I think today that the fear of real intimacy, where all risks are taken, is what made me avoid my father, even in his moments of death. For in those last moments of life there is no room for sophistication or hypocrisy or games or role-playing. But I wasn't ready for the bareness yet. My only chance now to meet my father is in other men.

Or in myself.

5

"I want to see you," Lee Strasberg said one day at the Studio. I was working on a scene with Anne Bancroft called *The Stronger*. A speeded-up tape-like dialogue flashed through my head. "Me?" "Yes, you." "Me or her?" "It's the same." "No. I'm an actress. I can choose my own character. I don't have to be me." "No, no, no. You have got to be there all the time, Viveca, guiding, choosing the route. Without you there is no character on the stage. I must see you, *and* her." Help!

A fairy tale told me as a child about boys and girls going down into the water: as they emerged, black spots appeared on their naked bodies for each lie they had told. When the last two girls emerged, one was all white but the other had a large black spot. She was caught! Secrets were revealed! Lies! Now, Lee wants to see her! Help! Daddy! Help!

It was a common phenomenon, making Lee the daddy-figure. But he would have none of it. He barely noticed you outside the sessions, but then he was there only for you, involved only in you and your talent. It felt marvelous. Nobody had ever taken you seriously like that; not even Daddy, who used to pick you up and kiss away your tears. Lee was interested in my tears, too, but only for the work. "Tears are an actor's gold mine," he would say. But I wasn't ready to separate professional intimacy from personal intimacy. It was too threatening. The work had opened up areas within me that were hidden, secret, fragile, revealing a little girl with a black spot. I was not ready for that! Not yet!

The Stronger by August Strindberg. What an appropriate play for me to be working on. "If I am strong, you are weak," and vice versa—the constantly repeated theme in his plays, in his life, too. The seesaw game played in my family, between me and G.T. and now between me and Annie. Or was it just me? It didn't seem to bother her.

The Stronger: a twenty-five-minute one-act play. Place: a cafe. Time: mid-morning Christmas Eve.

Two actresses meet. One is married. One is not. One is a mother. The other is not. Both are in love with the same man, the husband. Annie played the mistress, Miss X; I, the wife, Madame Y. I was married; she was not. I was a mother; she was not. In the play, the wife talks. The mistress is silent. She seems so much more interesting, more mysterious. Wrong! "You are silent because you have nothing to say," the wife tells her. The wife is often performed as chatty, but then talk coming from a woman is often labeled "chatty."

I wanted the opposite. I wanted my wife to talk in order to break the spasm of tension between them, in order to open up the secret. All secrets! I wanted her cockiness, covering her fears, to vanish and turn into courage once she broke through the lies and dared to discover the truth. I wanted my wife to face panic, hate, tears, fury, screams, fears, and, out of the disaster, to become marvelous, strong, spirited, even have a sense of humor.

I had worked out her scenario. The husband and she had made love to each other that morning. It had been better than in a long time, better than ever. Afterwards, the kids had crawled into bed with them and they all had breakfast together! Those were the best times in *my* home life with G.T. Love, family, and work! All one thing! Together!

"I will never give him up. Never, never," the wife says earlier in the scene to the mistress. I loved that line. (I, who had left three husbands. The fourth one hadn't left me yet.)

I knew I wasn't fabricating something. I had read a letter from Strindberg to Siri Von Essen, the actress who was to play the wife in *The Stronger*, also his wife in real life, when it was first performed in Denmark. "Play her that she is the stronger," the letter states. "The softer one bends and rises again, the harder one bends and breaks." Madame Y's last line to the mistress is: "Thank you for teaching him how to love. I am going home now to love him."

He had his own reasons for wanting her to forgive him. He had had an affair with a young Danish girl, and her father sued him. Siri stood up and testified on his behalf in the courtroom. Their

marriage didn't survive anyway. Did Strindberg not know how to
bend? It takes two, and Strindberg's women didn't know that, although they might have felt it. But it is not enough. You have to
act upon it or you don't believe it.

A richer ending *is* possible for the scene today, for both women
to become "the stronger" through facing a truth that has lain like
a rotting boil between them. A beginning of self-knowledge, of
sisterhood, not for a moment robbing the scene of human qualities.

It had been a turbulent session at The Studio, but a good one.
Funny too. There was no reason for me to panic. It wasn't that I
didn't know how to work, but something had interfered. Something I had no control over! Patterns, patterns!

I knew I was in trouble already in the morning when I was getting dressed for the scene at the Studio. The kids were off to
school. There was nothing to stop me from getting ready. I couldn't
make up my mind about how to look. I tried on one outfit after
another until I was exasperated and wanted less and less to be
beautiful, or gutsy. Christ, Viveca, I said to myself. You decided
to make her gorgeous, sexy, vital, curly hair, high heels, hunting
for love with the man she's married to. Not plain! And no self-
pity, no defeatism! Come on, Viveca. Stick to the concept.

Arriving at the Studio in time, I bumped into Annie. God, did
she look together!!

I was nervous, shaking down in the stomach, where I still had
my uterus. "Nervousness is a tremendous source of energy. Use
it," Lee would say.

Oh yes, one part of me understood. But another didn't. She
couldn't think. She was in a panic.

"The difference between a great actress and a good one is that
the great actress has humor," Orson Welles said to me one day. I
was doing Cordelia to his Lear. Brecht calls it objectivity. It's all
the same. It is also the sign of a mature person. Orson talked about
himself, of course, and so did Brecht. They knew, like me, but
couldn't always cope, like me, afraid of admitting weakness, like
me. The morning after the opening night of *King Lear*, the reviews
came out and were devastating. Orson Welles went so far in his
fear of facing his fragility that he decided to break both his ankles.
Did he really? The truth only he and his doctor know. He arrived
at the theater Sunday evening in an ambulance, both legs in casts.
He insisted on canceling the performance and appearing alone, in a
wheelchair, for those who didn't return their tickets, reading the

Bible. Orson Welles! The great, the daring, the brilliant. Fragility, thy name is man, too! His objectivity, his humor went out the window. Just as mine did, over and over again. "You don't know how to work," he had said to me another day. He was right—also about himself. It's a slow process. Maybe never-ending.

The production could have been great, but wasn't quite. Too bad, for his concept was gigantic.

We performed *Lear* again the following night. Orson arrived at the theater in an ambulance, his legs in casts, playing his Lear in a wheelchair, which he continued to do all through the run. His performance improved extraordinarily, as if confinement forced him to use a deeper, more private part of himself and give up the image of the giant Welles.

What he had thought of as weakness turned into strength. It wasn't that he didn't know how to work. Something had interfered!

It was my suggestion to have a fist fight with Annie in *The Stronger* that morning at the Studio. "I love it," she said, with a glint in her eyes. I had forgotten that she was in one every night on stage in *The Miracle Worker*. She knew every trick in the book. She was in tip-top shape as a fighter. I brought an umbrella, the suffragette's weapon to the performance. Symbolic, I thought, and funny! I struck her, *lightly!* (After all, I am an actress.) The next second I found myself lying on the floor. What happened to the symbolic weapon? Don't know! Lost it! In a flash of a second, Annie had grabbed my hair. I immediately sank to the floor. It was a perfect choice, a funny one, too. If only I hadn't felt that I copped out on fighting for what was mine. Couldn't see that having a fist fight with Annie was good whether I won or not, as long as I functioned fully.

While all this was going on, Madeleine Sherwood, who was the waitress serving us chocolate, struck out at Annie in my defense. They got into a fight! Neither of them gave up an inch. Finally, Lee interfered for the scene to continue. It was a wild session, and all through it I stayed on the floor sobbing. A terrific choice!

"Tears are an actor's gold mine," Lee used to say. But my father had told me, "A soldier's daughter never cries."

I was bitterly complaining after the session to Mendy Wager, an actor friend from the Studio. We were having lunch at the greasy spoon. "What's the mater with you, Viveca? So you didn't win the fight. How could you, with Annie? But you made a terrific adjustment."

"My goddamn tears became my only tool. I have others. They disappeared. 'A great actress accomplishes the tasks she has set for herself,' Lee says. I want that! I copped out on my own strength, Mendy," I cried out, choking on a piece of toast. "And it isn't the first time."

"I see," Mendy over the pea soup. "If you want to break a pattern and you can't yourself, you have to go to the shrink!"

Annie went to the shrink. Every day. She coped better than I. She made choices quickly and clearly, and she did not get into a panic even if her choice turned out not to be the right one. She had a sense of her own worth. I had lost mine.

The stronger she seemed to become, the weaker I got. There was only either/or. The seesaw game!

It was obvious what had happened that day. Annie became my sister—the stronger, the good one—and I, the weaker, the bad one! Lee became the daddy-figure, the judge. The stage, an arena for survival instead of a place for creativity. I couldn't get out of the war that had begun way back in time in my family when my only defense was to withdraw, to become the victim, like my mother.

"Once I give in to her, that goddamned suffering child-woman, she won't let me go," I mumbled to Mendy, for I was sick and tired of the child-woman. But child-woman did not care, for as long as I dared not face her, even embrace her, she was in control. I was her prisoner; she was my jailer.

"I want to see you," Lee had said. He meant the whole of me! I wanted it too, now. I went into analysis.

Should analysis be part of an actor's training as a way of improving his craft? Why not? The actor is a mirror of life.

I am my own instrument. My inner life, my emotions, my experiences, my past, my will power, my soul, my body, my voice are my violin. I am millions of tones, millions of nuances, and I must know them all, accept them all. How else can I use them? Anything unresolved, unclear, will muddle the tone.

It is no accident that so many actors today seek analysis. Life in the American theater is often brutal and fierce. It competes with European theater and its artists without being given the same care and financial support, meaning love—for love is also money. It is tough, for the theater in America is still treated as a charity case, feeding itself from leftovers from the rich man's table.

The actor is part of the system. Unemployment is high. Employment is insecure. Pay is low, sometimes even nonexistent. "To be or not to be" means to eat or not to eat. Under those conditions, it is difficult for the actor to function, and analysis helps him cope, helps him protect the creative impulses.

"How do I find the right shrink?" I said to Mendy that morning over the pea soup, after the session at the Studio. "Besides, I am broke, as usual."

"Everybody who needs analysis is broke," Mendy said with a laugh. "When you're ready, you'll find one."

I had forgotten all about the analyst who told me that first summer with G.T., "You have had three marriages; the fourth one won't work either unless you straighten yourself out." It had surprised me that I had cried all through the session. I wasn't ready then; I was now.

A few weeks later I ran into one! I had been asked to be part of David Susskind's show, "Happy Marriages." Ironic, since I was on my fourth. We were an astonishing group. Artie Shaw, married five times. An Indian woman, a writer, married once (since then, divorced). She told us an Indian custom. When the wife has a lover, she puts her shoes outside the bedroom door so as not to be disturbed. It is respected! Jules Feiffer was newlywed. (He is no longer married to her but remarried to another lady.) Then there was the psychoanalyst, Harold Greenwald, married once and forever (so far). Ruth, his wife, is a fabulous lady. We became great friends. I kept talking about wanting to be close to my man, illustrating it by pressing my palms together. Greenwald moved them gently apart. "There must be space in between," he said, "in order for the flow, in order to be able to breathe." It was a live show, in front of millions of people. I was moved. He made me aware of something I wanted deeply.

We went out for drinks afterwards. "I need help," I said.

"Come and see me," he said.

I did. Again, I astonished myself by crying bitterly like a child over my marriage, my life, my career. Why? It wasn't all that bad. It was puzzling. Greenwald listened warmly. He suggested I see a woman, Madame E.

I did. I fell, exhausted, on a sofa with white dowels so like my childhood bed, in the quiet room overlooking Washington Square, with Madame, my French female analyst, sitting by the window, an old quilt over her legs, listening to me. Listening, listening. To my tears, too. I couldn't stop crying now when someone was listening.

I learned that life is not a fight. That I don't have to be the stronger or the weaker. That there is something in between—the middle ground.

I learned that I can let go. That I can be who I am. That I can't be who I am. That I can be part of the universe. That I can't be part of the universe. That it cannot go on without me. That it can go on without me. That I can go on without it. That I can't go on without it. That I love my father and that I hate him, too, but I can still love him. Reality makes it possible.

That George can't live without me. That George can live without me. That I can live without him. That I can't live without him. That I can live without the children, and they without me. That I can't live without the children, and they can't without me. That . . .

That I can make choices about myself. That I can't make choices about myself. But that I can make choices about myself. *That* is what I learned.

That I can change k to c without giving up of myself. That I did change k to c and gave up of myself. But not totally. *That* is what I learned.

Analysis is like the movement of birth, the movement of life. Exhilaration, pain, wonder, quietness, tenderness, thinking, remembering, understanding, fury, nothingness, stillness, waiting, awareness, denial, defeat, loss of awareness, movements, hope. Forwards. Backwards. Forwards backwards forwards. Sometimes noticeable. Sometimes not. Waiting, waiting, waiting. Strength, weakness, anger, lies, tears. Lots of tears. Waiting. Nothing. Thinking. Waiting. Movements. Hope. Understanding. Forwards. Backwards. Forwards, backwards, forwards, hope. Each time an extra inch, like the movement of birth; hoping birth may come, and it will come . . . hope will come, defeat or not, black spots or not.

I don't know if I will ever be finished with analysis. What does that mean, "to be finished"? I only know that it doesn't hurt so much anymore. I am even joyful. And I find it continually interesting, this exploration of self, and therefore of "you," for I can see and hear others better now.

Analysis paid off almost immediately as far as my work was concerned. I began to take the initiative. "You can do it," Madame said.

I began to believe it.

"Let's do something together," I said. We were having lunch, a whole bunch of us, after a session, at the greasy spoon.

There was a gentleman from South America visiting. "Come to South America," he said.

"Yes, why not? Let's form a group and go."

Tad Danielewski became the natural leader. It wouldn't have

occurred to me at the time to assume part of that position, nor would it have mattered, for Tad, quite naturally and beautifully, shared it with me.

We called ourselves The New York Company. We were Betty Field, Ben Piazza, Morgan Stern, Rita Gam, and myself. We did three evenings: *The Zoo Story/Miss Julie*, a play by John Van Druten, and an evening of Tennessee Williams. Ben Piazza and I did scenes from *Sweet Bird of Youth*. Alexandra del Lago became my favorite part. I felt dangerously connected to her. Dangerously, for I still dared not take the risks she does in spite of her defeats!

Our program was very ambitious. We were the first English-speaking company ever to visit Buenos Aires and we were a success. Yet I was still unaware of our accomplishment, above all about my own contribution as an actress.

As usual, I had trouble coping with competition. Rita Gam was more assertive than I. Tad confronted me one night. "What's the matter with you, Viveca?"

"I'm no good, Tad. They love her more than me."

"You're crazy," he said. "You're a great actress. Don't ever compare yourself with Rita or anybody else."

Tad was not only a friend but also a brilliant director.

He reached for the moon and he got the shows on. And at times we did reach the moon.

On top of that he had organized a deal to do *No Exit* as a film. We shot it in a studio outside Buenos Aires during the day while playing at night. We got little sleep and no pay. It didn't matter.

When I saw my rushes, I knew that the work at the Studio had paid off. The film opened in New York during the newspaper strike and received no reviews. It died a quick death, and there was no one there to pick up the pieces (and in those days I had little initiative in that direction). But we won the Silver Bear in Berlin. And a small distribution company, Brandon Films, got hold of a print. Every single university that I have gone to has played *No Exit*. It never seems to go out of style. Who picked up the check?

After four weeks of filming and performing in Buenos Aires, we continued the tour. When school was over, the family joined me in Rio De Janeiro. I had learned my lesson!

I don't know what all this traveling did for G.T.'s writing. Did he put his work second? He never spoke about it, but now, when I write myself, I find moving around impossible.

We lived in a hotel overlooking the ocean and we walked on the beach and breathed salted air filled with music. People were gallant and graceful, and you live only one life.

Our last stop was Mexico City. We played in an old, beautiful theater where you could be heard whispering. The reviews were glorious, the houses filled, flowers, and, again, grace all around me.

The South American tour was my first taste in taking the initiative as an actress. *Brecht on Brecht* became the next!

<h1 style="text-align:center">6</h1>

Brecht on Brecht became G.T.'s and my first independent venture of importance together. "Here is something for you to work on at the Studio." G.T. handed me a couple of pages: *The Jewish Wife,* a twenty-five-minute scene from the play, *The Rise and Fall of the Master Race* by Bertolt Brecht, so complete it makes a one-act play in itself, a hair-raising account of the power of corruption. How the need for survival makes you sell not only your soul but also your wife. "I can't talk when I look at you," she says, the Jewish wife, to her Aryan husband, explaining why she has to leave him and Nazi Germany.

I had never worked on Brecht's writing before. I barely knew about him. It was a tremendous discovery for me. After a couple of sessions at the Studio I knew I must play it. I went to Lucille Lortel, who ran the ANTA matinee series at the Theatre De Lys.

"What do you want to do along with it?" she said, needing a two-hour performance.

"It's up to you," I said.

"Why don't you ask G.T. to put together some songs, poems, scenes," she said, being creative about it. It was a fabulous idea way ahead of its time. Those kinds of evenings were rarely done.

G.T. immediately took to it. "I'll call Lotte and I'll ask her to sing, and maybe Annie (Jackson) and Eli (Wallach) would like to read some poetry," he said. Everybody said yes immediately. Everybody always said yes to G.T.

I was teaching for Gene Frankel at the time. We asked him to direct, and Wolfgang Roth, a brilliant stage designer who worked with Brecht in Berlin as a young man, to design our set.

Bertha Case, Brecht's agent, called G.T. one evening. "Come over and listen to a tape," she said, "from B.B.'s testimony at the Un-American Activities Committee investigation in Washington. It might just be what you want for the evening." She was right.

Four weeks later we performed *Brecht on Brecht*. It was magic every evening when Brecht, in his croaking, German-accented voice, introduced himself: "My name is Bertolt Brecht. I am living at 36 West 10th, 1898 . . . eh, eh, eh, 89." The bastards made him nervous. He got mixed up about his own birthdate. "What got me at last, mediocrity," he said in one of his poems.

The effect was chilling and wonderful. We were six actors sitting on the stage on high stools. There was a large picture of Brecht hanging behind us.

"He always had love affairs with his actresses," Lotte told me one day. "He would have had one with you," she added dryly. One evening I came to the theater looking glamorous.

"Would Brecht have liked me tonight?" I said to Lotte.

"No," she said. Nobody can say no like Lotte Lenya.

"Why?" I dared to ask her.

"I'll tell you a story," she said. "Brecht was having an affair with a well-known actress at the Deutsches Teatre. She was very glamorous. One week after the affair she looked like all his other women—plain!"

I never met Brecht. He died in 1956. But I met Helena Weigel, his widow. She became the Artistic Director of the Berliner Ensemble, their theater, after his death. Somehow their infidelities— and I hope she had lovers, too, although I hope she didn't try to change their looks, but let them be as they were—did not interfere with their cause. I saw it with my own eyes.

I was fortunate to be invited to the Brecht Dialogue, 1968, in East Berlin. People from all over the world came for a week to see their theater, to learn, to listen. It was a glorious experience, an inspiration for both G.T. and me. "In our new theater, we shall at last act according to the classic principle: change the world, it needs it." This rang in my ears as we walked home through a dark East Berlin after the last performance.

Yes, the cause held them together.

Did it split us up? In work you can't lie? It wasn't that we lacked opportunities.

It became obvious the moment Lucille announced *Brecht on Brecht* that we were a hot ticket. The box office phones started to ring. She quickly scheduled a second performance. Then Clive Barnes gave us a rave review. The Theatre De Lys was available. Lucille was willing to give us a break. She suggested we talk to Cheryl Crawford, the producer. She immediately agreed and all rights reverted to her. Since the show had already been produced by us, we could have either co-produced it or perhaps even produced it totally on our own. It still didn't occur to any of us, not yet. Cheryl, however, is a first-rate producer and did a superb job.

We all took the same salary, minimum Off-Broadway. (Less than the stagehands. We had three move the six stools during intermission. We only needed one.) However, all the actors received a percentage, and if the week was a hot one we sometimes made up to $300 a week. It didn't make any of us rich. I didn't care. I went to the theater every night. I was on stage every night. We were a hit, and G.T. and I were doing it together. Everything was suddenly within reach, and this time our success had come with very little effort. We brought each other good luck!

London wanted us. An American-born female producer cabled us. "I want to bring the whole package of B-B over . . . Love . . ."

"How fabulous, Georgie. You always wanted us to live in London. Maybe this is a beginning. We are a team now. We are coming on strong with our own show, 'Made in the U.S.A.' "

"Let me put my agent on it," Georgie said. I had funny feelings in my stomach. I never did like his agent. Even more so, I didn't think he liked me.

Letters, cables, talks. "They think we should do it at the Royal Court, instead. George Devine loves the show. It's really classier, I think," G.T. said one day.

"I see." I continued to feel peculiar.

The next week, the agent came from London to see the show. The agent said nothing after the performance. Didn't he like me? He was British and they don't like accents—only their own.

My fears were confirmed. I was soon informed that Lotte was going to London, not I; that G.T. was going to London, not I. It was to be a British production starring Lotte Lenya, under the direction of George Devine and George Tabori.

I was furious. Suddenly I, who had started this project, had no say. I had given up my power on paper, for I was married to the man who was in power. On paper. Only.

"Lotte doesn't want to come if you're part of the production," was the explanation given me. "She wants to be the one and only."

"Yes? Lotte? Lotte is going to do *The Jewish Wife?* Does she have all that say?"

"Yes. They don't want to do the production unless Lotte is in it."

Even now, fifteen years later, thinking about it, I see red. I wish I had *then*. And screamed! I didn't. Finally, I managed to confront Lotte. She came to the house. She and G.T. and I sat in the living room. "Is it true that you don't want to go to London if I am part of the production?"

"That's right, Viveca. It's either me or you. If you want to go, I'll stay home, please," she said in her broken English.

"But they want you, Lotte. They don't do it if you are not part of the production. So, it means I don't go, right?"

"Right," she said.

I looked at her. She looked at me.

Lotte Lenya, that strange, ugly, sometimes bitter, sometimes wonderful woman whom I had been working with for months down at the De Lys, sharing a dressing room night after night, sharing magic moments on the stage. Lotte, whom I thought had our interests at heart, made it quite clear that she felt no comradeship. Like Mother Courage, perhaps, her life had been too tough.

But then I copped out, too, that day in our living room. I should have said to G.T., "Georgie, you're the writer, the co-director. You've got the power to say, 'I could never go to London without Viveca!' And Georgie . . . if they don't like it, fuck it all. . . . We can have our own production any place, any time. We know it now! Who needs London at such a price?"

But I didn't. And he didn't. And the anger grew. It didn't help much that the production in London was a flop and closed within a few weeks.

It did help some that I stayed with the show, and I could let go of my fury on stage, especially when I knew that G.T. was standing in the back of the house. He must have known I was talking to him when I cried out, "Let's not talk about misfortune, let's talk about shame!" But, like the Jewish Wife, I couldn't tell it to him straight and *that* didn't help. Like her, I was afraid of the answer.

It didn't help either that G.T.'s attitude was masked as impatience. "Why don't you stop holding a grudge against me?" It would be years before he could admit the betrayal, or that I would insist on airing it, which was my betrayal. It was too horrendous for someone whose father was killed by the Nazis and had done nothing about it yet. It was too horrendous for someone who had ignored her father when he was dying and had done nothing about it yet.

Journeys, journeys.

We were at a standstill in the marriage, G.T. and I, and I could think of only one way to get through the mud! Oh, there might have been some need of revenge behind it, giving it back to him the old way, the female way. It seemed safer than breaking through sound barriers. At this point all I could think of was to live! Be joyful with a man! Not be depressed! Survive! I had learned my lesson.

Cancer, the sickness of the discouraged, someone said.

A year or so after our wedding on the beach, I remember a feeling . . . it struck me like a sledgehammer . . . I have no right to live . . . I buckled under, leaning against our bed. Two months later, I was in the doctor's office.

"If discovered early, it is not fatal. You are a young woman. You must be saved," the doctor said. I barely heard him. "We have booked a room for you tomorrow morning for a biopsy. Let me explain to you about the operation. I will show you some pictures." He did. I was in his office on Park Avenue. The leather chair was soft and comfortable. Music was sweeping through the walls from the waiting room and the pictures were beautiful in deep sensual colors. I could see the cancer creeping in to the uterus. Invading it. But I couldn't react. I was in a fog.

Had I brought it on myself? Was the effort of a fourth marriage too much? Hurting people? Dragging the children from California to New York? Changing fathers once more? G.T. was very romantic, but being a father and a husband is very real. I had begun to withdraw. Here it goes, the same goddamn pattern. Am I getting frigid? Thoughts went through my head like knives. Then there was the struggle of making a living, and, above all, making it as an actress, wanting it with my whole body and soul. Had I taken on too much?

The rain was coming down in buckets as I wandered that day down Lexington Avenue toward home. I was dressed in my brown leather coat. I had had it made by a tailor in a small town in Austria while doing *Four Men in a Jeep*. I had just met G.T. for the first time at the London airport to discuss an outline of his and had wanted to make a deal with him. I wanted to become an independent actress! I fell in love with him instead. And here I was, seven years later, walking down the avenue, the rain mingling with my tears while G.T. was away in Austria making a film with Anatole Litvak, and I might never get done what I wanted to do with my life.

Instead of picking up the phone and telling G.T. I was afraid of dying, as if it were a sign of weakness, I sent him a wire that I was to have minor surgery for a day and not to worry. When he received the wire he thought I was pregnant with another man's child and was having an abortion, he told me later. How incapable we both were. As if our love weren't for real, or couldn't be trusted enough to take the truth.

Damn it! Eighteen years of hide-and-seek eventually destroyed it.

The day after, the doctor called and confirmed. "Cancer cells have been found."

I called G.T. I wasn't so strong anymore. "Come home." He was in the middle of the film. It wasn't easy for him to come, but he did.

The night before the operation we gave a party. After everybody left I sat down and looked at G.T. Questions never asked, never to be answered, went through me like knives. My womb, as the doctor had put it, had fulfilled its function. But like everything else in my body, might it not be used for different reasons at different times, reasons, in spite of our enlightened age, still unknown to us? Was I ready to give up the cycle of menstruation? I liked the swollenness, the heaviness of my body at the end of each month and then the release, the flow, like the cycle of nature dividing up the seasons. And what about my sex life? And what about my nerves and the muscles in my back that had to be cut off? Was it really true that my womb was of no more use? I had dared ask none of those questions. My best friend, Sophie, had died of cancer.

"My God, it's happening to me," I thought. "It's not a film. Will I ever come back?"

G.T. hugged me. I was glad he was there.

Two weeks later I was home again. He carried me up the stairs over the threshold into our bedroom.

The snow was still on the ground. I could see the trees through my window, black and bare, stretching themselves against the winter sky. I started to cry, as if I were in mourning.

It is a proven fact today that sixty percent of all hysterectomies were unnecessary. If mine was, I will never know. It didn't occur to either one of us to go for a second opinion. That was due to ignorance. My womb is gone, like some of my teeth or my brown hair. But I can't replace my womb, nor dye it nor put caps on it. But I can learn to live without it. I must.

I was wild that spring.

On the plane back to Madrid after my father's death, I started to flirt wildly with the man sitting next to me. I felt free, so free. My father could no longer judge me. My womb was down the Hudson River. G.T. was in New York with the children. I could fly again with the wind, be special, fulfill my dreams. Not be defeated like my mother, or stuck. Yes, I had felt stuck with responsibilities toward plays, people, children, husbands, bills, and bad reviews. I was sick and tired of the woman in mourning, of the woman in pain. I wanted to be joyful! I started to fantasize about having lovers. I thought it would never happen between me and G.T.

Robert Ryan was playing John the Baptist. He was dark, serious, unfulfilled, hungry like my brother, like me. We were sitting on the terrace with the deep blue-black Spanish sky above us and dark mountains around us. It might just have happened that night. Then the phone rang.

It was G.T. calling from New York. "Just wanted to tell you I love you," he said.

I laughed. "I know. I do, too." I went back to Ryan. "It was my husband," I said. And I knew nothing would happen that night. Nor did it any other night.

"It's not possible for me to love a married woman," Ryan said later. "I don't want to be responsible for breaking up a marriage."

Perhaps he was talking about himself. A few years later his wife died of cancer, and he followed two years afterwards.

He needn't have worried about me. It became clear, years later, that I never had such intentions. I was through with changing marriages. Maybe I knew it all the time—that it was just a desire to live and love, and I surely had that right.

That fall when I couldn't get over my fury with G.T. for replacing me in *Brecht on Brecht* in London, I wanted a lover! Again! I received an offer to go to Hawaii to do *Hedda Gabler* at the university. Four weeks in Hawaii! The setup was perfect. I handed in my notice at the theater.

Oh yes, I was wild about the part, I wanted to explore it, and, oh yes, we needed money as usual, there were millions of legit reasons to take the job, and, oh yes, when I stepped off the plane and felt the soft embracing silky air of the island caressing me I knew I was in for it. Oh yes.

I met Jake the next day. He was a history professor and a Peace Corps man and played Elvstedt, my lover in the play. I took one look at him and knew it was going to happen. He was sweet, loving, yet tough and human.

Our first night we spent in a romantic hotel on the island. I placed flowers from the door to the bed, waiting for him. I was ready for him and he for me.

When I left the island I thought my heart would stop. We wrote to each other daily. The love affair lasted six months. By then it was apparent that there was not enough room in my life, except for a romance in Hawaii, and when it became apparent to me that he wanted and needed more from me than that, the affair broke up. A change in my pattern! A step forward for Viveca!

G.T. found my diary. "You have a lover," he said. I was in a panic. He was standing by the mantelpiece in our bedroom, where he stood years later when he told me about his girl. "No," I said. "No, no, no." I found myself denying it passionately.

"A man's pride is in his penis. Don't ever tell him you have a lover," a man had said to me not too long before.

"Bullshit," I had answered. "Women get over it. It's a question of ego, that's all."

"Women can forgive," he said. "Men can't. Not yet."

"Bullshit," I said again. But, confronted with the reality, I lost my conviction.

"No, no, no," I repeated. "It's notes, notes for my screenplay." I was writing a screenplay, *I Want . . . I Want . . . I Want*, about a woman who wanted only to love and a young girl who wanted only to be an artist. I wanted to get it out of my system. "I love you. There is nobody else." It was a hundred percent true. At that moment I was only a woman who wanted to love her husband, like millions of women, like my mother.

Obviously it would have been better if I had said what I also felt. "How dare you read my diary! My secrets are mine! I do with them as I wish!" "As with my body," quoting him from his own writings. For, oh yes, his fears had come through.

Or "Let's talk about why, Georgie. Let's share our pains, our fears, or angers." Yes, it might have been better, for he had been courageous enough to ask the question.

And in a way it had nothing to do with it. It had nothing to do with it years later, either, when G.T. had the girl from Berlin.

The line between betraying someone and fulfilling oneself is thin. An intimate tie between two people is complex, and once you begin to speak the truth, it usually either brings you closer together or further apart. And I suppose that's really what it's all about. I wanted to talk to G.T. about it all, years later, when nothing was at stake, or at least so it seemed. We were sitting around the green dining room table eating scrambled eggs. It was the first time he visited us in New York after the separation.

"I didn't understand then why I began to want other men," I

said. "But I do now, and it didn't have to contribute to the break-up between us. It was all about something else," I said. He tensed up.

"Don't tell me," he said. "I don't want to know anything about it. Don't tell me. I loved you for eighteen years." And gray-pink silence crept in between us once more. It takes two!!

Why can't men allow women what they allow themselves? What do they allow themselves? And why do we feel we must obey them? All my life it seems I have been afraid of men's rage and judgment, for I felt I needed them in order to survive, more so than they needed me. That was my betrayal against myself.

"You always acted as if I were betraying you, or about to betray you," G.T. said to me a year or so afterwards. He was visiting from Germany again. He had brought his new girlfriend, Uschi II, along. The subject of *Brecht on Brecht* had come up. It would have to. It was I, of course, wanting again to clear up the past with him, with myself. We were sitting on the beach on Long Island.

"Let's go, just you and I," I had said. "I need to understand about me in relation to us. I don't know exactly why. I know I need to be free from us. Perhaps it has nothing to do with you. But I won't see you again for another two years."

Nothing seemed to be at stake. But I felt the tension in my stomach, as if I still had no right to speak my mind. As if it meant attacking him, and therefore he would have to defend himself. And war between us would be unavoidable.

I didn't want it to happen anymore, marriage or no marriage, and so I went on. "But you did," I answered. "In my book you did betray me and I, you, by letting you. You were a shit and so was I. Isn't it better that we admit it, at least now? It will bring us closer to each other in a new way, Georgie. Don't you need it, too?"

He looked at me quickly. "My God, he's frightened," I thought, getting frightened myself. Ties are stronger than we know or want to know. I knew it well from the night before.

I hadn't thought it was going to bother me, seeing her, Uschi II. After all, she was not the one who came between us. Yes, her name was Uschi. She was also twenty-six. "She is sweet, loving, and young," he described her to me. It was before I met her.

"And you are sweet, loving, and old," I thought. What's the difference? It made me angry.

"I am in flight," he continued. "I am living at her place now, in Bremen." He had his own theater there now, his own group. He was very creative. "I envy you your house," he continued. "I can't seem to settle down. It seems every time I change a place I change women." I wasn't angry any longer. I understood now.

"She looks like Lena," he added.

"More like your mother," I thought when I met her later that day; we were driving out to Long Island. And I really didn't think it was going to bother me. I had my own love life, now.

We drove out together to East Hampton, late at night, in my Rabbit. I was sitting in front. Kris was driving and G.T. and Uschi II were sitting in back. I turned around and what I saw *did* bother me. Uschi had slid down in his lap. He was holding his large hand —he had beautiful hands—over her tiny, gracefully shaped skull. Her hair was cut like a boy's. She was fragile and beautiful in her sleep, and the way he looked at her expressed enormous tenderness. Dazed, I turned around very slowly and for the rest of the journey I looked straight ahead and when we stopped at a diner later for a cup of coffee and I saw his right arm move very gently toward her left, I went out by myself looking at the sky.

I was lonely, lonely, lonely.

The next day, being aware of all that, sitting on the beach with G.T., watching the waves go back and forth, endlessly, I added carefully, "Georgie, I'm not attacking you. You don't have to defend yourself. I'm only trying to air what happened between the two of us. For my sake, perhaps, more than yours. I need it." As I said it, the tension in my stomach began to leave. And when G.T. said, "Yes, I should have fought for you; I chickened out," I said, "I chickened out, too, for I didn't dare to insist on your fighting for me."

Fought for ourselves and our own honor, I was thinking as I walked by myself on the beach later in the afternoon, not wanting to give an inch anymore, not wanting to be a martyr for anybody. The price is too high; I knew that now.

7

I discovered the beauty of the Berkshires the year after *Brecht on Brecht*. Two young men, Paul Giovanna and Bob Seidenberg, were running a summer stock theater up in Stockbridge. They asked me to play Lea in *Cheri* by Colette and Jenny in *Threepenny Opera*. We rented a cottage by the lake. We went to sleep with the moon shining on the blank, black water and woke up with the freshly green birches gently hitting the open windows. It helped soothe our childish wounds.

The summer was ideal in many ways. Giovanna and I had decided to do our own adaptation of the book by Colette, not wanting to use Anita Loos' which had been done on Broadway a few years earlier. We wanted a more intimate version of the love story between the French coquette and Cheri, the young man who could easily be her son. The love story between two unconventional people who let conventions split them up. The production was done beautifully in Vanity Fair costumes and a black platform set. Only the sheets on my bed were pink. We were naive about the rules of the business. We hadn't even asked permission to do the adaptation. We figured if it was brilliant we would get the rights. We *did* get brilliant reviews and with victory in my heart I set out for Paris to acquire the rights.

I saw everybody—the lawyers, the friends, the agents, and finally Colette's husband, an elderly, charming French gentleman. But even in French rejection is painful.

"No, Madame Lindfors. *Regrettement mais non, non, non.*" I still try every year because I am crazy about the project but I might as well rerun a tape. "No, no, no, Madame Lindfors. *Regrettement, mais non.*"

It was my first experience with the ten percent system. Colette is dead. The estate is now in the hands of the survivors and the agents. Unfortunately the world suffers and will not see the play, and I don't get to play Lea. For me that's a disaster.

But it isn't over yet!

To do Jenny in *Threepenny Opera* with Kris playing Filch was sensational. It was Kris' first professional job as an actor. He was only nine. I had said to Giovanna, "Please get him a small part so I can keep an eye on him." Giovanna gave him the part of Filch, "that impoverished frimp who is so eager to become a qualified professional beggar," as Brecht describes him in "The Old Hat," a poem about an actor's search for the right hat for his character. Kristoffer had heard Eli Wallach do it as part of *Brecht on Brecht.* He used to stand in the wings night after night.

I watched Kris before each performance dirty his gloves a bit more or add another hole to them, or to his pants, to show "that Filch was sleeping in some dark hole under a bridge," or put a toothbrush in his breast pocket to show that "he hadn't given up the essential props of civilization." I realized how much he had listened to the poem.

When he was fourteen he quit school. "I want to act," he said one day to me, "and I can't learn that in school. I would like you to come and discuss it with my principal."

My face fell down but I said, "Fine." He had worked with me during the summer doing *The Guns of Carrar* by Brecht. I knew he had talent. I went to school. I was impressed by the way they dealt with the decision. The three of us came around, after two hours, to agree that if he wanted to become an actor and quit school, he should be allowed to try. If a year later he wanted to go back to school, he could.

I was thinking, as I walked out of the school, that had I been allowed to follow up on *my* desires when I was fourteen I might be less ambivalent about making decisions at the age of forty-six.

He went with me on the road. It was after the Berkshire Festival summer. I was still more stubborn than scared and had formed my own company. We toured the campuses for three years. We were only five actors but the program was quite ambitious.

The Strolling Players with Viveca Lindfors Presents A Revolutionary Evening: *Guns of Carrar* by Bertolt Brecht and *Cuba Sí* by Terence McNally; and *Three Boards and a Passion* (a title derived from Dumas' answer to the question, "What is theater?"). A dramatic chronicle consisting of scenes, dialogues, memoirs, letters, speeches, criticism relating to the theater.

One afternoon in the South, at a girl's college, we were doing *Three Boards and a Passion* for the first time. Kristoffer had a monologue. Within a half a minute he had that audience wrapped up in an exchange between them. He was charming, sexy, deep, and passionate. The girls were screaming and swooning. I laughed, cried, sitting on the stage. He had that wonderful quality—joy, vitality, passion, intensity, that special charisma that would make him the star he is today. I, a mother, his mother, an actress, his fellow actress, was part of it all.

After the tour, he was immediately hired by the Shakespeare company in Stratford, and the following fall—he was fifteen by now—he was offered the lead in David Merrick's production *Penny Wars* on Broadway.

On opening night I stood in the back of the house, the old Lyceum Theatre where I had played *Anastasia* when Kris was just a baby. I couldn't sit down; it was too exciting.

Don had brought his whole family up from Los Angeles. They all sat in the fifth row.

Kris's performance was extraordinary. At the curtain call the audience wouldn't stop applauding him. I had known all along about his talent. For Don it was the first time!

Things had been rough between Don and Kris ever since the divorce. Don dropped out of the picture to begin with, but when

Kristoffer was three going on four he wanted to pick up the father tie again.

I was about to leave for Italy to do a film and planned to take Kris along with me and Lena. She was on Easter vacation. John went to the country with his best friend, Chevy Chase. My God, Chevy Chase—gorgeous, brilliant, beautiful; always in trouble, either with school or his mother or stepfather. He spent more time at our house than at home. Just as I was getting ready to leave, I got a letter from Don. "I am going to marry Doe. I have a home now and would like to have Kristoffer come and visit us. Nana, too, of course."

I had a few ungenerous thoughts like, "How dare you marry another woman!" but I was essentially happy about it and about his interest in Kris. I didn't quite know how to explain to a two-year-old that there is another man someplace, in California, who is his real father. What does "real" mean to a two-year-old? Whoever plays with me, holds me, touches me, feeds me, walks me, loves me, is real. I knew about that, having been a mother who had come and gone a lot. I don't know how much Kris understood, but he got on the plane with Nana quite happy and returned a few weeks later equally happy, it seemed. So happy that it was agreed upon that Kris would go back again, during the summer, for another couple of weeks. I was essentially happy, too, for I wanted Kris to have a relationship with his real father. I didn't want to bring up another child alone. I also needed time for myself and my work.

Three days before the trip, Kristoffer started to say, "I don't want to go." I didn't take it too seriously to begin with, not until he couldn't explain at all but only cried.

As we drove out to Kennedy Airport, Kris dressed to the hilt in his cowboy outfit, it got worse. "I don't want to go. I'm not going." He was crying. Guns and boots didn't help.

"Kris, they love you. They are waiting for you. You had such a good time the last time. Why?" There were millions of smiling snapshots of Kris with Doe; Kris with Don. Did he not have a good time? Yes, but suddenly there was a new set of parents in his life, giving love and claiming love in return; even commitment.

A two-year-old going on three has no defenses against those claims. "I have a daddy already. Do I have to love another as much as him? I can't. Not yet." Thoughts like that must have gone through his head. Had he been older, he would have been able to tell us. But he was only two, going on three, and so he kept repeating, "I won't go. I don't want to go. Please, Mommy, I don't want to go." By the time we got to the airport he was crying desperately. I couldn't get him to board the plane. He started to kick. "I won't go. I *won't!*" I began to feel terrible.

"I can't force him on the plane," I said to Nana. "I don't have it in me. I am going to call Don."

Nickles and dimes in a stuffy telephone booth with a crying child in my arms, how did it all happen this way? "Don! I feel terrible. I know you're all waiting for him, but I can't get him on the plane."

"What's the matter with the kid? Just put him on the plane?"

"I don't know what's the matter with him. I just know he won't go. He's in a panic, Don. Maybe if you could come here, to New York, for a few days . . ."

"For Christ's sake just get him on the plane. It's my legal right to have him here. He was fine the last time."

"I'll try once more." I did. The same thing happened, but worse. By now, Kris was so wrought up he could barely talk. Everybody in the airport knew what was going on. I went back to the phone. "I'm sorry, Don. I've made up my mind," I said. "I realize this is an imposition for you all, but I simply won't force him. That's all. I'll call you when I get back to the house." I hung up. I did with my child what I thought was right! Kris was happy, so happy.

I knew I was going to wind up dealing with lawyers and psychiatrists. I didn't care. I did, of course, but Kris stayed with me that summer.

Eventually we all had to deal with it, Kris particularly. For the knowledge of a real father became a threatening fantasy in his life. A boogie-man hiding in the closet; a boogie-man that has more power than any human being. It became Kris's struggle, and eventually ways had to be found for visits to California.

To begin with, the pattern of Kris visiting Don was like clockwork: two days after arrival he was sick with an earache and a sore throat. Eventually, with the help of a shrink, he dealt with the panic.

"What's the matter with the kid?" was always the reaction. Don never trusted Kristoffer's feelings, never took them seriously, never accepted that they were of him, his son—a unique and special human being. Was it the mirror image again? Had no one ever taken Don seriously?

"If I don't take myself seriously, how can I take my child, who comes from me, from my flesh and blood, seriously?"

But that night at the Lyceum Theatre, with Kris playing a lead in a Merrick production, changed something for Don.

We all met in Kris's dressing room way up on the fourth floor.

We had to climb an old, iron spiral staircase to get up there. I saw in Don's face that he finally had discovered what a superb son he had. It was hard for him to express it. But as we climbed the old iron staircase down again and he kissed me goodbye at the stage door and started to walk away through the dimly lit stage alley, I sensed that he wanted to tell me something. After a few steps he turned around. I could barely see his face, but it was the same Don that I had loved, still love, curly-haired and with a smile, as if he had a sweet secret. "You've done a great job with the kid, Viv," he said.

"Thank you," I answered, feeling tears well up in my eyes.

Then he disappeared into the streets and out of our lives again for some time, and I climbed up the old iron staircase once more to Kris's dressing room that used to be Leontovich's while we were playing *Anastasia* and Kris was only a baby.

The tears I was wiping off were good ones.

Maybe for Kris, becoming an actor began that summer when he was afraid to visit Don when he was only two and I began to drag him along to the theater because I had no choice. He got used to falling asleep in dressing rooms, watching actors put on make-up, watching the play from out front. He became a Golden Coach child.

I have a watercolor made by an anonymous artist of me as Jenny and Kris as Filch in *Threepenny Opera* that first summer in the Berkshires. It is hanging over my desk. Kris reached only up to my bosom. Now we are doing the Old Hat together as a vaudeville team in *My Mother . . . My Son*, and he gets more laughs than I. Some nights!

"What a perfect place to have a theater festival," I said to G.T. at the end of our first summer in the Berkshires. "We can have a theater of our own and the family a place to spend the summers together!" The dream again!

It was impossible not to fall in love with the area. Stockbridge is located near Tanglewood, with its music, and near Jacob's Pillow, with its dance. It is an old, traditional, summer stock house, filled with signs of a historical past. It is surrounded by lawns and woods, with an old, red, L-shaped barn in the back of the property, a small restaurant in one end, storage space for the sets, and even a small experimental stage, ideal for reading new plays or a children's theater in the other end. I spoke to the local people and the idea was well received.

We organized a committee. G.T. became the artistic director. I became his assistant (!) together with Alvin Epstein. The fourth member of the group was a well-known PR man from Lincoln Center. He was to handle the business part of it. The project was born.

We had a glorious time.

We worked eighteen hours a day from January on. To develop a company, we ran workshops three times a week in a loft on Spring Street. By February we had chosen the four plays for the season: *The Skin of Our Teeth* by Thornton Wilder, *The Cretan Woman* by Robinson Jeffers, *The Merchant of Venice* by Shakespeare, and *Waiting for Godot* by Samuel Beckett.

We were aware of the need to develop a relationship with the community. Once a week one of us went up to Stockbridge and conducted a workshop from February until the season opened in June. People came from all over the area, regardless of the weather, and it snowed and rained a lot. Together we read and explored the plays chosen for the season. It was as stimulating for them as for us. The three-hour drive home at night seemed like thirty minutes.

On weekends we talked people into being part of the Board and raised money. Bill Gibson and Arthur Penn both lived in the area, and it seemed natural that they should be part of the venture. We offered Penn any choice of plays to direct. He chose *The Skin of Our Teeth*. Annie Bancroft played Sabina, and Estelle Parsons the wife.

The second production was *The Cretan Woman*. I played the woman. Marty Fried, at the time a fairly young and unknown director whom I had met at the Actor's Studio, directed it. Frank Langella played the stepson opposite me. And it was during the rehearsals that Marty fell in love with Lena, and she with him.

The most astonishing production as far as artistic statement was concerned was *The Merchant of Venice*. G.T. directed it. In his continuing search for traces of information about his father's death, a victim of the Nazis, G.T. had found an old, yellow flyer advertising a performance of the play in Auschwitz by a group of inmates. (The Germans' need of order back-knifed them. They filed their crimes as methodically as their accomplishments.)

The play, as it was performed in the Berkshires, opened on a bare, raked stage, bare except for the body of a thin, naked dead man, lying stage center. While a military orchestra joyfully plays "Lili Marlene," two men in prison clothes carry him out. A large photo of Hitler is then brought in and hung in the background.

Last, a group of German officers take their places in the audience in the front row. The stage is set up. The play can begin.

A group of inmates enters carrying large pails of water. They start to scrub the raked floor, crawling from way back, slowly, toward the audience. But *The Merchant of Venice as Performed in Auschwitz,* as was our title, ends in the courtroom scene. One of the German officers gets up on the stage and insists on taking over the part of the judge. With the script in his hand, the Nazi tells the Merchant, the Jew, to get down on his knees and ask forgiveness— as is indicated in Shakespeare's text. The tension is unbearable. The rest of the inmates, sensing that their life and death is at stake, have entered the stage. Will he or will he not submit? The Jew playing the Merchant looks around, then slowly goes down on his knees. But he is not alone for long. Portia, played by me, is the first to join him. One by one, the other inmates follow. We slowly start to crawl toward the front, as did the inmates in the opening of the play. As we reach the edge of the stage there is a sudden black-out. When the lights slowly come up again, left on the stage are only piles of our clothes.

G.T. did the play again, ten years later, in Munich. A perfect setting. Circles, circles.

The festival ended with the Beckett production. Gene Frankel directed it simply and beautifully. The season was over. The seventy-three percent box office proved that we were successful, artistically and commercially. The only question left, insane as it sounded, was whether we, as producers of the theater, would be asked to stay on to produce another season. We had, to this date, no contract to continue. The decision was in the hands of the Board now, a board that we ourselves had formed.

It became obvious already in the spring, before the season began, that the fourth member of our group, the PR man, was more interested in securing a position for himself than for us as a group. He had not secured a contract for us—not only for seasons to follow but for this season. I confronted him. "It's hard as well as inefficient to work without the security of a long-term agreement," I said.

"Well, you won't get it," was his answer. "The season will prove whether you are able to handle it or not."

My stomach turned over. I was never good at being put to a test.

The power still was in our hands had we wanted to take a strong stand. I doubt that we could have all been replaced, but neither George nor Alvin wanted to deal with the confrontation, partly because there was no time—they were busy doing what they were supposed to be doing—and partly because there was no money to hire a lawyer.

My stomach turned over again because I knew I couldn't fight the battle alone and that conflicts unsolved would poison the air. They did. That was our contribution to the failure.

In August G.T. and Alvin finally joined me. We confronted Bill Gibson and said that we wanted to find someone to replace the PR man for this season and the ones to follow, but that, above all, we needed a contract in order to go on and plan for the next season. Bill mumbled that the Board would probably only accept us as a total group, but at the meeting in the end of September we would be allowed to offer our proposal. Our proposal! I was stunned. How dare they put themselves in that position? My stomach turned over again, for I knew well they dared!

The defeat was obvious. The festival no longer belonged to us. And the season wasn't even over yet.

On top of it all, Kristoffer came down with appendicitis. I called the doctor at six o'clock in the morning. Four hours later he was operated on. Had the summer been too much for him? Too emotional? As for me? He had acted in two productions and had had a wonderful time doing so. But it was impossible for the children *not* to be part of our struggle. I sat by his bedside as he was waking up from the anesthesia, wondering whether I had done the right thing in involving them all in our survival fight. And why had it become a fight?

It wasn't over yet. Even the last days of the beautiful Berkshires summer were spent working with the lawyer, preparing our proposal for the Board. Instead of listening to music in Tanglewood, walking along the lake, bicycling, swimming, playing, loving. It was hard on family life.

George and I drove up for the Board meeting at the end of September. We had moved back to New York. The children had started school and we were involved in new projects. George was writing a new play, *Nigger Lovers*, and was preparing a production in Berlin of *Cannibals*. I had a contract to begin my college tour group, Strolling Players, five actors touring the provinces. It kept me going and this time I made sure I was in charge, after the experience of the summer. And it wasn't over yet.

I was not allowed to go to the meeting. George represented the group. "It is because I am a woman," I said to my woman friend through tears. I couldn't stop crying all morning, desperately, loudly, and uncontrollably. "A year ago I started it all! It was in my hands, and here I am waiting for *them* to decide whether *I* am in or out."

"Partly, Viveca, partly." She stayed with me, this wonderful woman, like a sister, all day in the house in the woods where we had spent the summer. She fed me, talked to me, listened to me, while waiting for G.T. to come back from the meeting.

"I felt it all summer long, that it had something to do with me being a mere woman. That I had to prove myself a hundred times more than anyone else to make them believe that I, a woman and an actress, would not necessarily screw things up. It's not fair!" I couldn't stop.

"I know, but life is often not very fair so don't blame yourself."

I looked up at her. "I feel it's my fault, too," I said. I still have endless nightmares about this kind of situation, where I am not wanted, not included, dismissed, and then the guilt, as if I, a woman, should be punished for stepping into man's territory.

"Perhaps that is what you bring to the situation, but not only, and it is life, Viveca. Nobody is perfect. It's that feeling of defeat that hurts you. There is no reason for you to feel that way. Look at the situation clearly."

"Yes, I know what you're saying," I answered. "You mean 'Just because they threaten me, I don't have to feel threatened.' Is that what you are saying?"

"Yes, yes, it's got to begin there."

"Oh God, how long?"

"You must strengthen yourself, Viveca."

"I know, I know. I don't have to pick up their vibes. But I need their support! I'm still fragile about my independence."

"I understand. That scares them, too, Viveca."

"So why can't they simply go by simple rules of fairness and morality? Without it, there is no theater, no life, no love."

But she would answer, "They would like to, but perhaps they can't. It's all too new to them. Patterns are changing and it's violating for them, too. In the meantime, Viveca, deal with yourself. Maybe they will come around, and if not, Viveca, there are others who love to work with you, and other theaters, too, as beautiful as this one."

At lunchtime, G.T. called; they had turned down our proposals. They had turned down the PR man's proposal, too. Arthur and Bill were taking over the festival. "That's what it was all about," I said to her. I couldn't stop crying. "They discovered the beauty of hav-

Don Siegel and I, Paris 1949. The chestnuts were in bloom outside the American Embassy when I married an American.

They flew me to New York to be photographed by Hausman. A few weeks later, I saw myself stacked on the pavement outside Schwab's Drugstore on Sunset Boulevard. A month later, I was fired by Warners.

With Rita Gam in the film version of Jean-Paul Sartre's No Exit, *one of my favorite films—hardly ever shown!*

Mandy Wager, myself, Lotte Lenya, Anne Jackson, George Voskovec, and Dane Clark (who took over for Eli Wallach) in Brecht on Brecht—*a marvelous success at the Theatre de Lys.*
(PHOTO: HENRY GROSSMAN)

The first picture of the Tabori-Lindfors family in the house on 95th Street. We had just moved in, too.

Eugenie Leontovich and I in Anastasia, *Lyceum Theater, New York, 1954* (PHOTO: INTERNATIONAL NEWS PHOTOS)

Judy Collins and I in the Peace March in Washington, D.C., 1968

We were five players traveling to colleges—The Strolling Players—my own group!

I Am a Woman—*1973 (PHOTO: BJORN LARSSON, RSC/KAMERABILD)*

Teaching—maybe directing (PHOTO: R.T. KAHN)

My Mother . . . My Son *with Kristoffer—my son, the actor! I see myself in him.*

Natasha, Katrina, Lena, and I, with my mother's portrait hanging above us, in the cottage on Long Island

My eldest son John and his first born, Nicholas John

Back in Hollywood—25 years later! Filming Welcome to L.A. *for Robert Altman. Loved the work and the freedom involved. From left: Geraldine Chaplin, Lauren Hutton, Sally Kellerman, myself, and Sissy Spacek* (PHOTO: LION'S GATE FILMS)

In The Way We Were *(with Robert Redford and Barbra Streisand), I played Salke Viertel, whom I knew in New York. The viciousness of the McCarthy period was easier to handle in retrospect.* (PHOTO: COLUMBIA PICTURES)

ing their own theater in their own backyard to use for their own purposes! It was all so obvious!"

"Maybe, Viveca, maybe. But in the meantime . . ." I didn't hear her. I was crying too hard. The Berkshire Theatre Festival that we had started with so much hope in our hearts—it is impossible to imagine how much hope—no longer belonged to us.

Summer was over and fall was here when G.T. and I drove down the Taconic in the early evening. Nature was brilliantly beautiful. The colors of the trees were turning bleeding red. I was wounded and open to beauty, to pain, to love, to us. How can we love each other again?

The dream had fallen through. We knew things about each other that we could no longer deny. We were no longer perfect in each other's eyes, difficult between lovers, lovers that still are children. And we were. It was getting darker between us.

G.T. had had a second gallstone attack, this time more severe. I had been filled with compassion for him. He seemed so surprised that I still cared. "My God," I thought to myself, "he no longer believes in us."

Did he not want to share a theater with me again? Or life?

Something had changed between us.

"Every time we work together it turns out to be a disaster. Why do I insist on it?" I had asked myself. Perhaps he had asked himself the same.

Nigger Lovers was the last play he wrote with a part for me. The rehearsals had been awful. No communication. Only misunderstandings between us. It didn't help much that the play flopped. It was an enormous box office success before the reviews came out. The next day the house was empty. However, by the weekend, the box office began to increase again. But it was too late. The decision to close was already made.

It was devastating for G.T. The only good thing was the story about the rats.

The last matinee, during the first act, I heard strange noises, like a baby squealing. "Who takes babies to a show like this?" I asked the stage manager as I walked off the stage.

"Not babies, Viveca," he said. "Rats!"

"What?"

"Yes, the basement has flooded. The rat poison is in the water and the rats are drowning, half-poisoned."

"Oh, my God." The image was enough to make you sick.

After the last curtain, I was called to an Equity meeting in the green room. The deputy was a Black actor. "I spoke to Equity. We have the right to close the show because of the danger of the rats coming up on the stage. I want to cast a vote to cancel the show for tonight," he said. I had started to laugh but stopped myself quickly, realizing that for him it might not be so funny. Perhaps he grew up in the slums of Harlem where small children die from rat bites.

"Come on," I said. "We have a good house tonight!" But I didn't protest much because I didn't believe for a second that the vote would be in his favor. It was. Two minutes later, the evening performance was cancelled. Our last show! I was stunned.

"Am I allowed to call another meeting?" I asked the company manager when I had gotten myself together.

"You are, but you'd better hurry up."

The audience was in the lobby. The sign was just about to go up about the cancellation of the show—not explaining why, of course. That would have been too embarrassing, particularly for the theater owner, the real criminal in this case. The theater—and this is not unusual—was kept in a disgusting state—no wonder the rats were taking over.

"Look," I said to the actors. "We are doing a show about fighting for a better situation between Negroes and white in the South. . . . We are also fighting the critics. . . . And you want to give up our last performance because of some dying rats in the basement? Well, I will not be kicked off the stage by some fuckin' rats. Come on," I said. "We are actors! We have an almost full house! The producer [Lynn Austin] has a chance to make up for some of her loss. We have a chance to perform. Shit, man, let's not give up!" I was passionate.

We took another vote. The answer was, "Yes, let's go on." Ta ta!

The rats did *not* come up during the show. They didn't even squeal. They must have died quietly during the performance. It was one of our best. The reality of the situation brought an intensity to the play that we had not always found. And I had fought for what I believed in!

Why couldn't I fight for my marriage?

Why fight? Did I feel I had to?

Nigger Lovers was a love story between a man and his dog, a female European bitch. I played her, Stacy Keach, him. In the end of the play he shoots her, and, by mistake, during one rehearsal the gunshot went off right at my temple. I went hysterical. I felt that G.T. wanted to shoot me out of his life for good. Was that true? I never asked him. He never told me.

8

I am driving up the Taconic again. The first time in two years. And it is all coming back to me. My God! I didn't really want to think about it all. Not today.

Lena is with me. Kris too. G.T. is already up there doing a workshop production of *Pinkville*, his latest play. Marty is assisting him. It is going to be a family weekend! And I want to be joyful with my man. Yes! I want to love him tonight. Yes!

"He is your husband, not necessarily your producer, your director, your mother, your father, your sister, your brother," my analyst had said. Yes. Yes. Yes. I am learning. I have to.

"You want a straight relationship with your husband," my new analyst said. I had changed analysts.

"Yes," I had cried out. "With him, with you, with my director, with my children, my friends, myself. Above all, myself. Yes, myself." I started to cry, but I felt hope for the first time in a long time.

Madame's constant advice, "Sit back and let the men do it," hadn't worked for me for a long time. It only caused anger and anxiety, as did "Viveca, you are beautiful; let them adore you, love you, take care of you." It sounded more fitting for a fading heroine in an eighteenth-century French novel. It had little to do with being a woman in the 1970s, me.

It was painful to leave her, for she had been like my mother, and maybe that's why I had to leave her. I needed a more vital woman image.

To love, to exist in a new way as an equal, was a feeling so strong in me during those years, the last in my marriage, that, although, it felt at times violating to pursue the change, it was even more violating not to. I could see why my mother never dared to go through that period. It seemed easier to get ill and become a cripple, for the attitude "Oh, she's such a difficult woman" made me shrivel and give up my conviction in no time. Not only with G.T., but with men in general, and women, also. But once the journey begins, there is no return. The price is too high.

We are driving through the main street of Stockbridge. How I love this village! "Let's stop at the theater." We look at the posters. I am stunned. It is right back to a commercially run summer stock theater. I wander into the house. I am stunned again. The brilliantly designed thrust stage by David Hays is gone. It is back to a regular proscenium stage!

"The failure of the festival didn't only lie with us, but with the local people who didn't defend their theater, the big shots who played their own ugly power games. It's a bloody shame, and what a waste," I think, sitting in the back of the house.

"You have to be in the same place in life. You can't go wrong then," Paul Austin, my director for one of the shows in the Strolling Players, said to me the other day. "You can put up with each other's weaknesses, or peculiarities, even substitute for any lack of action that might be useful, but not essential to the creative result. But the attitude about life has to be somewhat the same. You can't go wrong then." It has to do with morality. Yes. And courage of commitment.

Lena is putting her arm around me. She probably senses what I am thinking. She is with child now. The family is growing. I am becoming a grandmother, and Kristoffer is on his way to becoming a sensational young actor. I knew. He had been with me on one of the tours. We wander out of the theater that once had promised to be a summer home for us all.

Yes! Strolling Players was successful. Five actors touring the provinces. We drove, we acted, we even walked one snowy night in the Midwest when we ran out of gas. I felt strong again, independent, creative. I had taken life in my own hands, and this time I had chosen my partners more carefully.

Was G.T. threatened by my newly found strength, ever so fragile? He knew so much about so many things in so many ways. I adored his genius.

"I hope he will be around for the *Mother Courage* production. I am still nervous about working with a new director and a new production concept. It's his adaptation, so why wouldn't he?" I am thinking, walking up toward the red barn where we once had planned the Children's Theatre. It was rented out, now, to the producer of *Pinkville*. Yes, I still need his help. Why shouldn't I? I am his wife and we rarely see each other lately.

The rehearsals were over. There were only a few good-looking young boys and girls hanging around. Always are in the theater.

"Where is Mr. Tabori?" I asked. "Oh, I think he went back to the house," a young girl answered. Was she smiling peculiarly? I am suddenly overcome by a creepy feeling that there is another woman around. One that is more intimate with G.T. than I?

I began to feel like I did two summers ago, like one of those women I am often asked to play in mediocre films or television— middle-aged women, victims, gray women, always turning out to be the heavy without explaining why. Oh yes! Women over forty are the worst written characters in the media.

"Who am I? One of them? A mutation?" I asked myself.

The redhead girl turned out not to be the only one. There were phone calls from Diane, a brilliant Black actress, and then there was Mia, and God knows who else the year that followed, the year Lena got married. I still didn't pay much attention.

Today it bothered me. The feeling didn't leave me. "Come on, Viveca. You've had lovers, too. It's just your own guilt."

My God! I had even brought Jake home for dinner. How insane! What did I want, that G.T. would understand me as my father did? Would I understand him as his mother did? I hadn't discovered my jealousy yet. I was about to.

"Marty is waiting for me at the coffee shop. I'll meet you at the performance." Lena is gone. Kristoffer has found some friends.

I am walking over to the rooming house alone. I know the area well. I could even love it again. So why am I not here now?

When G.T. had asked me at the beginning of the summer to join him during the rehearsals, I had said I couldn't. "I'm still allergic to the Berkshires." There were other reasons. We had rented a house on the beach. I had started working on *I Am a Woman*. I was looking forward to work without pressure of time or involvement, walking along the beach, feeling the sand under my feet. I knew none of that would happen if I were part of George's rehearsals. It's impossible not to get involved.

I used to be jealous of G.T. for closing the door, taking time for himself, doing what he wanted to do for himself. I wanted it now. When I did, jealousy, possessiveness, feelings of being left out, not being part of his journey, seemed to disappear. I wanted to keep it that way. Fumblingly, I tried to explain all this to G.T. He said he understood. Somehow I didn't believe him. He hadn't been very persuasive, either. I began to torture myself. "Oh, why can't I work up here? I should be with him. Don't I love him? What's wrong between us?" But the desire to change my pattern, not to pay a price for love any longer, was more intense. We had been married for eighteen years. We should be able to trust each other and our love, accept each other, exist separately or together. After all, we are both working artists.

I didn't go.

Did G.T. notice the change in me and ask himself, "Why put up with it?"

When I got to the rooming house, I realized that none of G.T.'s things were in the room. It seemed totally unused. "There *is* another woman around! Don't fantasize, Viveca, either in pink or in black. Are you worried about him leaving you for a young girl? It's beneath him and you!"

It wasn't. Still, I am glad I didn't know about her, for tonight I wanted to know about us only.

Lena and I were sitting together during the performance of *Pinkville*. Marty and Kris and G.T. stood in the back. I put my arm around Lena. It was no play for pregnant women. It was about Vietnam, about violence, fear of taking a stand, bending to authorities, anger for being trapped, and betrayal. It was brilliant. I knew it would move to New York at the American Place Theatre, and probably go on to Germany, as *Cannibals* had.

Cannibals, mildly received in New York, had been an enormous hit in Berlin. It must have been an extraordinary experience for G.T. Those he hated now loved him. I hadn't shared his moment of glory. I didn't go to the opening. I was working, filming *Puzzle of a Downfall Child*.

I could have found a couple of days to go to Berlin but I didn't want to distract myself, besides the expense. Was it careless of me? In retrospect, yes. Lena went. Did I feel left out in spite of its being my choice?

I paid little attention to G.T.'s involvement with the Germans. If I had I might have understood his need for confrontation with his past, where hate mingled with love and fear with courage. And they were more essential than confrontations with me, with us, with love. But I wasn't ready to open my own blackness yet, and so how could I be generous with his?

Moving to Europe had always been a wish of G.T.'s. Eventually, I could see that with the work offered him now it became even more tempting. Germany offered him contracts, money, security, a theater of his own, and a kind of respect that G.T. felt he never received in this country. Then there was Uschi Number One waiting for him, adoring him in a way I no longer could or would. She was the daughter of a Nazi, and he was a Jew whose father was killed in a concentration camp.

Journeys, journeys.

But I knew none of that watching *Pinkville* that evening in the Berkshires with Lena. Kris and G.T. were standing in the back. I did wonder about the violence in his work and the fury and why I was getting none of it myself. I, the wife.

Tears withheld are like old wine in bottles. If not aired they explode . . .

After the performance, we went back to the rooming house. G.T. explained about the empty closets. "I'm staying with Jeffrey, a friend, up in the hills. It's quieter there; he has a pool. That's why none of my things are here."

I believed him. I wanted to believe him. I was hungry for him, for us. I hated it when I saw him take some sleeping medicine. Why does he lately . . . I resent it. Within ten minutes he would vanish. I began to feel the pressure of time. I resented that, too, for I knew something was between us, not only anger—I knew that was not to be ignored.

"Georgie, we are in trouble. I am scared. Let's go to a marriage counselor. We must do something. I don't feel married to you any longer. Please, please, let's do something." I was much more desperate than I had known.

I had said things I hadn't even dared to think to myself.

By now we were in bed. Suddenly he sat up and in a mean way (the medicine had already begun to work) said, as if it were all my fault, "All right. Let's try, but this time, let's really commit."

Thoughts were rushing through my mind like burning flames in a storm. "Has he given up on us?" And my heart sank into my stomach. I put my arms around him. It will always be mysterious for me to understand how two people can be so far apart and then suddenly so close together. Within a few seconds we made love, deeply, passionately, openly. The only way, it seemed, to break through the sound barrier. The ancient way!

When I woke up in the morning and put my hand out he was gone! Where? We had been so close. Was he rehearsing at eight AM or just taking a walk? Why hadn't he left a note? How could he be so careless about us now?

I got dressed and walked through the flowery wall-papered walls in the dainty New England house. The daffodils and the roses and the carnations didn't sweeten my senses. I ran into the landlady, a lonely, hysterical woman. I asked her if she had seen G.T. She looked at me strangely and began to talk about the phone bill.

"What bill?" I asked.

"It's a very large one," she explained. "A lot of long distance calls to Germany. I can't lay out the money."

Germany! I knew he was planning a new production in Berlin,

but why didn't he make them pay for the calls? "It's not my business. Deal with him directly," I said to her as well as to myself. She smiled as if she knew a secret. It made me even angrier. I walked out and down the road to the coffee shop in the middle of Stockbridge. By now I was crying. "After such a night, such openness, how could you just take off? I hate you," I mumbled through tears, calling him every name in the book. "You can keep your super elegant Hungarian hypocritical face to yourself. Why did I come up here in the first place? I could have had a beautiful weekend all by myself on the beach. You can go and fuck yourself."

"Daddy was crying," Lena told me as we were driving back to New York. " 'Mommy doesn't trust me,' he said."

It was unfair of him to put it on me. The girl was living up the road, in the hills, at Jeffrey's. "I was lonely," he explained seven months later. So he hadn't understood.

"I want a woman at my feet, not an equal," he said, the day before he left for a new life without me. It was a cold February morning. We were having breakfast again around the green dining table. I wanted to kill him but then I also wanted to love him, and that was still my dilemma.

He kissed me goodbye on the street where we lived for eighteen years—the writer, the actress, and the three children. Only Brandy my dog was with me. I was wearing my silver fox coat, the one that was stolen from me a week later . . . the bastards. "I'll be back," G.T. said. Brandy and I saw the car turn the corner and walked upstairs to the third floor into his study opposite our bedroom. As in a crummy TV drama where the camera closes in on a close-up of the empty closet, I saw that there was nothing left, not a jacket, not a sweater, not a pair of pants: just one pair of dirty underwear, slightly yellowish where his penis used to rest. We knew he would never be back.

I hated him. I wished he had died, that the girl had died, that they were struck by lightning, swept away by winds, and crushed by falling down trees. I wished that I could have killed them both in an orgy so wild, so insane, that nothing would be left except me, me, me.

"He's gone . . . he left you . . . he's gone," a voice in my head kept repeating. I realized for the first time that I was going to be alone the way I had never been alone in my entire life. And I started to shake, rebelling against it. I made it across the hall into my bedroom that now was only mine. I picked up the phone and called a friend I knew would listen, with whom I had just made three small films. He knew me well.

After a while I began talking to him about the work I was doing on *I Am a Woman*. He said, "It ought to be a good time for you; maybe you will finally do your own thing."

Two weeks later I received a cable from my sister. "Mother dying. Come home." I left the next morning. I didn't want to be late this time.

Besides the work on *Woman*, Brandy and the house were my only solice that summer. They embraced me, replacing G.T.'s arms at night. I didn't dare even to leave for a weekend on Long Island despite the heat in the city. Coming home was even worse. To turn on the lights and realize he wasn't there, wouldn't ever be there, to go to bed and put my hand out and realize he wasn't there, would never be there, was disastrous.

Brandy had already gone through the shock of loss when Lady, his mother, died. He was one of nine puppies from Lady's last litter, the only black one.

After Lady's death, Brandy followed me around like a shadow. He wouldn't stop shaking. I understood him now. I thought, if I don't stop myself, I'll get Parkinson's Disease. I felt lost, like a falling star without any connection.

In August I was in South Dakota visiting Kristoffer, who was on location doing a film, *Rosebud*, and I met an Indian painter. I had read a letter that same day, written to Kris from G.T. It was sneaky of me and I was asking for it. It was Kristoffer's letter! I only got through the first two lines, then I buckled over. "I have never loved anyone but you and Uschi," he wrote. "Bastard!" I yelled. "Did you have to deny it all? Eighteen years? You fucking bastard!" The betrayal seemed horrendous.

I met the Indian artist that same evening. He told me about their philosophy. "We believe that if you use the earth, it belongs to you. If I use you and you me, we belong to each other. It's quite simple." He had explained to me about the word "Indian-giving." "When the white man came here the Indians signed a piece of paper in exchange for some land. Then they left and returned some years later and killed us for being on the land. They called us 'Indian givers.' Their philosophy was a different one."

When I returned to the city, I asked an English girl living on my top floor (I was afraid of living alone that spring and summer, but also couldn't stand having anybody intimately involved around me, so I took in some boarders) to pack his manuscripts, letters, for I knew too well what it would do to me if I did it myself. Down it went into the basement, packed in boxes, neatly, even a pipe I found and a picture of his father and his keys to our house, now only mine!

Out with the carcass . . . out with it!

My first lover after G.T. came from Israel. A Jew! His name was David.

I received an offer to make a movie in Madrid. It was still fall when I left New York and 95th Street. The trees in the gardens outside my bedroom window were still bleeding red.

I love Spain. I love the Spanish soul. They want the darkness as I do. They trust it as I do. Without it I can't face the lightness. I love the stone houses, the bareness, the white tones and the people in black. I love their warmth. I love their ancient stone streets. I could walk on them forever.

David was sitting next to me in the bar in Madrid one afternoon after shooting. As usual, I was writing the diary, letters never sent off. "Are you a writer?" he asked me.

"No, I am an actress." He seemed disappointed. "What do you mean!" I said. "We are the mirror of humanity. Life rarely comes up to the intensity and clarity that we reach on the stage! And the risk is less. I am in control!" I laughed at myself. "It's a gorgeous profession."

It intrigued him. "Would you have dinner with me tonight?" "Yes," I answered quickly. I had made up my mind to go with whatever, to join life, to take any risk. It had been a sleepless night, a black one, too black.

The attraction between us was obvious. It increased over the dinner table. When we wandered back to the hotel he stopped me under a Moorish arch. He put his hands on the wall, around me, so I couldn't get away, even if I wanted to, and I didn't. We looked in each other's eyes, then on each other's lips, until we were so close that we became one with one another for a second, for then he moved away a quarter of an inch, as if it were too much for him, and for me it surely was, and then he kissed me again and again and again.

I have never understood the phrase "a great lover." When two people are hungry for each other for whatever reason, they become brilliant lovers. We were for three nights. He left me early one morning and I have never heard from him since. I wasn't hurt, for I wanted to be a woman, not a child.

A week or so after the film was finished, I stopped over in Paris on my way back to Madrid to visit my cousin Rolf who lived in a gorgeous apartment on Frederick Le Play.

We were having breakfast—Rolf, Greta, his wife, and I. We had been out the night before talking about our parents. We'd had a marvelous time, so much better than when I was thirteen and he used to try to kiss me after dinner at his mother's house. At that time I preferred his brother, who was sad, complex, and more beautiful. Today I rarely see him.

Greta is a clear-headed, straight, loving Swedish blond woman. Everything is simple to her. You commit to a man for life. "He'll be back," she kept saying about G.T. to me over the breakfast table.

"But can I wait? Will it be worth it?" I asked, when the phone rang.

"Of course," she said, and went to answer. "Germany is calling for Mrs. Tabori," she came back with a triumphant smile. I ran to the phone. I had sent him my telephone numbers wherever I had been, but this was the first time he called me.

"Tabori here," he said. He sounded beautiful, just like in the old days. Warm, joyful, trusting. We decided to see each other.

"I could go home over Germany; I could see your production," I said. "I'll check on the airline schedules and call you back to-night."

I hung up the phone. I was crying. "It was Georgie," I said to Greta. I was in heaven. I checked all the airline schedules. I called him back around six in the evening. There was no answer. I called again at seven. I called at eight, at nine, at ten, at eleven, at a quarter to twelve. I called at one. I called at two, then I fell asleep. I started again at eight in the morning. No answer. I called at nine. A friend of mine, a Hungarian woman, Martha, tried at nine-thirty. She called me back. "He is in the bathtub; he will call you back as soon as he gets out."

When he called, I couldn't help asking the question, "Why didn't you answer the phone?"

His answer was clearer than I had imagined. "I pulled out the plug."

The rest of the conversation was of no importance. I remember sentences like "Things are as before. Uschi is with me. Nothing has changed." And answers like mine, "I am going straight back to New York, to my children, to my dog, to my life, to my work."

Another voice inside of me was screaming, "How can another human being mean so much to me when I mean so little to him?"

I got on the plane that afternoon and it continued to scream, until it became a hoarse whisper: "I hate you. I want you out of me, I want to get rid of you, you are like shit in me, poisoning me, like a big hard shit. I want you out. I want to shit you out once and for all, forever.' I got drunk and wrote page after page after page. Like Alice in *Dance of Death*, "I wanted to bathe. I wanted to wash myself clean." But unlike Alice, I wasn't going to get trapped again and wait "until death do us apart," for I knew I would be the first to go.

Fall was over when I returned to my house on 95th Street. The leaves were covering my garden, preparing the earth for winter to come. There was a letter waiting for me, with a message from my mother: "I wanted to be joyful but I couldn't."

First I thought that I would choke from fear for, like her, I wasn't sure I could be joyful. But then one summer evening in New York, I realized, as always, I was stronger than I had wanted to know and that I was a different generation.

9

They were unknown, those two bastards that held me up one hot summer night in New York.

I came home one night around nine in the evening. I had noticed them already up on Lexington Avenue—two flamboyant, tall black men. I had a funny feeling in my stomach about them, but that summer I fought hard to ignore my fears, any fear. Thinking about the work always helped me. By the time I put the key in my door I had forgotten about them.

Suddenly, I hear a voice, "Don't scream, lady." My heart went straight down into my female organs, fighting a four-year-old's paralysis. But not this time, baby! I don't take any more orders! Not me! I turned slowly, slowly, slowly, as if in a trance. They were on top of the steps, framing me in against the door, the bastards. It was dark where I was standing. It had been only three months since they broke in and stole my purse. They must have known I was still living alone with no man in the house, only a dog, and Brandy was getting older. He didn't even see them. He was across the street, trying to shit.

"Don't scream, lady," one of them repeated.

They didn't count with my newly found woman's voice, weak still, but aware, ready to defend itself against authority, orders, anybody's—male or female.

From deep down inside of me it came, out of a will long suppressed but a will that no longer would allow *anyone* to take anything away from me that was mine! No young blonde or dark bitch to take my husband away; no tall black bastard to take away the key to my house, *or* my will to scream.

It came, first in a few stuttering words, like burning lava pushing itself through cracks of its prison, "I am going to scream," I heard myself say as if in another place and then I repeated it once more. "I am going to scream." And then it came, *my scream*. It seeped through my body, my soul, my veins, my voice. From the gut it came, strange, weird sounds. *My scream*.

I screamed to Stefan, "You bastard! Why did you tell me you didn't love me after we gave each other so much?" I screamed to Rydeberg, "Why did you hurt me? Why did you have to dismiss our love with a few lines in a letter, as if I were a thing, not a woman who loved you?" I screamed at my sister, "Why did you try to dominate me? I had to hate you in order to leave you, in order not to be like you. Do you understand?" I screamed at my mother for never having been the woman she could have been, the image that I needed, and for loving her and not being able to free myself from her. I screamed at my father for not taking my side against her, not trusting me enough, out of some stupid convention, and for setting false images of what is a loving woman when I wanted to be a daughter only. I screamed at George for giving up on us, on our dream, and for copping out by choosing a girl the age of my own daughter. I screamed at the movie producers in Hollywood who told me I was too old to play a loving woman on the screen, opposite a man older or as old as I. I screamed at my brother for telling me I was too shallow, that I would never be a great artist when I was just afraid of my own strength.

I screamed and I screamed and I screamed, and the hate became clearer and purer and then vanished like a fallen star.

The bastards turned around on their sneaker-covered feet. I saw them disappear in the darkness across the playground into 96th Street. Brandy sat on the sidewalk now, howling, and the neighbors finally came out. I was shaking, for I had used something in me long unused. I was back on virgin territory. I screamed because I wanted to get back to her—the child, the animal, the woman who had taken her life into her own hands about everything—love, work—yes, everything! Once! Long ago! And then had done it again and again and again. I wanted to get back to her, the she I had been! Would always be! Was already in that flash of a second when I happened, and the wonder in me was alive!

❧ VII ❧

I Am a Woman

> "Two mice fell into a pail of
> milk . . . One screamed help and
> drowned . . . the other started to
> tread water . . . In the morning she
> was on top of butter . . ."
>
> OLD SWEDISH FOLK TALE

I AM LYING IN MY bamboo-decorated room at the Lenox
Hotel, watching the snowflakes swirl and dance, gently rocked
by the wind back and forth, momentarily distracted from their
task of slowly covering the earth, the trees, the black asphalt, the
red rooftops. By evening everything will be white. It's a good
sign. We are opening *I Am a Woman* tonight.

"Art makes the unbearable bearable," I wrote in my diary by
my mother's deathbed. It's been five years since she died, since
G.T. left. Since the work began.

I shudder when I think of women my age going through what I
went through without any other involvement than themselves, the
past, and a painful present. I was lucky. I could use my dilemma
to create a play. It became my number one Survival Kit!

Today I know I am not alone in my struggle. My entire sex is in
search of new, healthy images. I see the women in the audience
standing up at the end of the play, as I, the woman in white
swirls her cape around her triumphantly in celebration of being
alive, her other arm raised high in the air, mask in hand, as a
symbol of free spirit. I see the women in the audience raising their
arms too, waving back to her, to me, as if they need to affirm for
themselves the possibility of becoming one total being. Later, during the dialogue following the performance, the question comes,
constantly repeating, as if on cue: "Why did you do this evening?
And how?" I tell them, for I identify with them all. I know well
the fear, the ambivalence, the disbelief of being able to carry
through any task that has belonged to man's territory.

I wrote of this in the introduction to the published version of
I Am a Woman under the heading "Woman + Actress = Me." "I

269

was in a dilemma. A dilemma fabricated by society leading to a neurosis of my own. A dilemma I could no longer stomach. A dilemma that led to conflicts in my marriage as well as my work. And so the play came from many sources, many needs, spiritual, psychological, as well as realistic."

The simplest of my drives, at least the most concrete one, was that I wanted to make a living in a way that permitted me to respect myself. I had discovered that the college market accepted and paid well for the kind of work that I was interested in doing. It seemed like a better solution than to run around looking and auditioning for commercials or mediocre TV dramas. To begin with, I had done a solo Brecht evening, *VL on Brecht*. It was successful and I loved doing it. I always ended the performance with an open dialogue; it became almost as important a part of the evening as the performance.

The booking agent suggested I put together another one-woman evening.

I knew I wanted to express myself as a woman and began to look for a literary figure to center the evening around, influenced by the male success of Hal Holbrook's *Mark Twain Tonight* and Emlyn Williams' *Charles Dickens*. Perhaps I wasn't as attuned to women writers as I am today. Perhaps my accent limited me. Or perhaps I just wanted to act certain glorious parts I would soon be too old for. In any event, I quickly gave up the idea and began to assemble my favorite monologues, poems, newspaper clippings. I called the evening *I Am a Woman* and tried it out in a few places. Kevin Kelly of the *Boston Globe* saw it in Provincetown and gave it a rave review. I began to have visions of projections, of costumes, of music, of lights, of props. I knew the script needed work. I decided to look for a director and co-arranger. I went to Paul.

I met Paul Austin when I started the Strolling Players college tours. I asked him to direct one of the shows. It was right after the Berkshire summer and I was in no great shape, but Paul was extremely supportive. He respected my will and desire without for a moment losing his own. It seemed natural that I would ask him to help me with *I Am a Woman*, and I will never forget his astonishing answer: "I would love to. I have often been cruel to women and I would like to understand myself in regards to them."

Later, I heard him explain to an interviewer, "When fifty-one percent of the population is treated as a minority, there are a great many social and personal crimes being committed. There is no choice but to try to change this."

270

I had never thought about it that way, and when Paul suggested that we read everything about the women's movement I wasn't even sure I was interested. I was a "sexy dame," and women's liberation was for freaky ladies.

Oh yes, I was conditioned. Even the idea of a one-woman evening scared me. Images of elderly unsuccessful actresses touring the provinces, reading poetry in flowing gowns, came to my mind. Every time I mentioned this, people laughed. "You see," I said, and laughed too, "you thought of me and my evening in the same way. We are all conditioned."

But today I think of those women as forerunners to the movement, heroines. Like Nora in *A Doll's House*.

I was much more of a freak myself than I had known, or had ever wanted to know, and it had nothing to do with being sexy. The best part of it was I began not to care. I wish Garbo had understood. How insane that she retired at a time in her life when her creativity was at its peak. It might have grown way beyond her own imagination—ours, too.

As a woman actress I was luckier than Garbo, than Monroe, than Sullavan. The fight was all around me.

After one of the matinee performances in Seattle, our first commercial date, I met with a group of women from NOW. We talked about the movement. I said, "I am happy it came at this time in my life. Fifteen years from now it might have been too late." A lovely white-haired lady around sixty-five stepped forward, hugged me, and said, "No, darling. It wouldn't." We both laughed. That evening, I thought of her when I performed Barbara, the lady who delivers the lecture on the female orgasm in my show. "It's never too late, darling," I ad-libbed. It got applause.

Under the protection of the work, I began to ask myself the questions so much in the air. What is "me"? What is "conditioning"? What is health? What is neurosis?

I read. I listened. I watched. I was astonished. I, together with millions of women all over the world, began to understand myself.

It was an extraordinary coincidence that at this time Paul and I should be working on a theatrical evening called *I Am a Woman*. As if on cue, articles began to appear, poetry, novels, anthologies —about women, by women. People were marvelous, making suggestions. *Ms.* came out with its first issue. Women were finally speaking up for themselves, raising their voices, exposing handwritten diaries hidden under napkins, among the kitchen silver or the children's toys.

On the NBC-TV special about the changing relationship between men and women, Barbara Walters interviewed me on the subject of sisterhood. "I used to put women second," I said, "including myself since I am one. If I had a date with a woman for dinner and a man called me and invited me, I would say yes without even checking with her first, diminishing us both. The worst part is that she too would understand and agree I did the right thing."

"What are you doing about it?" Barbara asked.

"Just working on changing my attitude," I said, "or the ghosts return."

It begins in the womb between mothers and daughters! I was thinking of another incident with Lena, now a mother herself of two girls. "My God, I am coming back," I had thought, and I clearly didn't like it. It also had to do with Natasha, my grandchild.

I was sitting on the old chest in the hall of Lena's apartment, the same chest that had stood for years in my mother's house. God knows what it had listened to there. Marty was telling me about the play he was directing. Lena was wandering back and forth, making order in a household were disorder is unavoidable—two children, little help, work, no money. Suddenly a voice broke through, filled with indignation, about being robbed of what was hers. "Someone drank my tea! Someone drank my tea!" As if screaming was the only way she could be heard.

It was unlike Natasha, but there was trouble in the house between Marty and Lena, and Lena had moved out for a few weeks. It was a courageous decision, made in order to become clearer about herself. She was back now, but for how long? The children might have asked themselves. For them, it was scary. I found myself more concerned with them than with her—they let me in on their pain and she didn't. When she was a child, obviously I didn't hear her, and now she is proud, my daughter.

Natasha came running to us, the three grownups, the wise ones with the power to set things straight or set things crooked. "Someone drank my . . ." That's when a few drops of tea with milk and honey spilled on the rug.

"Damn it, Natasha. You spilled tea on the rug," Lena's voice, desperately furious, interrupted her.

Natasha turned white in the face. "But somebody drank my . . ." The voice had already lost some of its guts, some of its conviction.

Lena's voice, now stronger but not yet strong enough to be able to listen to someone else's scream, but wanting to stay in control, "Get a rag immediately and clean it up. Immediately! Did you hear me?"

Natasha's eyes seemed blacker than ever. For a second her mouth quivered. The indignation of the mother erased all her own sense of rights. Then the fear, "What if she disappears again, what if she's so angry with me that she will never, never, never come back?" Oh God! How well I knew that feeling!

Natasha knows I understand. Lena doesn't. I left her for nine months when she was a baby and never really understood to make up for it. I have changed since then. She doesn't believe it yet.

When I said, "Lena, she has a legitimate complaint; someone drank her tea," Lena turned on me in fury. "Don't diminish me in front of my children."

"Diminish?" I repeated. And I, too, like Natasha, in a flash of a second, forgot what the moment was all about. In a second I was in a box, shattered, side-tracked. Diminish? Am I diminishing her? No! Where? When? I forgot about the incident with Yulin and others like it and about all the times I had acted a diminished woman in front of her—as my mother had in front of me, and hers in front of her. And that was my problem, for there was no reason for it anymore!

Natasha, white in the face, feeling she had created a conflict situation, ran into the kitchen, picked up the rag, ran back, wiped up the tea spilled on the rug, then moved tearfully, carefully toward Lena with the rag in her hand. And like an angel, she put her arms around her, as if she knew and understood what trouble Lena was in. She took the risk of being excluded once more from her. "I love you, Mommy," she said. The voice was tiny, but *there.* I felt my insides shaking, for someday I wanted to be able to do what she did. Not out of fear, but out of love, as she had.

God, I hope she can hold on to her love and still understand that she is in the right. Not lose that sense of her own right. I have had such trouble doing it myself. Is that when Lena meant by "diminished"? If so, it must have been threatening to her, this image I gave her.

I understand her now in retrospect. I, too, wanted to destroy every part, I thought, of my mother in me when I was Lena's age.

My mother always apologized for herself, for her life, for her painting, but even if it had been out of survival that I denied my love for her, it was as painful as it was impossible to accept, for I had loved her intimately, sensually, and passionately once, and that part of me never understood the separation. I had had to trace my way back to that love, for the confusion colored all my intimate relationships and I surely wanted to stop the spasm. Nor do I want to pass it on to the next generation, this image of a diminished woman, or one that diminishes—they go hand in hand with each other.

Inge, my new analyst, is a woman, too. She listens carefully, never threatened by my anger or pain as my mother was. On the contrary, always ready to clear up misunderstandings between us, something my mother had no knowledge of how to do. I.B. lives around the corner the way my grandmother did. There is a fire in the fireplace when the snow lies on the ground outside in her garden. And when the weather is warm, the smell from the flowers and trees fills the room. She helps me open locked doors to my past, allowing air in so that I dare to search the murky corners and still am able to breathe. Se has become a reality in my fantasy-filled existence. There is peace between us, as it must have been once in my mother's womb. There are many forms of intimacy. Yes.

I am beginning to trust women. I'm beginning to know how to love them. My daughter is one. So am I.

"I am woman . . . hear me roar . . . in numbers too big to ignore . . ." is playing on the radio in my Boston hotel room under the announcement. LINDFORS SPARKLES . . . SHE HAS GONE FAR AND PENETRATED DEEP . . . DON'T MISS HER . . . I am back in reality. It's time to get to the theater. I could dream all day. A hotel room can be very seductive in its unfamiliarity.

I love this old twentieth-century hotel. A divine lady sings show tunes in the bar every night. It is said she was Cole Porter's sweetheart and that they were supposed to get married, but he died. Now she sings his songs every night. She must be at least seventy-five. Her hair is white, as white as her spirit.

The snow is still coming down outside on Independence Street. Boston is one of my favorite cities. It reminds me of the America I dreamed of. I am going to walk all the way to the theater, feeling the snowflakes on my eyelashes.

The theater is located on a small street. I am laughing as I turn the corner. VIVECA IS COMING BACK is printed on the marquee. I opened twenty-five years ago here in Boston in the Shubert Theatre a block away on Main Street in *I've Got Sixpence*. I had just fallen in love with G.T. The neighborhood has deteriorated since, like our love. It's even unsafe today. Last night, after rehearsals, when the kids came out from the theater to go home, they found the windshields of their cars smashed. The important question became: Will the insurance company pay for the repairs? Nobody makes more than a hundred dollars a week working in this theater. How will they get home tonight?

I wander into the house. Everybody looks exhausted. They have been working around the clock. I feel two, four, six arms around me—Dorothy, Jerry, and Esquire, the Boston Repertory Company. "We are sold out for two weeks and we want you to play two more. Can you stay? They love you in Boston."

I laugh. "I have to think about it." They had finally raised the money for *Woman*. They are building their own theater with the profit. For a moment I began to feel like Mother Courage, violating something human in myself. Always leaving my children . . . and now the grandchildren.

"Do you have to go?" Natasha, my granddaughter, asked me the day I took off for Sweden, looking at me with her big black eyes, just as big and black as my son John's thirty years ago. I remember the sense of surprise that I meant so much to him, but I don't remember what I answered. To Natasha, my grandchild, I said, "Yes, I must go to work." She understood. We hugged each other. She was running a fever. I felt her tiny, thin, hot body against mine. I longed to take her along, the way gypsies would, and protect her against all harm.

"Okay, we will give you until Thursday," Jerry says cleverly, having sensed my hesitation. He is one of the producers and has so far done a superb job. I knew, of course, my answer would be yes for I, too, know about being an artist *and* a businessman and having to grab the moment. Natasha will have a different relationship with me, her grandmother, from mine with my grandmother. As John had a relationship with me different from mine with my mother. And I will use my dilemma when I do *Mother Courage* the next time, I am thinking.

For better or for worse. It's been my choice all along. Sometimes it is agony. Sometimes it is glorious. For sure it is life.

"Up the revolution! Women on top!" The sound of my own voice is booming out over the loudspeakers.

It was Paul's idea to use sound as another voice in the evening, creating a bridge taking us from one woman's land to another's. Sometimes using my own, sometimes sound effects, sometimes David Horowitz's score, haunting, yearning, loving, angry, tender, and always suggestive, mirroring the feelings of the women.

I sit down in the back of the house, watching Paul, my director, my co-arranger, my friend, at work. We have gone through some turbulent years together, good ones, too, and a lot of changes.

I have sometimes been criticized for not choosing a woman director for *I Am a Woman*. I am not sure I was ready at the time for that, or whether someone was available with Paul's quality. And I was not about to discriminate for the sake of revenge.

Although my relationship with Paul was strictly a working one, the road was as rocky at times as in a marriage. "You always think that I am taking advantage of you because you are a woman," he said one day, and I answered, "You always *do* take advantage of me, *because* I am a woman." We stood glaring at each other, both of us knowing we had spoken the truth.

Trying to understand the movement. Drawing the knowledge from it, but as equals, Paul and I began to experience an unspoken sense of faith in each other's talent and taste, a human intimacy that led to complete acceptance of each other. Love! Our needs complemented each other. His was to understand the darkness in woman . . . It was mine to explain about it . . .

Yes, Paul and I have remained friends.

We began working on the script in January, 1971. I was in the middle of the break-up with G.T. With the guidance of Paul, the turbulence turned into creativity.

We had decided not to write any of the material ourselves, but rather let each piece take us into unexpected places, more complex, than we would have been able to invent ourselves.

People were marvelous, making suggestions, sending us poetry, scenes, clippings. My files kept growing. The story line slowly formed itself.

Obviously our needs to understand the changes within ourselves and around us influenced our choice of story line and material, but only partly, for we wanted it to be a journey of many women, not only mine, emotional, as well as social, with the kind of clarity that follows from that combination. "Without blaming anyone," as the Polish Pope said the other day, "but I do have to tell the truth."

The first part of the journey took the woman into the past, with the voices of the present piercing through, moving the story forward. The second part took her into the present, making her see the future, take responsibility for it, politically and emotionally. And for herself.

I was about to throw out a file on the Women's Strike for Peace when my eyes caught the tape containing the testimony by the Vietnamese freedom fighter during the Peace Conference in Paris. We were approximately seventy-five women, women belonging to Women's Strike for Peace, from various countries that were fighting in Vietnam, and the women from North Vietnam. We lived together in an old French castle half an hour outside of Paris. We slept together in the same rooms, ate at the same tables, and became sisters with the women from the country we were officially fighting a war with.

She was nineteen, soft-spoken, and beautiful. Her face was young and unlined; only a scar across her upper lip gave a hint of the horrors she had experienced. Some days she was dressed in a fatigue uniform, other days in a Vietnamese long cotton peasant dress. Sometimes her hair was braided, sometimes loose, often a flower stuck in it lightening its darkness. One young woman from Texas became her closest friend during the week. They were inseparable, always holding hands, as if Ngo Thi needed to affirm that there could be love in spite of the hate between the two countries.

The afternoon she delivered her testimony I was ill upstairs with the flu. But I knew from seeing the faces of everybody later that day that something extraordinary had happened. I asked one of the women to give me the tape and a translation. As I read it, I knew I had to find a way to use it. I forgot about it until one day— I had cleaned up my office—I saw it lying in the garbage can ready to be picked up. I saved it. Lucky! It was Paul's idea to use her voice on tape and me as the translator. The most moving moment is when Ngo Thi breaks down. Her first words, after she is able to speak again, are: "I had to fight. I had to fight two, three times every day." At that moment the tape stops and I become her. It's deathly quiet in the house whenever, wherever I play it.

The moment is clear, so clear. It is not in her nature to fight. It is not in human nature to fight. It is not in my nature to fight. As an artist I wanted to express this: I wanted to say that war between countries, violence between people is against our nature. I was finally able to express a point of view as a woman! No blame. Just the truth!

After six months, Paul and I had completed a four-hour version of *I Am a Woman* and ahead of us lay the shaping of it into a two-hour performance.

We were offered a workshop in Hartford in October. We accepted and went into rehearsal.

We gave four performances in Hartford over a period of two weeks. We learned that the show was rocky, but that it could work. With the money we made we paid for the sound, the costumes, and other things we needed. Everybody was generous way beyond any pay. I'll never forget seeing Joe Eula standing in the costume shop in Hartford, steam coming out of the dye pots, pieces of material hanging around him, tones from deep rose to light flesh color, to be dried, to be checked under the lights, to be examined, to be tried over and over again. He lovingly created a costume for the working actress and the woman on her journey. Leotards with a skirt tied around the waist; a brown traveling cape with a slouch hat. Props, some old and some new. Sparingly, he helped me create images of the thirty-six women.

It became our method to mount the show with the money we received for performances. By the time we opened in New York a year later, the physical production was financed through the work.

By now we had formed a corporation of *I Am a Woman*. I was often amazed at how complicated even a one-woman show can get, both from a technical as well as legal point of view. We finally learned to stay away from anybody—accountant or lawyers, producers or partners—who doesn't want to work as hard at their task as we do at ours.

We eventually became experts. Clearing rights, dealing with thirty authors and their representatives, taught me as much as I want to know about it. Most of them were wonderful. The only flat no we had was from Françoise Gilot, Picasso's wife. We wanted to use the chapter in her book where she brilliantly and funnily, charmingly and ironically describes how Picasso tries to seduce her. "No, no, no," she repeated in her French-accented English. "I will not be part of an evening of bits and pieces." We finally had to give up. It's ironic because she really was a victim of Picasso's male chauvinism and she ought to have been happy to be part of an evening like *I Am a Woman*.

We could live without Gilot's piece. But not without Anne Frank. And the ten percent system almost did us in.

The story of her diary is symbolic of the story of her life.

This exquisitely handwritten diary that kept her spirit and her body alive for as long as it did was found after her death by her father and taken to a Dutch publisher who, with great care and love, published it in hopes that the Dutch people might learn something from Anne's spirit.

The words soon turned Japanese, French, Swedish, Italian, English, even German. Yes, the diary and Anne's words, like stepmother violets, spread themselves in the most unexpected places, surviving wind and storms.

In New York, a play was written based on the diary. Suddenly there were new groups of people in charge. People who had nothing to do with the original writing of Anne, the original beauty of the book, people who were strangers to Anne, but people who knew how to tie up rights. It falls under the heading of greed. It's ironic. As if the angel and the devil were continually drawn toward each other; everything Anne stands for is about the human spirit defeating greed, power hunger, and ego.

I went to the agent, a woman, representing the play for permission to perform the words from Anne's original diary. I got an immediate no, no, no. Which in English hurts as much as in French. After endless correspondence, legal letters, expensive letters beautifully typed up by secretaries, and with the help of friends and telephone calls, finally a yes was accomplished. The writers of the play, the Hacketts, put their foot down. They understood. I went through the same ordeal for the record, for the book, and last but not least for the CBC-TV special. It almost killed the deal. "But why?" we all said to the agents, to the authors, to their friends. "It's only five minutes altogether. Anne's words are essential to our evening. We can't do without them. Please." "No, no, no!"

We didn't give up until one day—I was down in Mexico performing *I Am a Woman* at a college—when I received a call from Norman Campbell at CBC. "We are sorry, Viveca. The agent called this morning. 'If you use the words of Anne Frank, I will sue you,' she said rather loudly over the phone an hour ago," he quoted her. "I am afraid we have to cancel the taping," he added!

The project was dead.

I took a long walk to cool off. It was a hot day, but not as hot as my temper. I started to kill her. I cut her up. I stabbed her. I flushed her down the toilet. My violence not unlike the violence of the Nazis, the difference being it happened in my head. My way not to go insane.

However, the last shall be the first. As I got back to my bungalow, the phone rang. My secretary was on the other end of the line. "She died this afternoon."

"Who died?"

"The agent, a few hours after she screamed no, no, no at the CBC."

"My God," I said. I looked up to heaven and, lo and behold, through the clouds, I saw Anne talk to her! "Come on, lady. Why did you make it so hard?" And she starts to explain. It comes out, "gobble, gobble, gobble," like crazy talk, because in heaven that's what *that* kind of logic sounds like. She will have to learn to talk like a human being again. I began to feel sorry for her. After all, she was a mutation. Aha! That's why she was in heaven. She had to pay a high price for her independence, just like my aunt, just like Nora in *A Doll's House*, or Alice in *Dance of Death*, or like so many women of that generation.

The next day, we continued negotiations for Anne's words. Maybe she helped us. We got the rights! The show was done. Ta, ta! It paid off! Lesson learned: Don't take no for an answer.

We wrote to all the regional theaters, and our first commercial date was Seattle's Repertory Theatre, beautifully situated in the middle of the festival grounds. Our opening was glorious. The reviews were raves, and by the end of the run we sold out.

We left Seattle in an exuberant mood. Cleveland had come through with an offer for a week, the Arena Stage in Washington for three!

In Washington, for the first time, a reviewer, and a major one, attacked me. It was an obvious anti-female review. He attacked my sagging breasts, my age, and my Swedish accent. There was nothing I could do about it. I had this strange feeling reading his review that unless I gave him his image of a woman he could not accept me. My breasts *are* sagging! I *am* over fifty and I *have* breast-fed three marvelous babies. Before, my breasts were more beautiful, but some men don't mind them the way they are. I wonder what his look like, and he hasn't even fed anyone. I won't ask him what other parts of his body look like. Sagging, perhaps?

And, oh yes, I have an accent. I was born in Sweden. What is wrong with that? I am not the only one in this country born someplace else and into another language, or a dialect. Why do we all have to speak the same way? Are we not mirroring life on the stage? What is so great about perfect English speech? And to whose ears? Could it possibly be his problem?

I was still in a panic. That night I had to go on portraying Anne at fourteen and Brenda at sixteen. Harold (my lover) told me over the phone, "Fight the bastards. Organize the women." He helped me find my fury.

Harold often encourages me in my strength. "You can handle it," he says. He became essential to my fight in Washington. It began that night.

We had played a week of previews to standing room only; for the first time the house was small and the atmosphere cold. When I got to that gorgeous, freaky lady, the Madwoman of Chaillot, I ad-libbed, "It doesn't always look so good in the morning, especially if you have read your review in the *Washington Post*." The house roared and broke into applause. The ice was broken. During the open dialogue we discussed the effect of a review and the right of an audience to do something about it; that power can shift. It worked. Letters began to bombard the newspaper.

The women were terrific. They marched. They threatened. Barbette Blackington organized her own picket crowd in front of the *Washington Post* and demanded equal space for a brilliant reply she had written. She got it. Audiences began to build. In Washington, D.C., sisterhood became a practical reality to me.

Our next step had to be New York. To begin with, we wasted eight months through the incompetence of a commercial Broadway producer. Everything became money and business. The haggling almost killed the baby.

Finally in October we faced it, and when Gene Frankel at the Theatre of Space offered us a workshop production, which enabled us to keep artistic control in our own hands, we accepted.

The script was frozen now. We thought! Two days before the opening in New York, I happened to read the introduction to *Pentimento* by Lillian Hellman, where she explains her own need "to see and see again." Like the woman in the play. Like me. Like so many of us today. It became our opening speech. It replaced Anais Nin's brilliant piece, "The Ragpicker." We hated to lose it but had no choice, for it was clearer and "Nothing is lost but it changes," sings the Ragpicker.

Anais understood. She had become my friend, and "the city of Fez" from her diary is the closing statement in the show.

When I was doing *Courage* in Washington, I had discovered her diaries. I fell in love with them. They would be waiting for me in the rented apartment near the theater after the performance. I read hungrily until I fell asleep. They told me what I needed to hear. I discovered a voice within me that I hadn't listened to before. Anais' voice, a woman's voice, women's voices! Mine!

Before I returned to New York, I quoted a few lines of hers on a television show. The next day I received a call from her editor. "Would you like to meet her?"

"Where does she live?"

"New York."

I was surprised. I had pictured her living in Spain or in Paris.

A week later I had returned to New York and was in the middle of facing the break-up of my marriage. I went to her apartment for tea on Washington Square. Her husband, Ian Hugo, met me at the door, a tall, distinguished looking gentleman who soon became one of my dearest friends. A sublime man, a filmmaker and artist. He served me tea. A few moments later, Anais appeared, like a wind of grace. I felt strange. I told her, "I have been reading your diary. I feel I know you so intimately, more so than you know me."

She looked at me curiously. "I have seen your work. I know you, Viveca." From that moment on we were friends and stayed friends until death, savagely, cruelly, and unjustly, took her away.

At her memorial service I read from "The Ragpicker." "Nothing is lost but it changes." I am glad that she did see *I Am a Woman* at the Theatre of Space. She came to one of the very first performances and helped spread the word, and we depended upon word of mouth.

There was little money in the budget for ads. The women came to my rescue again. Dorothy, Jan, Kathy, Susan, and Mary, and many more. They did everything from running errands to being my dresser; pasting posters all over New York, legally and illegally; driving their cars with balloons and posters in the windows; even running the lightboard when one electrician dropped out. It paid off.

We opened *I Am a Woman* a snowy night in January in the Theatre of Space, which once used to be a church. The critics arrived one by one. *The New York Times* gave us a rave. Interviews began to appear. By the end of the run we were playing to standing room only. From then on, we haven't really stopped.

After a four-month run in New York we went on a nationwide tour. And later that year an invitation came through from Sweden, the country where I was born, where my life as an actress had begun. And here I am now eight weeks later in Boston, U.S.A.

"We wanted to wake the wonder in us all, the wonder in Anne, age fourteen, the wonder in Anais Nin, age seventy," Paul said during a dialogue in the beginning of the run. The wonder in me, too. Did we? Yes! But differently from what I had expected.

Doug is checking the lights. I am watching him paint the stage in pink and blue and dark green tone, cold white ones too, bringing out in the brilliantly sculptured Ironset by Suzanne Benton faces of women, or a hand, or even a crotch. It's magic. I am glad we got it through customs.

"All this traveling, Viveca. How do you do it?" Paul suddenly asks me.

"I spoke to Kathy last night and this morning I woke up in a hotel room. 'Kathy?' I asked myself. 'Who's Kathy?' Intimacy is not my strongest point," I laughed, "and traveling doesn't help much. I can't take them all along with me as gypsies or the court musicians would have. But would that really help?" We both started to laugh, because the night before we had been sitting around talking about love and work and all the complications in combining them. On the other hand, we had said, if you don't live life, how are you going to portray it? Being an artist is mirroring life.

"Obviously it has nothing to do with generations or age," I said. "A man in the audience, at least fifty-five or sixty, asked me one evening during the dialogue. 'Do you believe that intimacy is possible without possessiveness?' It was very quiet in the house. The question obviously hit home with us all. I took a deep breath and said clearly, 'Yes.' Then I added, 'I am not quite there myself yet. I like my newly found independence, but I am still fragile about it.'"

"To love in a new way . . ." Paul says, "we all want that . . . not only women . . . men, too.' He is interrupted by Doug's voice over the loudspeakers: "Paul! I need you!" "These are turbulent times," Paul adds and disappears down the aisle. . . .

2

"Not until I turned eighty did I give up a yearning for the love of a man," my Aunt Else, my favorite aunt, said to me one day in Stockholm. We were sitting in her kitchen, drinking champagne, the very best. She was just past eighty now, elegant and beautiful as always, her eyelids painted blue even though she didn't know I was coming to visit. We laughed and cried together as always. She always moved me, Aunt Else, and crying with her was and still is always as nice as laughing. "Love," she said, with a champagne glass in her hand, "is the only big thing in life. To live alone is unnatural, Viveca."

"I know," I said, and laughed and cried again. "Why is loving a man so much harder than loving you?" I asked her, sipping the champagne.

"Oh, Viveca," she said, "we are women and can forgive. Men have not been allowed to make a mistake. Ever! The real problem comes up when they realize we know they have made one. We become their mirror, their bad conscience, and sometimes they even leave us in order to justify the crime. Oh, Viveca! That's when you have to be the wise one and love them no matter what."

"How?" I asked.

She didn't answer that one. She just laughed and drank some more superb French champagne. She knew I had to answer that one myself.

I had met Harold eight months after G.T. left—a handsome man in his sixties. I fell in love, passionately and generously. I wanted to go with him to the end of the world! But I knew better. He was more careful committing himself. Once he did there was no holding back. I began to feel trapped by his demands to be his woman, his partner.

"What do I tell the hostess?" he would say if I didn't want to go to a dinner party that he wanted to go to. "She'll think we are breaking up."

"Tell her I am at home reading a book," I answered.

"We'll be an uneven number at the dinner table. Or she'll have to find another woman for me," he continues.

"Why? Do you go to dinner parties in order to have sex with your table partners?" I would answer.

Sometimes he would take along another woman. Sometimes he wouldn't. "Does that upset you?" someone asked me once in an open dialogue following the performance.

"No," I said. "I trust him. The thing I worry about is that if I don't give him what he's asking for, *I* began to *feel ungenerous*. I am struggling to hold on to my love for him. For I don't like to be alone! On the other hand, I can't pay a price for love. No more."

I wasn't always so gracious about it in life. The old ghost feeling, being invaded, was back. "Your love is becoming a burden for me," I cried out one day through tears. The old female weapon. It was still difficult for me to be straight any other way. Better that way than not at all. "You must accept me as I am. You don't have to understand me, but accept me. Please. For your own sake, too."

It felt good to take the risk and say it, and it didn't split us up.

"It's not that you don't want to love," Inge, my analyst, said. "It's that you don't know how."

"At least I have lost all my illusions about peaceful old age," I answered laughingly. "I am fifty-seven, H.T. is sixty-three, and we are still battling like children about God knows what," I said.

"Tell me about it."

"Why do I stay with him at all?" I say.

"Tell me." She is very precise. "Maybe you're still afraid of intimacy?" she continues, since I don't answer.

The question makes me furious, because I know all about it. Intimacy is not just making love, but sharing thoughts, feelings, bad ones as well as good ones. It goes hand in hand. You sit on hate; you sit on love. It's the question of saying yes and saying no. "Tell me about it," Inge repeats. I try, for I can't handle it. Yet.

It was Friday night, leading into a together weekend. We had finally arrived at the decision to spend it at my house. For H.T. it is quite a trip. Subway, bus, taxi! He was a good sport about it. Maybe it was my guilt that started it off. Now it has to pay off for him, I began to feel that he felt. How, is the question. Do I have to tell him I love him? I need him? I miss him? I am happy he is there? I hate playing the game of the loving woman! Why can't we just exist with each other, as if we were living together!

Scene: An hour later, her bedroom. Bedtime.

She brushes her teeth, cleans her face, lies down on the floor to do her exercises, curing a bad back. He cleans his teeth, takes out his front tooth, puts it back. She loves it that he doesn't care. He is a peasant like her! He crawls down in bed, makes a few cracks about the exercises. She takes it in stride. When she is ready, she crawls down, too. She puts on her nightgown, determined not to be allergic to any pressures or anything. He puts his hand up her thighs, says, "Please take off your nightgown. I like to hold you and feel your skin."

She, friendly, "Yes, but I need the warmth because of my back. I get cold if I take it off."

Silence follows. She has begun to feel ungenerous! He tries again. "I'll keep you warm, dummy. Take it off and let me hold you for a while. Then you can put it back on."

It was a good suggestion, but she doesn't hear it for she is involved in thinking that *he* is probably thinking, "Christ, I came all the way up here from the Village and for what?" Besides, she wants to exist with him as if they were living together all the time, which, of course, they are not. On the other hand, she tries *not* to feel too guilty about the whole thing. Is it possible that she's out to prove something? That he is? "You can feel me through the nightgown, you dummy. And I can feel you, too." And that too is a good suggestion. She's trying to be funny. "I don't like the idea of falling asleep in your arms without the nightgown and then having to get up and put it on again." That is true, too, no doubt.

He, his hand still on her thigh, "Don't you know about skin?"

She gets fed up now! "Christ! I do know about skin." She turns around and moves over to her side of the bed, thinking, "It always has to be his way, always." Silence, for he is probably thinking the same.

He says, "What's the good in coming all the way up here to have you turn your back on me?" And she answers—knowing it was coming. All the time! "Shit, man. You're hassling me. That's why I'm turning my back on you. Stop hassling me and I won't." Accept me. Me! Me!

The battle is in the open. After five minutes he gets up, gets dressed, slams the door, and leaves. A few minutes later he comes back up the stairs, walks into the room, opens the door that he just slammed, and laughs. That's what is great about him. He carries no grudges and is basically a yes-to-life man. "I love you," he says.

"I love you, too. Come back to bed." She is laughing now. "Please."

He asks, "What about breakfast tomorrow morning? I am getting up early at 7:30. When are you getting up?"

She, on her guard again, answers, "I'm not sure."

He, "I don't like to have breakfast by myself. If I am going to stay, I want to know if you are getting up."

Shit! He is bargaining again. But she is determined to hold on to this position. "If I wake up, yes. But I really need my sleep." She has been traveling and performing, traveling and performing, and needs rest. "Let's play it by ear." She is annoyed now that he doesn't consider her health, and he is annoyed that she doesn't care about his welfare.

"If I can't hold you without a nightgown and can't have breakfast with you, I might as well have stayed home."

She answers, "Yes, I can see that." By now she is exhausted.

He walks out, slams the door again, a bit harder.

She tries to go to sleep. Can't. "It's the problem of living in separate places," she mumbles to herself. "If we were poorer, we would have to move in together. If we were richer, it wouldn't matter. We would have a limousine and a chauffeur waiting for us, taking us back and forth any time we want to." The image makes her dizzy. Now it has become a battle of power, and bloody half-assed. I wanted to love! I hate to be alone!

I should have taken the nightgown off. I should have agreed to have breakfast with him. Shit! She dials his number. "Hello," he says. "I love you, you dummy," she says.

He laughs, "I love you, too."

She: "We are so childish."

He stops laughing, "No, I am very mature. What I am asking for is a perfectly normal thing." End of conversation.

She, exasperated, thinks, "Who needs this kind of night, this kind of man?" She finally goes to sleep.

Half an hour later the phone rings. He: "I can't sleep. I love you."

She: "I know. It's all ridiculous. I love you, too. We need sleep and here we are."

He: "Yes, you might as well have come down to my place and we would be asleep by now."

"Or you could have stayed here," she says, knowing, of course, she shouldn't have said it even if it were true. It's the end of the conversation.

"God, it was three o'clock in the morning!" I said to Inge that day in her quiet living room—office. She laughs. I do, too. Now! It all doesn't seem so serious any longer. "Why couldn't I just have told him, 'I love you, you dummy. I'll take off my nightgown some other time,' and laughed and none of all this nonsense would have happened?"

"Yes. Say no and love him anyhow." Inge said.

"Yes, why can't I?"

I hadn't that morning.

"How can I share life with a man I don't live with? It's too easy to just walk out. Besides, I am sick and tired of romance. It's the little things in life that matter, not the big ones. I want something else, something deep, something simple, something real. I am going to look for a man who wants what I want. I am splitting," I had blurted out. I was talking to Susan, my tenant. Susan laughed, a terrific throaty laugh. She never laughed *at* me, but at the situation and with me. She was standing in the hallway in her green robe, leaning against the red wall. It was early in the morning. We always ended up in the hallway—two women discussing the essence of life, or the cleaning woman, or the kids, or Duffy or Brandy, or the job, or loving men. Oh yes, the last was the most common issue!

"I know what you're saying," she said. "I don't exactly know what it was that turned it around for David and me, but ever since we got together the last time, it's been terrific. It *was* different! All the other times we got together passionately, hungrily. But this last time it was harmonious, Viveca. As if we finally were aware of how terrific it was to love each other and how awful it had been without each other. It's been fabulous ever since."

Susan was only thirty-five, but very wise. "Thank God for women friends," I thought. I started to feel warm again.

"You can put up with a lot, Viveca," she said, "once you know what you need."

"Meaning want?" I said.

"Right," she said. "But it's a slow boat to China," she added laughingly. "Be patient."

Susan walked into my apartment three years ago, took one look at it, and said, "Can I have it?"

"Of course," I said.

"I am separating," she explained. "We bought a house up the street two years ago and I had just finished redecorating it! Now we are splitting!"

"I am sorry," I said.

"He's a terrific guy," she said. I admired her generosity.

A few days later she showed up with a paintbrush and paint, ready to go to work. She brought Jamie, age six, her daughter from an earlier marriage, Alice, a strange old cat, and Duffy, a white fluffy little thing who brought love into Brandy's life. The two became inseparable.

"Do you mind if David moves in with us, too?" she asked.

"Of course not. Who is David?"

"It's my husband."

"Oh, he's back?"

"Yes," she laughed.

A few days later I met David. He carried lots of boxes and seemed terrific. A few weeks later, he moved out again. And then he moved in and then he moved out. It went on and on and on.

"David moved out this morning," Susan would say. "This is it.

I am going to look for somebody else." I said nothing, having just seen him walk out the door with two suitcases as I had seen him do three weeks before and three weeks before then, always carrying the same papier mache statue (it was light) of an Irish priest that stood in the room facing the garden. It became a familiar sight. I was fascinated by the intensity of their struggle and the risks they both dared to take, wanting to get to the bottom of their problem.

"It was my stupid guilt," David said to me sometime later that year. He had been married to another woman for twenty-three years and had six kids with her.

"It's understandable," I said, "and I admire you for taking the risks." And then I told him what she had said to me in the hallway about their getting back together so harmoniously the last time. "She was happy, David," I said.

"I know," David said. He was deeply moved, as was I, for five days later she was dead! That day in the hallway was the last time I saw her.

I was upstairs in the bedroom resting, getting ready for a trip to Canada. I didn't even know that the ambulance had come and taken her away. I had stopped in to say hello and good night to Jamie. She came running toward me in her usual courageous yet intense way, similar to Susan's. "Mommy's heart is going tick-tick and the police took her to the hospital." I tried to hug her but she wouldn't let me. I hated to leave.

Two days later, at 6:00 in the morning, they called me long distance in Hamilton, Canada. "She's dead. Susan is dead."

"She's dead? No, no, no, no. Why? Not Susan. No. Why?" Sadness. I miss her. Anger. Did she have to die?

I loved her the way I had loved Sophie. Like Sophie she had everything I expected an American woman to have when I was a young girl in Sweden. She was tough, yet sensitive, a superb spirit, pretty, too, in a lively way. I hope part of her soul went into me, part of her spirit. I think of her courage and it gives me back mine.

"Susan had accomplished more of what she wanted in her life at the age of thirty-five than most of us ever will," her brother said to me a day later.

"What?" I asked.

"Love," he said. "She knew how to protect love."

When I came home from the airport in the evening, the house was filled with friends. David's friends, Susan's friends, singing, crying, talking. It was like a river of emotions at the bottom of my house, carrying David and Jamie over the insane days between an ambulance taking Susan away to facing that she was gone. Was she really? I saw her in the apartment, in the corridor, all over the house. I couldn't get her out of my sight.

I read Walt Whitman at the service. " 'Has anyone supposed it lucky to be born? I hasten to inform him or her it is just as lucky to die and I know it. I pass death with the dying and birth with the new-washed babe, and am not contained between my hat and boots.' Susan is talking through me. It is up to us to continue living as she did, as if she were still here," I said, after I finished the poem.

H.T. was holding my hand through the rest of the service.

3

"Magic time, Lindfors; it's all yours," Doug's voice rings out over the loudspeaker, bringing me back to reality. "Two hours to curtain." It's my turn to prepare. The snow is finally slowing down.

I love my dressing room in this shabby little theater. It has everything a star's dressing room should have, in spite of its faded elegance: red velvet-covered furniture, thick Arabian carpets, an old gaslight which is on the wall burning. An old faded photograph that I found in Sweden is hanging over my make-up table. It was taken during dance class thirty years ago, a few days after I was accepted at the Royal Dramatic Theatre School. I am wearing a leotard, as I do now for my *Woman* show. I am watching myself in the gold-framed mirror. In the friendly light, my body hasn't changed much. Yes. My breasts have. I don't care, but I do miss my reddish-brown thick hair. It is slowly turning gray now. It's been six months since I stopped coloring it. There are just a few faded crumpled ends destroyed by chemicals left. Coming forth at the roots are a few streaks of dark healthy hair, still. I haven't seen my old color in years. Mask off, Viveca!

I look at the photograph.

I didn't know that I was beautiful in those days. Beauty helped to get my career going, but it was scary until I learned to depend upon my craft, rather than my looks. The mouth was fuller then. I seemed hungry for life. I didn't know that I was, above all, hungry for myself.

I start putting on my make-up. My God! Nobody looks at herself as much in the mirror as a working actress. And I do mind some of the lines in my face, the bitter ones. It's the non-living that makes them, and I do mind those—I do!

Doug is calling places over the loudspeaker. The show is about to begin. It's my time, now, my part of the puzzle.

Paul knocks on the door, gives me some delicate flowers. He disappears quickly. He is an actor, too, and knows I must get in touch with the bareness in me, the ancient core that is me. My mother, my grandmother, my aunt, my father, my brother, my sister, my children, my grandchildren, and my lovers. All those people I was in touch with, but didn't always know I was in touch with . . .

I must have been born with that feeling but didn't always know how to cherish it. I must hang on to it for dear life now, for my own sake and everybody else's, I am thinking as I take my place in the dark on the stage.

"Let my life be bare. Let me wake every morning to create. Let me live without fear of losing self. Let me love those that I have chosen to love. Let nothing stand in the way. Let my life be bare." The haunting melancholy music rises, then fades quickly. The lights come up on me slowly, and I remove the mask from my face and begin the journey once more of one woman and many women. My journey, too.

Yes, I am less afraid to be alone today. Yes, I am less afraid of life today.

4

Home is still the Swedish-red-painted brownstone house on 95th Street. Slowly, through the years, through rain, through snow, the color has turned beautifully Mediterranean red. In the spring, when the green vines climb all over it, my house looks like a Matisse painting.

It is filled with colors. The door and window panes are deep green. The door to my apartment is blue. And the door to the garden apartment, the tenant's apartment where Susan lived, is deep red.

Most brownstone houses like mine have four stories, two rooms on each floor. One faces the garden and the other the street. When I wake up in the morning I can look out to my right and see my trees in the garden. If I turn my head to the left I can see through the corridor, with the blue-painted railing and the red-carpeted steps going up and down, the room opposite my bedroom with the child's drawing on the wall. And through the windows I can see the trees on the street. I am surrounded by trees.

Some of the trees are taller than the house and were there long before the white man put his foot here and named our hill Hellgate. It's comforting to think that those same trees were here at the time the Indians used the land. The trees are my friends. They tell me about the wind, the time of day, the weather, the season; when I see the green buds at the end of the branches I know spring is coming, and by the end of May they will completely cover the garden, shade the house, and, when my apple tree suddenly turns pink overnight, I know summer is here.

The nights during the summer are magic, especially on weekends when everybody goes away and the silence is not disturbed by the sound of air conditioning and traffic. On a Sunday night on my terrace I can hear the crickets in New York. And in the early morning I hear the birds. I love my house on 95th Street. It gives me a sense of peace and wholeness.

We were five women living alone that spring of 1971 in our houses on the 95–94th street block. The men left. The women stayed. We were all the same ages, between 40 and 55. The men were older. One disappeared to a native island and a native female. Two men died of heart attacks. A famous artist left his artist wife, who became famous on her own, and married a nurse instead. G.T. went to Berlin, dealing with his past. Or changing his future?

I watched the women in their houses turn off the lights at night, pull the curtains, and I wondered how they coped with their loneliness. Helen, the artist who went on to fame and fortune, painted her house in gorgeous, soft pastel colors. "I am painting him out of my house, out of my life, Viveca," she said. I wondered who else wanted to paint their men out of their rooms, their beds, their souls, their bodies . . . and who wanted to paint new ones in.

I finally bought myself a new bed. The old one began to show signs of the years and what it had gone through—husbands, babies, dogs, sickness, meals served in bed, love-making, hate-making. . . . The best times in my family life always took place in "our" large bed. Everybody loved to be in it.

Sometimes I share it, sometimes I don't. Once you get over the fact that nobody is there when you put your hand out, you get dangerously independent. I am not always sure it is a healthy lesson. How to exist with someone is a better one. But there is a time and place for everything.

So far, my house on 95th Street doesn't seem to be too large for me. There is always some grownup child of mine, with his or her child, or wife or girlfriend or husband visiting the guest room. And

Susan, John's wife, got pregnant with Nicholas John in my large bed and almost gave birth to him nine months later in it.

Lena and the children will be staying with me until their house up the street is ready. Natasha and Katrina will be able to walk through gardens and climb my trees onto the terrace. I will see them grow up. I will have a chance to conquer with the grandchildren what I didn't with my own!!

Lena and Marty are separating. It will be eight years this New Year that they married in the garden room that now belongs to the tenant's apartment. Natasha and Katrina don't know about it yet. They only sense that something is lacking and worry.

"Mommy and Daddy are having a talk," Katrina said one day, her face pale and serious. We were out in the country house on Long Island.

"Yes, it's boring," I said. "Let's take a walk," trying to cheer her up. I should have known better. After all, she is my grandchild.

"No, I'll wait here," she said, and sat down on the steps to the house, preferring to worry about the grownups, to stay and stick it out.

"We haven't told the children yet," Lena said later.

"I don't envy you that moment," I said. We both remembered it . . . "They are the worst."

It's been hard on Lena. I knew she thought that it would never, never happen to her marriage, that hers would be different from mine. It is and it isn't. I used to think the same about my mother, and it *was* different, yet the same. Lena is in love, and wants to go all the way as I did, once.

"Will it ever change, Mother, the pattern?" Lena asked me the other day. We were out on Long Island.

"Yes, I think so," I answered. "It already has. When I split with your father, and fathers, I thought only of the *gains* for you—a new father, a better one, I hoped. I never thought about the loss of the one you already had. I never paid attention to the fact that you loved them. The men didn't, either, or to their own love. You and Marty are handling it differently. Your children will not lose either one of you. Patterns do change," I continued. "You are creating new images of men and women as I did, as John does, as Natasha and Katrina and Nicholas Jan will."

When I took off in the middle of the afternoon I saw her planting flowers around the cottage. The children were helping her. She was planting perennial flowers only. "I don't want the annual ones," she said.

293

"It's lonely, lonely," Marty said to me one day. The feeling of being abandoned is turbulent and complex whether we are men or women. I find myself deeply rooted today in my home, in my children, and now my grandchildren. I don't think I could change roots any more.

When G.T. was home the last time and talked about living in Germany vis-à-vis New York (having a need perhaps to affirm for himself that he is better off over there), I said, "Yes, I can see why you moved. The work is more fulfilling for you. I would move, too, if somebody offered me a sensational opportunity. But only temporarily. The children are here and the grandchildren."

"Of course," G.T. answered. "You have invested so much in them." I wondered why he *hadn't*. Eighteen years he had been their father. It's a long time.

"It's a weird thing to become a parent," John said to me one day. Nicholas Jan was sitting between us, in New York, having breakfast with the two of us. "It really feels nice to have my son here. He loves me; I love him. I don't ever want to lose him," he said.

I almost lost Kris that spring and summer after G.T. left. He ran from me, from the situation. He couldn't stand my pain. I couldn't blame him. Nor was it easy for me to have anyone around that reminded me of the situation. Kris did. On the other hand, I knew if we didn't have a talk soon the silences between us would multiply themselves and I couldn't bear losing him, too. He was my flesh and blood.

"I have my mother's blood," he had said to G.T. at a family counseling session, an awful one that didn't seem to lead toward anything. "I used to think I wanted to be cool and sophisticated like you. I don't." But then, he also loved G.T. He had been his son for almost twenty years. Kristoffer's dilemma was that he, too, knew about Uschi for months. Before I did. Even spent time with the two of them in Germany. It lay between us like a cancer, before and after the secret was in the open. He felt he had to take sides, get involved, or identify. With whom became the question. He was only nineteen.

Thank God for the house on 95th Street!

He came home one day from California, for he had no place to stay. It was his birthday. He was going to be twenty. I knew, perhaps unconsciously, that if we didn't have a talk with each other now, it would just be another long stretch of silence, and that was unbearable.

I woke up early, six o'clock. I wandered downstairs. The counter was filled with cheese, bread, oranges. The eggs were boiling on the stove. The timer was ringing. The coffee was brewing. Kristoffer in the middle of it all, naked, gorgeous, tall, blond, brown-eyed. My perfect baby—now in the shape of a man.

"Happy birthday," I said.

"It's not time yet," he said. "I was born at 7:46. Remember?"

I laughed. "I don't. Who told you?"

"Don."

"I see. I am glad someone knew. I only remember that I *felt* you were enormous. I don't even remember your face." I continued, "It's funny. I see Lena in her children. I suppose that's how you're going to come back to me, too, when you have yours."

"I am never going to have any," he said.

"Well, that's how you feel right now," I said hopefully.

"No, I'll be a lousy father," he said as he wandered out onto the terrace. "I don't want to be number two or number three. I have seen you being a wife to G.T. You were a tigress when it came to us, the children. George came number three, after us, after the work. It scares me."

For a moment I went into a panic. "God, the ghosts are coming back," I thought. But only for a moment.

"Kris, you don't have to be scared," I said gently. "If you become as much of a father as your wife is a mother, the child will be a link between the two of you and competition will blow out the window. The child will be yours as much as your wife's. You will make up for what your father *didn't* do for you," I said.

"I'm afraid," Kris said, looking out over the garden. "I am afraid sometimes I don't believe in love. I'm afraid it's us," he looked at me. The screaming sound of an ambulance racing up Third Avenue provided us with a welcome pause. He continued. "I wonder what can be done," he said.

"We can talk," I said. "You can talk to me and I can talk to you."

But I didn't dare to continue that morning. It happened later that night.

His birthday party was still going on. I finally had gone to bed. I had a nightmare. I woke up screaming, as I hadn't heard myself scream since that mugging night. I thought somebody had been molested downstairs. I struggled out of bed, still screaming, down the blue stairs. I saw them sitting on the couch, Kris and two of his friends. They all three looked up at me, startled. I didn't even realize that I was naked, only that I felt furious.

I was still in the dream, feeling I had to fight to keep what was mine.

"Would you like some tea," Kris said very warmly. He took me up to my room and sat on my bed as he used to when I was little. I don't know how, but we finally got on the subject of his involvement with George and Uschi.

"How did it all happen?" I asked him.

"It was that Christmas before last, when Georgie and I went to Berlin. Remember?"

"Yes, I took you to the airport."

"Right. I was in terrible shape about love," Kris continued. "I had just broken up with Bonnie and I was doing my usual number —wanting to be so goddamn grownup about it all, and sophisticated. Anyhow, the trip was nice. We had a good time. We arrived in Berlin. There was this blond, good-looking girl meeting us. I thought she was a secretary from the theater. I didn't think anything of it. We drove to the hotel. I got a tiny, awful room and I felt lost. I unpacked and went into George's room. Not until I saw their clothes hanging together in the closet, his and hers, did I catch on. 'My father is having a girlfriend in Berlin!' G.T. acted charmingly, as if the whole thing was nothing. So I took the cue from him, didn't say anything, thinking, "Okay. So what?" Besides, what was I going to do? Make a big scene with him? Where would I go to Berlin—a strange town? I didn't speak the language. I didn't want to go right back to New York, having spent the money on the trip. I felt trapped."

"You were," I said. I could feel my anger rising like a wild horse. "He should have forewarned you. He could have said before you left New York, 'I want you to come to Berlin *but* I want you to know I do have a girl and if that upsets you and complicates your relationship with your mother then you should not come.' It would have been up to you to make the choice. And you wouldn't have felt so stuck."

Suddenly it seemed easy to accept each other again, no matter. It has been good ever since.

In the morning I walked up to the room on the top floor where he was staying, where he slept as a child. He was sound asleep, lying on his back, tall, strong, beautiful, like a young god.

"To be or not to be, that is the question."

I had seen his Hamlet at the Arena Stage several times. The last matinee performance, the speech was unbelievable. There was only a spotlight on his face. To see him struggling, achieving, finding what I am searching for, to see clearly the continuation of self gave me an almost religious stillness within myself. I saw it in my father, my brother, my self. Where I end, he will continue, I had thought that day in the theater in the middle of the audience. I was thinking about it again as I watched him sleep, one arm over his slightly turned head and one leg pulled up as if he were walking through air and would never give up.

5

"If I have to I can do anything . . . I am strong . . . I am invincible . . . I am wo-wo-wo-woman . . ."

It is the end of the show at the Charles Street Playhouse in Boston, U.S.A. Helen Reddy's words boom out over the speakers. I sing with her, swirling my white cape around me triumphantly in celebration of being alive. The applause is thrust against me like a wave, strong and full. I bow. It was one of those nights when we were all one. Men and women. Young and old. But I don't let them go yet. The note is too triumphant.

There was one face, a woman's—there is always one, or more than one! She was sitting in the first row, not too young, about thirty, hair pulled back in a bun, no make-up, courageous in wanting to shed all hypocritical roles, knowing the price of anxiety if she didn't. And she didn't stand up. Her face began to twist from tears of hope mingled with despair, pressing themselves through her body, like burning lead, until she could cry. I watched her, moved, for I had been there myself. I pick up the microphone. The house is quiet. "A last message from Anais Nin," I say.

"And so it was once upon a time that I stood up and broke, as if by a magical act, the evil curse of obsession. It seemed a miracle but it was the result of many years of struggle, of analysis, of passionate living . . . of many people, many places, many loves, many creations. From that point on I experienced emotional dramas which passed like storms and left peace behind them."

I take a deep bow. The applause comes again, slower, firmer. I stay down in my bow. For them. For me. For Anais. For us all. For the theater.

I wander down the steps into my dressing room. The snow is finally slowing down. Doug is coming behind me with the props, the costumes, all the paraphernalia left on the stage that belongs to woman on her journey—the brown traveling cape, the entertainer's

297

red wig, Marilyn's blond, the wife's hat, the moneybag belonging to the whore and Mother Courage, and last, but not least, the blue scarf symbolizing the purity of Anne Frank's spirit.

I take off the white cape, the cape of the loving woman, the total woman. I catch myself in the mirror. I look like my father. I have the Lindfors chin. I thought of him during the performance, and a flood of emotions were suddenly available to me. I know he loved me and would have accepted me as the woman I am, as his daughter.

There is no confusion about my image tonight. I feel completely ageless. "Maybe, after all, the split is healing. I am coming closer to myself."

I am handing Martha, my dresser, the silver mask. "Be careful with it," I say. She wraps it in the soft, silky, strangely blue, worn out, torn scarf, symbolizing the purity of Anne Frank's spirit.

"Where are you going from here?" she asks. "Home. It's been a long journey."

When I wandered out into the night the snow had finally stopped. The city was all white. I could see the moon, big and full, against the dark blue sky.

❧ VIII ❧

Five Years Later

*"Talk to me like the woman that
I am. Look at me with no
preconceived notions of how I
must act or feel and I will try
to do the same with you . . ."*

FRAN SANDERS
The Black Woman

WHAT IS LOVE?'' Natasha asked me one day. We were walking on the beach. It was a windy day, the end of the summer after the tour. After Boston. She huddled under my coat. She tried to keep up with my steps and I with hers. Suddenly, a sliver of moon revealed itself behind some dark gray clouds. We both stopped. It was stunning. It was so tiny, and yet so clear. We stood looking at it. Then we both made a wish.

She turned to me. "Moa, do I have to keep it a secret from you?" she asked.

"No," I said. "I am part of you, you are part of me. It doesn't make any difference."

"OK . . . you first, Moa."

"Mine is to be a loving and mature person," I said laughingly. She accepted it completely. "What's yours?"

"I wish for a kitten and a white horse," she said, very loud, very clear, over the sound of the waves.

2

"Lindfors," he said.

"Tabori," I said.

He called me from Marty's where he was staying for a brief visit. It was late fall now. "I am wiser," he said over the phone.

"I am close to another man now. It's that simple or that complicated. I don't know any other words," I said.

"Words are so exhausting," he said.

"Not as exhausting as deeds," I thought to myself, "or fantasies not acted out. That's worse."

299

"I think I am finally together," he continued. "I am sixty-one. How immature I was," he laughed. I laughed too. I couldn't have five years ago.

I went over for dinner. I had worked and didn't bother to change or to make-up. I didn't feel my age in comparison to Uschi who was twenty-six. An improvement.

"Lindfors," he said again.

"Tabori," I said again.

Some things just don't ever change. We hugged. The evening was very simple. Very quiet, almost as if things were back to normal. Only now there were three grandchildren born and I would go home to 95th Street without him. That makes a difference—whether one goes home together or not, goes to bed together or not.

I played with the children—they were with Marty this week—and G.T. played chess with John. I don't think he minded being beaten this time. That's an improvement. Nana did the dishes. Marty was watching the chess game. Lena was reading the paper. They are staying friends and not only because of the children. It was ghost-like and yet real. How sophisticated are we, I asked myself. Or have we really become wiser?

Later in the evening friends started to arrive. H.T., too. I couldn't quite cope with introducing him to G.T. I went into the children's room and read them a story. When I finally entered, the room was filled with friends from our past life, as well as this one. I saw the two of them talking to each other.

It felt strange to leave, but I did, and with H.T. As we crawled down in bed together and he held me quietly, tears—hot, salty, burning—rolled down my cheeks onto the skin of his chest. I don't know if he felt them, but his arms were around me as I fell asleep.

Nothing is lost but it changes.

Something had fallen into place between us up in the heavenly beautiful woods in New Hampshire. I had gone to visit him in his country house. I wanted to finish my book and be with him. Exist together. Accept his weaknesses as well as his strengths, and he, mine, I hoped.

Loving in a new way. Without paying a price for it! No more myths!

As always, it turned out different from I had imagined. As always, I forgot our fragilities were not the same.

"It's a slow boat to China," Susan had said.

"When my allergy hits yours, watch out!" I used to say to G.T.

I found myself right in the middle of it all again. It didn't help that I knew that our life patterns and history were long and different. H.T. is an intellectual and academic, used to a scheduled life. And I have always led an unscheduled life, a chaotic one. And there is nothing wrong with either one of them. Oh, I understood all this in my head, yet I demanded or needed from him complete understanding, even support. God, had I learned nothing!

The old ghost feeling in me about not being a loving woman popped up in me, confusing me whenever he made demands on me, demands I couldn't or didn't want to fulfill. If I needed to finish a chapter that was finally moving for me at dinner time, he got angry with me for having dinner alone. If I wanted to walk by myself or swim alone in the lake or have breakfast by myself on the steps in the sunshine, thinking about the next chapter or whatever, he took it as personal rejection. Or so I felt! It got worse and worse until I finally wanted nothing but to reject him.

I finally told him, furiously, "You're full of shit! You look for your wife in me." (He was married to her for twenty-seven years and had two children.) "I'm not her and will never be her. I've got my work! I want to come to you easily, without tension, without problems. Let me be! So I can let you be!"

"You mean," he said, "you don't want a relationship with a man. What you want is to have another dog, like Brandy."

I saw red. Red! "If you feel you are a dog with me, well then, I am not your woman, for I'm not a bitch. I already have one dog and he's quite enough." I wanted nothing but to split, to get away, to go home to 95th Street, except that it was too damn far away.

"Let's split," I said to him. "Fine," he said. I told him I would leave in the morning.

I said it! And I didn't die of a heart attack.

I went upstairs. I have my own room with a bed in the house in New Hampshire. I was amazed that I wasn't more afraid. For the first time in my life I was breaking up with a man because I wanted to, not because I was in love with somebody else.

I went to bed. "Okay, Viveca! Now that you're free, what are you going to do? I will attack life, deal with it, indulge in it, be part of it!"

A second little thought sneaked in, coming out of my gut. "Why can't you do that *with* him? Be free! You *do* love him and you *don't* want to be alone. And, after all, he is a terrifically supportive guy most of the time and when he isn't, just say no or do whatever you want to do anyhow! Don't be so Swedish! Love doesn't have to get you into a bind!"

My God! Was it the same old challenge again? Yes!

A cloud lifted. Love was possible again! I was finished with preconditioned emotions, at least for now! His or mine! Ta ta!

I went down to his bedroom, crawled down into his bed, felt his warm body against mine. I was hooked again! Wanted to be hooked again! Ta ta!

We didn't make love but we talked for hours about quitting. Why we wanted to. Why we didn't want to.

Everything was up front. "I have made up an image of a lover." I said. "I look for him in you and I don't see him. That's my pink glasses, graying my life, and I feel that you do the same. You want me to become your little girl. I don't want to be a little girl. Then I can't think, can't work."

"You don't have to become anything I want, if you don't want to," he said angrily. He was right. What was I afraid of? Losing him? Admitting that I needed him?

"Please, let's go to Inge and work on our fragilities," I said in the morning, knowing what the answer would be, and that's my problem.

"It's nothing wrong with me," H.T. said. "I don't have to go to the shrink. If we can't talk it out, you and I, why would we with somebody else?"

"But we can't, or I can't," I said. "I am too fragile."

"I doubt if you can with any man," he answered. He got me again. That, too, was predictable. I had walked right into it.

By now it was noon. I went for a walk. "How insane," I thought to myself, "that we struggle with all this beauty around us." It was another one of those heavenly New Hampshire days.

But the tape was going full force in my head. "I've got to get out of here. I'm leaving tonight." But another voice kept interjecting. "You are running away, Viveca, as always. At least H.T. stays and battles it out with you. Not like G.T. What do you want? No problems? Nirvana? Peace and grace only? You'll have it in the grave." I had no answer.

The tape sped on: "You got out of Sweden; you got to California! You got out of California, you got to New York! You got out of a marriage with Folke, and you got into a marriage with Don! You got out of a marriage with Don and you got into a marriage with George! You got out of a marriage with George and . . . Now wait a minute! *He* got out of it. I didn't want to!" Silence!

302

Ancient trees around me, the smell of green moss, black, blank water, stillness.

I find myself wandering back up the hill toward the house, barefoot, as the Indians must have done years ago. I am thinking of the Indian philosophy: If you use the earth, it belongs to you. If we use each other, we belong to each other.

H.T. in his underwear is standing by the fireplace. He is building a fire. He first picks up the wood from the open veranda. He picks it up from the pile that has been there the longest. "New cut wood doesn't burn well," he says. He cuts the trees himself and he saws the trunks into wood so he knows exactly from what pile to pick. "Kindling is best from birch wood," he explains. "They are hard and light easily." He begins to build the fire. He tears some old newspapers in long strips and lays them between the birch kindling. Last come the logs. "There must be air and space between, otherwise it strangles the fire," he says. He lights it and the flames rush through the open flue, through the chimney, and into the sky.

I feel the warmth coming toward me. I move toward him; I touch his bare legs. I put my head on his shoulder. I go inside his bedroom. I lie down on the bed. He follows me. I take my mauve shirt off. He takes his underpants off.

"Different colors," he says.

"Yes."

We crawl down. I lay against his body, feeling his strong shoulder against my chin. We lay very quietly and I begin to feel a yearning.

I touch one finger of his hand, rough from chopping wood, from lighting the wooden stove, from typing. I like all that about him. I touch one, then two, then three. I stick his strong finger into my hand. I begin to feel the surge within me, deep, low down, where I thought it was all dried up.

I don't care if we don't agree on everything. I don't care whether I think he acts insensitive or that he thinks that I am a domineering mother. I don't even care if he *is* insensitive or I am domineering. I know that someplace inside he is just like me! And I want to live!

My lips seek his. I feel them. I do, I do. It gets wilder. He goes inside me. I come and I come and I come. It doesn't matter that I have no womb. It does not matter at all. I am totally involved, totally satisfied, totally happy.

After lovemaking, we lay quietly. Through the windows I can see the ancient trees against the sky.

I want to meet you in the dark, and love you always. I want to

303

go further with you each time the danger signals flash like crazy
flames. I want to go further and deeper and deeper with you.

I was thinking about it all, shaking down the Lexington Avenue
subway. It is fall now. The trees are turning red again. I am on my
way down to court to legalize the end of the Tabori-Lindfors marriage. G.T. signed the papers before returning to Berlin.

I felt like in a dream. I almost missed the station at Brooklyn
Bridge. "It's my fourth divorce," I excused myself.

It was the first cold morning in the fall. The wind was blowing.
I walked into the courthouse and met my lawyer. "I have to go
over the questions and answers with you," he said. We did. It was
simple. The answers were either yes, yes, yes or no, no, no. There
was nothing in between. No room for ambivalence or thought.

"Have you been inhabiting with each other?" was one of the
questions.

"What does that mean?" I said.

"It means have you had sex with one another during the separation."

The answer was no. "He lives in Germany and I live here and the
only time we saw each other was last week," I said to Ganser. "I
am deeply involved with H.T., and G.T. has a new girlfriend,
younger than the one he had when he left me before. And don't
give me the line, 'good for him.' " "I won't," he said and laughed.

We went into the courtroom and when I heard them call out,
"Viveca Tabori," I thought, that's the last time anyone will ever
call me that. I sat down in the chair and answered the questions.
Yes, yes, yes. No, no, no.

"Can you identify your husband's signature?"

"Yes."

"Is that his signature?"

"Yes."

"Are you sure."

"Yes, I am sure. I was married to him for eighteen years. He *did*
write me a few letters, poems, and he always signed them," I said.

"Yes or no, please."

"Yes, your honor."

"The divorce is granted," he said and banged the gavel on the
table, mumbling something about women! I signed. Walked out.
The whole thing took five minutes.

There is something wrong about going through *this* ceremony
alone!

"That was painless, wasn't it?" said my lawyer as I met him outside the courtroom.

"Yes," I said. "Especially when you think how I felt five years ago at the utter thought that this could happen!"

"Time heals all wounds becomes true," he said.

"If you want it to," I thought. It's all about finding the want again. My own!

3

A STORY FOR MY GRANDCHILDREN

IN MY CHILDHOOD COUNTRY, across the ocean, far away from where I live today, way up north, where the winters are long and cold and dark and spring seems never to come, there grows through the cracks in the mountains and through the rocks by the salted sea, miraculously it seems, a flower called "styvmorsviolen," the stepmother violet. Its colors are intense and astonishing deep violet melting into black, or sharp yellow into white. The dark brown-green moss invisibly holds the flower down, protects it, surrounds it, yet allows for the mingling of its roots with the earth. The stepmother violet seems to survive in spite of the wind and the heat of the sun and the burning salt of the sea. It even spreads itself all over the world. Forever, it seems.

Index

309